My Life
in Baseball

My Life in Baseball

ROBIN ROBERTS

WITH **C. PAUL ROGERS III**

TRIUMPH
BOOKS
CHICAGO

Library of Congress Cataloging-in-Publication Data

Roberts, Robin, 1926–
    My life in baseball / Robin Roberts with C. Paul Rogers III.
        p. cm.
    Includes index.
    ISBN 1-57243-503-8 (hc)
        1. Roberts, Robin, 1926– 2. Baseball players—United States—Biography.
I. Rogers, C. Paul. II. Title.

GV865.R57A3 2003
796.357'092—dc21
[B]

2002045575

This book is available in quantity at special discounts for your group or organization. For further information, contact:
Triumph Books
601 South LaSalle Street
Suite 500
Chicago, Illinois 60605
(312) 939-3330
Fax (312) 663-3557

Printed in the United States of America
ISBN 1-57243-503-8
Interior design by Patricia Frey
All photos from the personal collection of Robin Roberts unless indicated otherwise.

*For Mary, a better coach
than even Cy Perkins*

Contents

Foreword

Robin Roberts. When I think of him, several images come to mind. I of course remember our battles in the fifties when he was the top pitcher in the National League and I suppose many would say I was the top hitter. With Robin there was no pretense, no trickery. He was going to come after you with that fastball of his that rose, hopped, or slid. And Robin could locate his fastball. I never saw another fastball pitcher with such good control. Or, put another way, I never saw another control pitcher who could throw so hard.

Roberts was also as competitive a pitcher as I ever faced. He didn't waste a lot of motion or argue with umpires; he just stood out on the mound and tried to get you out with his best stuff. He focused on the job at hand and with him you knew that he was going to be out there the full nine innings—or longer if the job required it.

I probably faced Robin more times than I did any other pitcher, save perhaps Warren Spahn. Robin was the Phillies' ace and was extremely durable. He took the ball in his regular turn for the Phillies for more than a decade. As his club's ace, he generally threw the first game of a series against the opposition's best pitcher. As a result, when my Cardinals played the Phillies we knew that Roberts would be coming after us and that we had better be up to the challenge because he certainly would be.

As much as I batted against Robin, our careers were even more inter-twined than you would think. Along about 1956 Frank Lane, the Cardinals' general manager at the time, proposed to trade me to the Phillies for Roberts, even up. I never asked Robin how he felt about the deal but I made it known that I wanted to finish my career in St. Louis. Robin was a natural in those red Phillies' pinstripes and I never could imagine myself playing without a couple of birds on my uniform top.

I first got to know Robin as my frequent National League All-Star teammate in the fifties. It seemed that every year he was the starting pitcher for the National League, no matter how recently he had pitched for the

Phillies. I was always impressed by how much Robin enjoyed the All-Star experience and being with the other top players in the league—as did I. Robin did not just pitch his three innings and head for the airport. I know that he started and pitched the first three innings of the 1955 All-Star Game in Milwaukee. The game went into extra innings and finally ended when I hit a game-winning home run off of Frank Sullivan in the bottom of the twelfth. There at home plate among my National League teammates waiting to congratulate me was Robin Roberts, still in uniform with his warm-up jacket on.

In more recent years I have enjoyed spending time with Robin and his family at the annual Hall of Fame induction weekend in Cooperstown. I don't believe Robin has ever missed the weekend in the 25-plus years since his election. It is a way that he continues to show his enthusiasm for and appreciation of our great game.

Of course, Robin's contributions to the game of baseball have not been limited to the field. Today he is one of the most respected senior citizens in the game and serves on the board of directors for both the Baseball Hall of Fame and the Baseball Assistance Team (B.A.T.), which seeks to help former players experiencing significant financial difficulty. During his playing days he took on an important role in the creation of the Players' Association. His leadership in the Players' Association could not have helped his playing career, but he was dedicated to improving the players' pension fund and establishing their licensing rights. Although few of today's ballplayers realize it, they owe a large debt of gratitude to Robin Roberts and others like him for their instrumental role in organizing the Players' Association.

Although during our playing days we were both involved off the field in trying to better the lot of major league baseball players, our true passion was for the game of baseball and for the competition it fostered. We were both fortunate to have the ability to play baseball for many years and make a good living from it. I believe we both thrived on the competition, whether it was against each other or someone else. Robin had that unique ability to find something extra in tight spots. When the chips were down, he was one tough competitor out on the mound.

I could tell that Robin enjoyed those tight spots and that he simply loved playing the game. He wanted the ball every fourth day, and he got it. He was quiet and just went about his business, but he delighted in every moment of it. He never forgot that baseball is a game to be enjoyed and that it is a privilege to be able to play. He respected the game and I certainly respected him as a ballplayer and a competitor.

As I have learned firsthand from our Hall of Fame weekends together over the years, Robin Roberts is one of baseball's great storytellers. He has an uncanny memory of the games, events, people, and places of 40 or 50 years ago when he and I had our battles on the ball diamonds in Philadelphia and St. Louis. I know you will enjoy going back to those golden years with Robin just as I have.

—Stan Musial

Acknowledgments

The authors would like to thank David W. Smith, Gregory L. Ivy, and Sharon Magill for their help in very different but important ways. Paul Rogers would especially like to express appreciation to Julie Patterson Forrester for her enthusiastic support of this project from the beginning and for her very able assistance in editing the manuscript. Thanks also to Jim Roberts for reading the manuscript. We are also appreciative of Tom Bast, Blythe Hurley, Linc Wonham, and Scott Rowan of Triumph Books.

Introduction

For many years, I have been a little hesitant to write a book about my life in baseball. I have always loved to tell and swap baseball stories, but in terms of putting them down in a book, I've often thought it is like when I miss a six-foot putt: maybe nobody cares but me. I guess I tend to think that my career wasn't all that important in the grand scheme of things. But the more I thought about how much baseball has meant to me and my family and how baseball has changed, for better and for worse, the more it seemed to make sense to write about my career and the changes baseball has undergone. I guess it helps that I really remember my life in baseball. As I hope this book indicates, I can recall events on a ballfield and conversations off of it from 40 or 50 years ago like they happened just yesterday. To me, it seems that they did happen just yesterday.

First, I can tell you that I remain an unabashed baseball fan. During the playoffs and World Series I watch every game I possibly can. To me, postseason baseball is the game at its finest: hard-fought games with only one goal—to win the World Series.

In the most recent World Series, Barry Bonds put on quite a show. But when the Angels won and were all mobbing each other on the field, I saw a shot of the Giants dugout. Barry Bonds was sitting with his son just glumly watching the Angels celebrate. As much as Barry Bonds had accomplished in that World Series, baseball is still a team game, and success and failure are measured by the performance of the team.

Alex Rodriguez is another example of how success in baseball is measured. His 2002 season for the Texas Rangers was probably the finest ever by a shortstop and, believe me, that is saying something. Still, he finished a distant third in the Most Valuable Player voting because his team played so poorly.

The only pennant winner I played on was the 1950 Phillies, known forevermore as the Whiz Kids. In those days the two leagues had a total of 16 teams with no divisions. St. Louis was the major league's westernmost boundary, and Washington was as far south as big-league play extended. Except for occasional barnstorming exhibitions, the World Series was the only postseason play.

Winning the National League pennant was a great honor and a very big deal. The Whiz Kids had a veteran pitcher named Milo Candini who won all of one game that year. Milo asked for a raise the next year—he told our owner Bob Carpenter that we wouldn't have won without his win. Contributing to a winning team was worth something. It still is in my memory banks. I played major league baseball for parts of three decades and pitched in 676 big-league games, but nothing in my baseball experience compares to the Whiz Kids' pennant in 1950.

As I watch and read about baseball today, I can't help thinking about how the game has changed. I'm not complaining, but oh what changes! In my 18-year career my total salary was $530,000 and I was paid well. My first year, 1948, the minimum salary was $5,000, which was what most rookies made. My first car, a Roadmaster Buick, cost $2,800, and my wife, Mary, and I spent $45,000 for a beautiful home on a large lot in a nice neighborhood in a Philadelphia suburb. My top salary, after winning 20 or more games six seasons in a row, was $58,000. It doesn't sound like much by today's standards and it isn't, but remember that the average annual household income in the United States in the mid-fifties was less than $4,000.

While the huge increase in player salaries can hardly be overlooked, the game on the field has changed in many ways as well. For example, when I played, on most teams the catcher was in charge of calling the pitches. That is certainly not the case now, even with veteran catchers. Today, the manager or pitching coach calls the pitch and relays it to the catcher so that he can in turn relay it to the pitcher. No wonder the games take so long.

Cy Perkins, who was my mentor and a coach for the Phillies for many years, used to tell me about when he was a young catcher for Connie Mack's Philadelphia Athletics. Mr. Mack told Cy, "Sometime you might have trouble deciding what pitch to call, and if you do, look over to the bench and maybe I can help you." One day Cy was catching in a tough situation with men on base and a 2–2 count on the batter. Cy wasn't sure what to call, so he looked over to the bench at Mr. Mack. In response, the great Connie Mack just shrugged his shoulders.

In contrast, when I coached baseball at the University of South Florida I had a young catcher named Scottie Hemond who became the number one draft choice of the Oakland Athletics. Before Scottie's first game he asked me, "What signs do we use for you to call the pitches?"

I said, "You've got to be kidding, Scottie. I don't call the pitches. I watch the game. You're the catcher, you call the pitches." It turned out that Scottie had never before called his own pitches. He did with me, though.

* * *

I hope to take you on a journey back to when the game was not that complicated, even though the play on the field may not have been as good as it is today. So pretend for a moment that you are with the 1948 Phillies and we are traveling by train to New York for a week. We'll play the Brooklyn Dodgers in Ebbets Field and then head to the Polo Grounds for a series with the Giants. We'll stay at the Commodore Hotel at 42nd and Lexington Avenue for the entire week. We have to pay our own way to the ballpark, but it won't break us because we will catch the subway for a nickel, transfer to the Brooklyn line for the same nickel, and arrive eight blocks from Ebbets Field, safe and sound. As we walk to the park from the subway station, the Dodgers' fans will yell dire predictions of what the Bums are going to do to us on the ballfield. If we win we'll walk back to the station by the same route. If we lose we'll try a different path.

After the game we'll decide how to spend our daily $6 meal money. The clubs aren't cheapskates—they also pay for our hotel, two to a room. For dinner my roomie Curt Simmons and I will take you to Chandler's, where the house specialty is roast beef. Curt will get an outside cut, large and well done. I'll have mine medium well. The meal is delicious and costs $3 with tip, and we'll walk both ways to help keep our legs in shape. Believe it or not, if we've played an afternoon game, we will be back to the hotel from dinner before 9:00. We may sit in the lobby and visit a little before heading to our rooms by about 10:00. After a sound night's sleep, we'll eat a good breakfast in the hotel, lounge in the lobby some more, and head to the subway once again with our nickels handy.

Of course, little by little things changed in the 18 years I played in the big leagues. When we made more money, we'd share a cab to the ballparks and to dinner. Later, the clubs provided a bus to and from the park. Airplane flights replaced 23-hour St. Louis–to–Boston train rides. Major League Baseball expanded to the West Coast and South. Teams built new ballparks with improved facilities for the players and the fans. We played more night games and fewer doubleheaders. More black and Latin players entered the league, following in the footsteps of Jackie Robinson, Larry Doby, Roy Campanella, Don Newcombe, and Monte Irvin. While I played, Willie Mays, Hank Aaron, Ernie Banks, Frank Robinson, Roberto Clemente, Orlando Cepeda, Bob

Gibson, Willie McCovey, Juan Marichal, Billy Williams, Ferguson Jenkins, and Joe Morgan all debuted on the way to Hall of Fame careers. The changes were positive; the game improved on and off the field.

One of baseball's great traditions is the passing on of its rich history from generation to generation. For me it was listening to Cy Perkins tell stories about legends like Babe Ruth, Connie Mack, Ty Cobb, Lefty Grove, and Mickey Cochrane. Last year I visited Billy Williams in the Chicago Cubs' clubhouse. Billy and I were teammates on the Cubs, and Leo Durocher was our manager. I was on the team for only three months, but Billy and I shared some funny stories from that brief time together. Don Baylor, the Cubs' manager, was listening to our stories, and after a while Don volunteered that he would have liked to have played during our time. But I suspect that Don played at the right time for him. In a few years he'll be telling stories and the younger guys who love the game will be taking it all in. In fact, he probably already is.

Of course, there was more to my life than baseball, starting with my wonderful parents, fine wife, and four sons and including my difficult transition from baseball to "the real world" to support my family. But my story is mostly about one of the lucky guys who ended up getting paid quite well to hang out in major league ballparks. Most of the story is even true, although sometimes I may exaggerate just a little. It starts in Springfield, Illinois, with a cricket bat and ends at the Baseball Hall of Fame in Cooperstown. Somehow I feel like I've never had a real job.

CHAPTER 1

Getting Started

The Roberts family was close-knit, and although we did not have much when I was a kid, we never felt deprived or thought much about it. Dad was a Welsh coal miner who migrated to Springfield in 1921 with Mom and my oldest brother and sister in search of work in the coal mines of central Illinois. He had served in the British Infantry in World War I and had been at the terrible battle at Gallipoli, although he was not in the front wave of troops that suffered horrible casualties. I came along in 1926, the fifth of six children. My middle name, Evan, was after my dad's younger brother who was killed on the western front in World War I before his 18th birthday. Growing up in Springfield, I was called Evan by everyone but Dad, who for some reason called me by my first name, Robin. As child number five, I was after Tom, Nora, Joan, and John and before George. My oldest brother, Tom, was very talented mechanically, like our dad, but died in an accident on a submarine in 1942 when he was only 21.

My first sports memory is of playing in our backyard with my brothers. We would take my dad's Bull Durham tobacco sack and fill it full of grass. Dad had brought a cricket bat with him from Wales, and we used it to hit the Bull Durham sack. Dad loved to pitch horseshoes, so we pitched a lot of horseshoes. My brothers and I would play football in the yard. I do remember that we used to whack the daylights out of each other. I was a real pain if I lost. I wanted to win every time and had a terrible temper when it didn't work out that way. I could put on quite a show.

Through the fourth grade I played ball mostly with my brothers and neighborhood kids. One weekend when I was nine years old we were playing softball down at the little grade school. Tom, who was 15, was playing shortstop, and I was playing about 10 or 12 feet behind him. A guy smashed a hard line drive right at Tom and he ducked away. I reached up and caught it and flipped it to him. I don't think Tom could believe that his little brother could catch such a shot.

On the other hand, Tom and my dad were great with anything mechanical, and my brother John was a fine carpenter, but I just did not have any ability in

1

those areas whatsoever. We had an old Model T Ford, but Dad didn't drive. Mom did all the driving, and one day while she was driving Dad to work, another car forced her off the road, knocking the car out of alignment. Dad paid $5 for a second Model T that didn't run. Tom and he combined the parts from both to end up with one running Model T. I stood and watched in amazement.

John helped Dad a tremendous amount in adding on to the house after Tom left to join the navy. They were always making improvements to the place—expanding the house, putting in indoor plumbing and the like.

Except for horseshoes, Dad had little experience playing sports. While my brothers and I were playing basketball in the yard one day, the ball rolled over to my father who was working in the garden. He kicked it back like a soccer player. My brothers and I never played soccer, but maybe that was Dad's other sport. I remember that the Bolton Wanderers of the English League was his favorite team. Dad tried to play baseball with us only one time. He picked up a bat and tried to hit fungoes to me. He took two swings and missed and called it a day, handing the bat back to my brother John.

People just have different skills and abilities and interests. I couldn't do anything with a motor or with a hammer and nails, but I could sure catch a ball, shoot a basket, or throw a football from a young age.

My first exposure to organized sports came when I entered fifth grade at our little two-room grade school, East Pleasant Hill. That was the year a new teacher, C. B. Lindsay, arrived. He had just graduated from Illinois Normal College (now Illinois State University) and was an energetic, enthusiastic young man and a gifted teacher. He made school interesting, both in and out of the classroom. He encouraged us to put on plays within the school and to participate in county dramatic and humorous readings and math contests. I enjoyed the county competitions and won blue ribbons in each area.

I took a particular liking to Rudyard Kipling, because I associated his poems with places like India where Dad had served in the military. I memorized "Gunga Din" and "East Is East and West Is West" in grade school and can still probably get through most of "Gunga Din" all these years later. At least I impressed Eddie Oswald, my catcher and roommate with the Wilmington Blue Rocks, a few years later with my Kipling recitations. After I had children of my own, we would ask the boys to read a favorite poem at dinner, and I would try to impress them with a few lines from Kipling. I don't think it worked.

The first time I had my picture in the paper, however, had nothing to do with academics, athletics, or poetry. One evening someone shot two people at a tavern near East Pleasant Hill School. The police chased the assailant right past the school. The morning paper reported that the gunman had thrown his gun away near the school. Tommy Fahrenbacher and I arrived at school early and decided to go look for the gun. The paper had suggested that the gun was thrown on the shoulder of the road, but we couldn't find it. Tommy decided that maybe the gun was up in the pasture. He climbed up the bank and over the fence and immediately spotted the .45 revolver.

Tommy put his red farmer handkerchief around the handle, and we carried it back to school. Mr. Lindsay took us to the Springfield police station right away. The police chief thanked us, and the *Illinois State Register* put our picture on the front page, the first time I hit the papers.

C.B. also loved sports, and he organized school softball and basketball teams so that we could play against other schools. In basketball we had only an outdoor cinder court, so we played all of our games away. I was in school with C.B. for four years, fifth through eighth grade, and played softball and basketball every year. He stressed good sportsmanship and good, clean competition, and I never missed a game. I took to basketball right away and could play softball well, too, so it was pretty clear from then on that I had a knack for sports.

At home during those years, I followed Chicago Cubs games on the radio. My younger brother, George, and I would put the radio in the window and stand outside and play the game along with the Cubs. When the Cubs were in the field we would put our gloves on and play in the field. When they came to bat, we would grab our bats, which had plenty of nails and black tape, and be ready. If Stan Hack was hitting, we would bat left-handed; if Billy Herman or Gabby Hartnett was hitting, we would swing right-handed. We would be out there every day, playing the game along with our Cubs.

My mother became a big baseball fan as well and would listen to the Cubs games. She was serving the family dinner when Gabby Hartnett hit his famous "homer in the gloamin'" against Mace Brown of the Pirates to catapult the Cubs into first place at the tail end of the 1938 season. Mom got so excited that she dropped a dish of potatoes.

Even though I really enjoyed listening to Cubs games, I never gave a thought to becoming a major league ballplayer myself. To me, guys like Bill Nicholson, who was my favorite Cubs player, were in another world, totally beyond my grasp. (Ironically, Bill would later become my teammate on the Phillies.) And my attitude did not change all through grade school, high school, and college. I was always focused totally on the next day or the next game and never gave a thought to the future. I just wanted to play the sport that was in season.

3

In addition to rooting for the Cubs, as a youngster I really admired Lou Gehrig and Byron "Whizzer" White, the star running back for the University of Colorado who was a Rhodes Scholar and was later appointed to the United States Supreme Court. A little later Otto Graham, who starred in three sports and played in the band at Northwestern, captured my attention. I think I was drawn to those people because of how they conducted themselves off the field as much as by their athletic success. They were all terrific role models.

Beginning when I was 12, I spent the summer playing baseball in a league that we kids organized and ran. There were two teams, four kids on a team. The most valuable player was Doris Koons; she was a five-tool player. We kept statistics in an "official" score book all summer. After every game we would figure our batting averages.

Later on I played basketball for Ferguson's Market. Our practices were at Kumler Gym, where the cost was a dollar an hour. We had 10 players so we each brought a dime. We just found a way to play. Our parents weren't involved, but my folks did enjoy watching me play.

In eighth grade, C.B. organized a sports banquet near the end of the school year. Grover Cleveland Alexander, the great former Phillies pitcher, was down on his luck and staying at the St. Nicholas Hotel in Springfield. The hotel was owned by a man named John Connor, who was really just looking after Alexander. C.B. knew about Alexander and asked "Ol' Pete" to speak at our banquet. Most people there did not know that Alexander was one of the greatest pitchers ever to throw a baseball, but I did know something about him because I was already following baseball.

Of course, Alexander won 373 games in his illustrious career, tied for third on the all-time list with Christy Mathewson and behind only Cy Young and Walter Johnson. He broke in with the Phillies in 1911 with perhaps the best rookie season ever, winning 28 games and losing only 13. He won 30 or more games for the Phillies for three consecutive seasons, including their pennant-winning 1915 season. That year he threw four one-hitters and compiled a minuscule 1.22 earned run average.

Alexander suffered from epilepsy and alcoholism that plagued him his entire life. In 1926, at age 40, he became the hero for the St. Louis Cardinals in their seven-game World Series victory over the New York Yankees, pitching complete game wins in Games 2 and 6 and then saving Game 7. Popular lore has it that Ol' Pete had celebrated his win in Game 6 in his normal way, thinking his duties in the Series were complete, and was significantly hung over for Game 7 when manager Rogers Hornsby called him from the bullpen to face Tony Lazzeri and protect a one-run lead with two out and the bases loaded in the seventh inning. After taking a strike, Lazzeri smashed a line drive down the left-field line that was foul by less than a foot. Alexander then struck out Lazzeri swinging and retired the Yanks in the next two innings to save the Series.

After the meal, C.B. introduced Alexander and you could have heard a pin drop, the room was so quiet. He got up and said, "Boys, I hope you enjoy sports, they are a wonderful thing. But I will warn you about one thing: don't take to drink, because look what it has done to me." Then he sat down. That was all he said, but I have never forgotten it.

Sitting at the banquet that night, I had no idea about the irony of my hearing Alexander's brief speech or how my baseball career would track his in many ways. In about 12 years or so, I would become the Phillies' first 20-game winner since Alex. That same year I would help pitch the Phillies to their first pennant since 1915 when Alex won 31 games. In 1958 I would win my 191st game in a Phillies uniform, breaking Alex's club record. I remember thinking back at that time to that eighth-grade banquet at East Pleasant Hill when Alexander had made his brief remarks. Finally, in 1976, I would become the second Phillies pitcher elected to the Hall of Fame, following Ol' Pete.

Phillies owner Bob Carpenter invited Alexander to the 1950 World Series to commemorate Alex's role with the 1915 club. I never got to have a conversation with Alexander, but, in another irony, C. B. Lindsay bumped into Alex outside Yankee Stadium following the last game of the Series. C.B. introduced himself and reminded Alex of their previous acquaintance in Springfield. Ol' Pete died only about a month later in a motel room in Nebraska. He was 63 years of age.

I had a brush with another great pitcher during my youth in Springfield. In 1936, when I was not yet 10 years old, Bob Feller came to Springfield to throw out the first ball for the final game of the Illinois State Amateur Baseball Championship. Feller was only 17 himself but was already a phenom with the Cleveland Indians. I was in the stands and managed to meet him and get his autograph on a slip of paper before the game. Unfortunately, I somehow lost the piece of paper during the game and never got home with my precious autograph. Since then Bob has replaced it with an autographed baseball.

When my dad came over from Wales, he mortgaged two acres of land and a two-room house, which he had to move to the property. As the family grew larger, he added rooms with the help of my older brothers. They pitched in and helped with the carpentry, the plumbing, and the heating system. As I mentioned, I was not much good with my hands and I really did not have any interest in learning. Dad even accused me of breaking garden hoes on purpose. I did break a couple, but not on purpose.

Sometimes when we were working on the house or around the property as I got a little older, I would get an offer to go play sandlot baseball somewhere. I would ask Dad if I could go play ball, and my brother John would say, "Get him out of here. He's not any help anyhow." So off I would go. I guess it worked out OK because later on, when I signed a professional baseball contract, I was able to build my folks a new house with my bonus money.

In ninth grade, I started at Lanphier High School in Springfield where my brother John was a senior. John was a good athlete and played football, basketball, and baseball there. But my first day, the principal came and took me out of class and said, "Evan, you can't go to school here. They've moved the boundary and you'll have to go to Springfield High."

So even though my brother was a senior at Lanphier, I had to go to Springfield High, which was way on the other side of town. It meant that I had to take a long bus ride across town back and forth to school every day. I was pretty small, probably about 5'4" and 104 pounds, but I played on the ninth-grade football and basketball teams. There was no freshman baseball team.

My sophomore year I had grown to 5'6" and about 125 pounds and went out for varsity football. I practiced every day but never got to dress for a game. It was quite a hardship because after practice I would take a late bus and get home about 7:30. My mother would ask, "Why don't you quit?" because I was not even getting to dress for the games. For some reason, I just couldn't quit. I kept thinking I would get to dress for a game, but I ended up going the whole year without dressing. I would watch the games from the stands after practicing all week.

On Sundays I would show up in a pasture and play tackle football with adults. I was 14 years old, and we played without pads. Whoever showed up played. I couldn't wait for Sunday afternoons; I really enjoyed the competition.

I also went out for basketball and was cut from the team after the second practice. Later on that year I played on a team organized by a young man named Herschal Moore, sponsored by Ferguson's Market, and made it to the finals of the school intramural tournament. We played that final game before a varsity game, and I had a good game, scoring 22 points. After the game, Mark Peterman, the varsity basketball coach, came up to me and asked, "Why didn't you come out for varsity basketball?"

I said, "I did. You cut me the second day."

6

He was also the baseball coach, and I made the varsity baseball team, playing first base for most of the year. One of my teammates was Ogden Wise, who had a cup of coffee in 1944 with the Pittsburgh Pirates.

After my sophomore year, the school board changed the boundaries again, so I could attend Lanphier High. I switched right away because it was so much closer and more convenient. My father worked as a night watchman at Sangamo Electric Company directly across the street from Lanphier High School. When my mother picked him up she dropped me off at school. I also had grown to 5'10" and 165 pounds by my junior year and had the size to compete at the varsity level. I started on the football team, where I played end, the basketball team as a forward, and the baseball team as the third baseman. We won the city title in football, defeating all four of our city rivals and winning six of nine overall. The highlight of the fall was when we routed Cathedral High, the defending city champions, 26–0. I then made all-city in basketball along with our leading scorer, Rudy Favero.

By my senior year I was about 6'0" and 185 pounds. That fall, 1943, we had a very talented football team under Don Anderson, our terrific high school coach. We won our Central Conference and swept to our second straight city title, winning all our games but for a tie against Cathedral. We had a number of fine athletes, but Billy Stone at halfback was truly outstanding. Billy went on to star at Bradley Tech and then played for a number of years with the Chicago Bears.

The highlight of the season was our game against archrival Springfield High, my old school, with the city title on the line. Both schools were undefeated, although we did have that tie against Cathedral. With a record crowd swarming around the field, both schools mounted multiple goal-line stands that left the game scoreless late into the fourth quarter. Billy Stone finally broke through for us, scoring on an 11-yard run with only 45 seconds left in the game to give us a 7–0 victory. I made the all-city football team and was offered a football scholarship to the University of Illinois at the end of the football season. At that point I was not interested because I was focused on the next season, which was basketball.

I also made all-city in basketball my senior year. We had a good team, finishing 17–6 and winning the regionals before losing in the state sectional playoffs. In the sectional loss to Jacksonville, Evemayer, one of their guards, stole the ball from me and scored the winning basket in the last few seconds. I could have died.

During the baseball season, the track coach, Cleo Dopp, asked me to come out and throw the shot put in the city championship because he needed someone for that event. I messed around with it and actually won the city championship, throwing the shot 39 feet 7¼ inches. That meant I got to go to the district meet, and I improved there to 43 feet 6 inches but ran into some real talent. The district winner threw it 54 feet. But my track coach was happy.

In baseball, I played third base and pitched every other game. I had started switch-hitting the previous summer and was a greatly improved hitter. I generally batted third or cleanup. We were short of pitching and I could throw strikes, so our coach, Ted Boyle, pitched me, but I really regarded myself as a third baseman. I had a good arm for third and could hit the ball.

I had a few memorable games. I defeated Cathedral High 7–1, striking out 10 and hitting a two-run homer. Against my old school, Springfield, I pitched us to a 9 to 2 victory, while striking out 16 in the seven-inning game and hitting a long home run. Probably the highlight of the year was defeating Taylorville in the sectionals, 5–2. I pitched and struck out 12 and hit a three-run homer off Johnny Orr in the fourth inning. (That is the same Johnny Orr who later coached basketball at the University of Michigan and at Iowa State University. His high school basketball team was 46–0 and won the Illinois State Championship that year.) I knew I could pitch but still wanted to play every day.

I guess it would be accurate to say, summing up my high school athletics career, that I could play and loved to compete. I was not an all-state player like Billy Stone but got some honorable mention and was an important part of my high school teams.

Although my dad did not participate in athletics with his kids, he enjoyed coming to see me play. He particularly enjoyed my high school basketball games. Because he was by then a night watchman just across the street, he could work the home games into his schedule and I don't think he ever missed one. My sophomore year in high school I played in a YMCA league for a team sponsored by Ferguson's Market, and Mom drove me around to all the games, or if I had a ride to the game, she would come and watch the game and drive me home. We must have played 30 or 40 games that winter in different gyms and Mom was always there. She also kept a scrapbook of my "press clippings," starting with the box scores of those YMCA games and following me all the way through high school and college and into professional baseball. The first scrapbook was an old typing manual. Mom simply pasted in the newspaper clippings over the printed pages of the manual.

Mom was a great cook. We never missed a meal, although I am not sure how my folks managed to feed six kids. Dad made $18 a week as a coal miner and a little more than that later on as a night watchman. We had chickens, rabbits, and pigs and a big garden to supply food for ourselves. We also had peach and cherry trees and a nice grape arbor. I suppose we were poor, but most people I knew were in the same circumstance so we really never thought much about it. There was a pride in being self-sufficient. Mom and Dad worked hard and did a great job of providing for us.

Dad had only two rules: dinner was at 5:00, and we were not to call or refer to Mother as "she." Other than that, if we did anything that Mother or Dad didn't like, they told us about it. Dad was also a stickler about good grades, especially in grade school. If we came home with mediocre grades, we really heard from him, and it was never the teacher's fault.

I mostly remember my home growing up as good food and a comfortable place to sleep. I had chores to do but got to play lots of sports. We just had a warm family feeling, everyone supporting each other.

Over the years I have met many people whom I respect and admire. But no one can compare to Mom and Dad when I think back to what they did to raise me and my brothers and sisters. I cannot explain how much they meant to me. It is a great memory for me the way that those two people kept their family together.

CHAPTER 2

Leaving Home

World War II was going full tilt when I graduated in 1944. I decided to join the Air Corps because I wanted to be a fighter pilot. I qualified for the Reserve Air Corps program. The army sent me to Michigan State University for six months, where I attended regular classes and received military training before I was to be inducted into the regular Air Corps. I reported to Michigan State on July 1, 1944. I was 17 years old.

I spent the month or so after graduation before I had to report to Michigan State playing baseball for Rossiters in the Springfield Municipal League, which was the local semipro league. I played right field and started for the league All-Star team in a game against the nearby Camp Ellis military installation. At the time I had to leave Springfield to report to Michigan State, I was hitting .382. Maybe that is why I considered myself an everyday player and not just a pitcher.

I did pitch one game for Rossiters that summer because a scout from the New York Yankees named Bill Essex came through and wanted to see me pitch. Even though I had only been playing the outfield, I did pitch and it happened to be against the best team in the league, Fitzpatrick Lumber. I lost 3–2. Afterward Essex came up and said, "I'd like to sign you to a Kansas City contract. We'll give you $4,000 for the year."

I explained to him that I was going into the Air Corps in just a couple of weeks and so that was the end of that. That was my first contact with a professional scout. I still don't know how Bill Essex found out about me.

I had never heard of Michigan State University when I got my orders to report there. I didn't know where it was or anything about it but took the train to East Lansing in time to report. Because I was good in math I was placed in math and science courses with some very bright people who ended up becoming executives and scientists. One was named Milo Radulovich. His grandparents were from Russia and later, because of the rampant McCarthyism of the early fifties, the McCarthyites tried to kick him out of the service because his father and sister subscribed to some Communist publication from

Russia. It became quite a celebrated case. Edward R. Murrow had him on his *See It Now* show, and Milo was finally reinstated in the Air Corps. Milo later had a book by Michael Ranville written about his experiences called *To Strike a King*. These guys were not only smart, they were nice people, and many became lifelong friends.

Michigan State had a beautiful campus with only 4,500 students. It also had great athletic facilities, and some of the guys in the program, including me of course, got to play a lot of basketball. The varsity Michigan State basketball players would come over to the gymnasium and play with us as well, because it was their preseason. My section had a good team, and we ended up scrimmaging the varsity and taking them to overtime.

Our reserve training program was to end in December, and we were not to report for our active duty until March 15. We were all going to go home for three months. Sam Fortino, one of the varsity players, told the Michigan State coach, Ben Van Alstyne, that we were available. As a result, the coach asked Joe Krakora, another trainee and a fine basketball player, and me to join the varsity. Michigan State was on the quarter system, with the winter quarter running from January to March, so the timing worked out that we could register for the winter quarter and play basketball for Michigan State.

Joe and I were both excited to play college basketball. Our first game was against the University of Cincinnati, and after about 10 minutes coach Van Alstyne put me into the game. I contributed 10 points off the bench in a 2-point loss. I started our next game and every other game in my career, 53 straight games. Coach Van Alstyne soon began playing the five starters (Sam Fortino, Bill Rapchak, Nick Hashu, Joe Beyer, and me) without substituting, and the press dubbed us the "Iron Man Five." I guess they were right; we played 13 consecutive games without a substitute. Although I focused on defense, rebounding, and passing, I did score 21 points in a game against Temple, which was within 2 points of the school record.

Early in the season we played the powerhouse University of Kentucky in Lexington. They were ranked number one in the nation and were led by their great center Alex Groza. We played them tough early on and actually led at the half, 24–18. But I knew we were in trouble despite the score. In the first half I was running down the court when Jack Tingle, one of the stars on the Kentucky team, hit me right in the chest with his fist. An official was standing nearby looking right at us, and so I said to him, "Hey, what's that?"

The official said, "Shut up and play basketball, you damn Yankee." Not surprisingly, Kentucky steamrolled us in the second half and ended up beating us 66 to 35.

Later in the season Kentucky came up to Michigan State for a return game. By then they had lost Groza to the army but were still ranked seventh nationally. Wouldn't you know, led by Fortino and Rapchak, we beat them at our place 66 to 50 in the biggest basketball upset I ever took part in.

Kentucky coach Adolph Rupp did not like to lose, and he was very upset on the bench as the game wore on. Once as I ran by the Kentucky bench, he yelled, "Hey, who's guarding fat ass?" I looked around and decided he couldn't have been talking about me. Bill Rapchak was playing a great game, and he had a much larger ass than I did. Or at least that is what I choose to believe.

After I got to the big leagues I looked up one day in Cincinnati, and there was Adolph Rupp. He said, "Hello, Robin. How are you?" After that, he would come to see me pitch against the Reds almost every year. I don't know if he was rooting for me or not, but he would be there.

On March 15, 1945, I traveled to Fort Sheridan, Illinois, to get inducted into the regular Air Corps. I was then shipped to Shepard Field in Wichita Falls, Texas, for basic training. After basic I was supposed to begin preflight training, but with the war nearing an end, most of the preflight programs were filled. As a result, I was assigned to a sheet metal school at Chanute Field, Illinois, which was only about 90 miles from my hometown of Springfield. It was a great posting for me because I could go home on weekends and see my family and hang out with my high school friends. I tried to play for the camp baseball team, but the officer in charge told me that they already had their team.

My barracks were right by the ballfield. I was sitting outside one day with one of my camp buddies, Howard Upp. I said, "You know, Howard, I can throw a ball over that left-field fence from home plate."

"You're kidding me," Howard said.

"No, I really can."

Howard was always looking for an angle to bet on something, so he said, "I'll get a lot of guys to bet us. You sure you can do it?"

I said, "Yeah, give me three throws. I might not be able to do it on the first one."

So we got most of the guys in the barracks to bet, and they were hooting and hollering, "Ain't no way you can do that."

Howard took all the bets, and I got good and loose. It was 335 feet down the left-field line, and I threw the first ball well over it. Howard collected his bets and was one happy guy. I don't know what he would have done if he had lost.

In September I tried out and made the Chanute Field basketball team. I never said boo to anyone, just ran up and down the court and scrambled for rebounds and loose balls. We played a couple of games against other bases in October. Of course, the Japanese had surrendered in August, and in late October the officers called us into a hangar and told us that we could stay in the service and go to preflight training or we could be discharged.

It took me about a split second to make up my mind, so I was discharged on November 1 and headed back to Michigan State. My brother John had been in the service since early 1943 and had flown 24 B-24 combat missions in the Pacific, earning the Distinguished Flying Cross. He wasn't discharged until November 15. I had been in the service for about a year, never left the United States, and got out two weeks before he did.

Discharged servicemen were immediately eligible for athletics, so Joe Krakora, who took his discharge as well, and I began practicing with the basketball team when we got to Michigan State in early November even though we could not enroll in school until the next quarter began in January. We just worked odd jobs, such as washing walls, to earn spending money and played basketball for the first couple of months.

We had a very solid team in 1945–46, with a number of veterans returning to campus and the basketball team. Although Michigan State was not yet in the Big Ten (it joined in 1949), we played a very tough schedule against Kentucky, Ohio State, Michigan, and Wisconsin twice each, as well as Notre Dame, DePaul, Syracuse, and Minnesota. On January 18 we played DePaul University in the second game of a basketball doubleheader in Chicago Stadium before a crowd of 19,317. DePaul had the great George Mikan who was, along with Bob Kurland of Oklahoma A&M, one of the first truly great big men in the sport. The three-second lane was only six feet wide back then, and George would camp near the basket and really dominate underneath. We played them very tough this night, and Mikan fouled out late in the game with DePaul ahead by only a basket. We tied the score with 40 seconds to play, but George's brother Ed Mikan tipped in a basket, and we ended up losing 58–52. We also lost two very close games to Notre Dame, a national power that year led by All-American Leo Klier.

We finished the year with a hard-earned 12–9 record, and most of our losses were close games. Afterward, the *Detroit Free Press* selected me as the Michigan Collegiate Player of the Year. Because 12 Michigan schools played college basketball, I was quite flattered by the unexpected honor.

That spring, 1946, was my first at Michigan State, and I decided to go out for the baseball team. I just showed up for practice one day after the end of the basketball season. The baseball coach, John Kobs, was surprised to see me because he knew of me only from my two seasons on the basketball team.

14

Coach Kobs said, "What are you doing here?"

I said, "Coach, I can play your game."

He asked, "What position do you play?"

"What do you need?" I replied.

"I need pitching."

"Well," I said, "I can pitch."

I really wanted to play third base because I'd played the position a lot in high school and considered myself an everyday ballplayer. But I wanted to play and not sit on the bench, so I figured I might as well go out for what the coach needed.

As it happened, the team was leaving for its southern trip just a few days later. I threw for coach Kobs, and he got rather excited because I was throwing as well as anyone he had on his staff. He told me to work out on my own and stay in shape and then join the team when it returned from its trip in 10 days. They won all nine games on their spring trip and so coach Kobs worked me into the lineup slowly. My first appearance was in relief against the University of Michigan, and I gave up a hit and run in three innings. That earned me my first start against Western Michigan. I got hit hard and took the loss but thereafter started contributing to what was an excellent ballclub.

I later threw a no-hitter against the Great Lakes Naval Training Station, winning 8–0. In fact, even though I walked 3, I faced only 27 hitters as my teammates turned a double play after each free pass. Great Lakes had a pretty fair club with Sammy White, who later caught for the Red Sox for a decade, and Mel Riebe, who made a name for himself in professional basketball. In the sixth inning George Ruttenbar, our center fielder, made a spectacular catch to keep Great Lakes without a hit. I wasn't really aware that they didn't have a hit until after the game, but it certainly was a nice feeling. I later learned that it was the first no-hitter in Michigan State history. Another highlight was when Marshall Dann, the sports editor of the *Detroit Free Press*, presented me with my trophy for being named Michigan's top collegiate basketball player before one of our baseball games. I finished my first year with a record of 4 wins and 2 losses and 4 saves on a very good team that won 21 games while losing only 5.

Our last game of the season was in early June at home against the University of Michigan. I pitched and lost 2–0. Classes were over and I had planned to head home to Springfield for the summer right after the game. One of my teammates, Pat Peppler, was going to play in Montpelier, Vermont, in the Northern League, a top summer college league, for Ray Fisher, the Michigan baseball coach. After the game he went over to talk to coach Fisher about when he was to report to Vermont. Coach Fisher asked Pat if he thought I might be interested in joining them for the summer. All of a sudden, Pat came running over to me and said, "Hey Robin, do you want to go to Vermont? Coach Fisher would like you to come with us."

I said, "Yeah, I'd love that," so I called my folks and told them I wouldn't be coming home because I was going to Vermont to play ball.

I was headed for a phenomenal time, pitching for the Twin City Trojans, named for Montpelier and Barre, Vermont. I was paid $175 a month for expenses, and all we did was play baseball. We did not have any outside or part-time jobs, and from June 15 to Labor Day we played almost every day, 60 games total. The weekday games were twilight affairs that began about 5:15, and we played in the afternoon on weekends. We had a good ballclub but lost the pennant to the Bennington Generals. I was strictly a pitcher and finished with an 11–8 won-loss record. I was erratic to say the least.

Late in the summer we were battling for the pennant, and I was lucky enough to pitch a no-hitter against the Keene (New Hampshire) Yankees. I was not lucky enough to win, however. Late in the game I walked a Keene batter, Joe Andrus. He stole second base and scored the only run of the game on two infield outs. I was a loser, 1–0, without giving up a hit. My opposing pitcher that day was Carl Braun, then a student at Colgate University but later a New York Knickerbocker basketball star. No one, including the public-address announcer, realized that I had pitched a no-hitter until the game was over. The announcer gave the game totals, and when he came to Keene he said, "One run and . . . no hits." That was how I found out that I had pitched a no-hitter.

I later learned that I was sometimes responsible for closing the governor of Vermont's office an hour early. Birdie Tebbetts, a big-league catcher and later manager of the Cincinnati Reds, once told me that before he married her, his wife, Mary, was secretary to the governor. She was a great baseball fan and saw me pitch that summer. Thereafter, whenever I pitched, she would, according to Birdie, close the office at 4:00 so that she could go home, freshen up, change clothes, and get to the ballpark by our 5:15 starting time. So I guess I did close the governor's office.

I was back at Michigan State for the fall quarter and for my third year of college basketball. I was named captain and, with Bob Geehan and Oliver White, we had another good club with a killer schedule. We played Kentucky, Stanford, Syracuse, Arizona, Georgia Tech, Marquette, Notre Dame, DePaul, Virginia, and Boston College as well as our normal games against Big Ten teams like Michigan, Minnesota, Wisconsin, and Ohio State.

The low point of the season and my college basketball career definitely came against Kentucky on the road. The Wildcats were 18–1 under coach

Adolph Rupp and were led by All-Americans Alex Groza, Ralph Beard, and Bob Brannum. I scored the first basket of the game and then watched Kentucky score 31 straight points. The final score was 86–36 and was the worst loss in Michigan State history. Even with that whipping we ended up with an 11–10 record and beat some good ballclubs, including Stanford, Syracuse, and Georgia Tech.

Although I played two sports at Michigan State, I was serious about getting a degree and a teaching certificate so that I could teach and coach. Until my second summer in Vermont, I really gave no thought to a professional baseball career. I always went to class and majored in physical education with a minor in history. I loved history and had an American history professor named Mrs. Ireland whom I thought was a great teacher. As it happened, Mrs. Ireland was a big sports fan and came to many of the basketball and baseball games. Fairly soon after I reached the big leagues, I received a call from Mrs. Ireland while we were playing in New York. She was in New York with her daughter and invited me to lunch with them at the Hotel Taft to listen to Vincent Lopez, who was a well-known pianist. After that, for five or six years I would meet her and her daughter for lunch at the Taft during one of our trips to New York.

My second spring at Michigan State I had a solid year on the mound, finishing with a 6–4 record and 86 strikeouts in 91 innings. I had two wins over Michigan and my summer coach Ray Fisher, and wins over Notre Dame and Northwestern. It turned out that I was the first pitcher to beat Michigan twice in one year since 1915. Coach Fisher was a tough loser; he really hated to lose and took it hard. One of the wins over Michigan was a 2–1 game in Ann Arbor. It was a tight game all the way. We were up by the one run in the bottom of the eighth when I gave up a one-out triple. I then struck the next two batters out, one of whom was Bump Elliot, the future athletic director at the University of Iowa, to preserve the lead.

Ray Fisher's wife, Alice, always came to the games in Ann Arbor and watched from a parked car down the left-field line, just like she did in Vermont. After the game I walked over to say hello to her as I headed toward our bus.

We all called her "Mother," so I said, "How are you, Mother?"

She said, "Oh Robin, nice pitching. We sure hate to lose, but you really pitched well."

Coach Fisher was standing across the way, and Mrs. Fisher said, "Look at that old rascal. He won't even come over here and say hello to you."

Finally coach Fisher came over and, with hands on his hips, said, "Lord a'mighty, if I have to lose it might as well be to you." That was quite a concession for Ray, to talk to someone who had beaten him in a ballgame. I had my hatred of losing before I met Ray, but he was a hard loser.

That summer, 1947, I went back to play for coach Fisher in Vermont. I thought he was a phenomenal guy. He could be tough as nails and really would get on umpires. He was a good coach who didn't confuse things. That summer Ray told a friend who repeated it to me, "Robin is going to be a good pitcher. I've had guys with better stuff, but I've never had anyone who wanted it more."

After attending Middlebury College, Ray had pitched in the major leagues with the old New York Highlanders (before they became the Yankees) and the Cincinnati Reds. In fact, he pitched for the Reds in the 1919 World Series against the infamous Black Sox, who threw the World Series. He started the third game of the Series and lost 3–0 to a shutout by Dickie Kerr. We asked Ray one time whether he could tell that the White Sox were throwing the Series. Ray had a great sense of humor and told us, "Well, they did some peculiar things. And there were some articles in the newspaper that suspected something was not right. But I'll tell you one thing. I pitched against the only guy who was trying."

Ray broke into the big leagues in 1910 with the old Highlanders and, in one of his first starts, beat Big Ed Walsh of the White Sox, 5–1. Overall he won 100 games in 10 years in the big leagues, perfecting the spitball along the way. He had an 18–11 record in 1915 for a New York team that finished in fifth place, 32½ games behind the pennant-winning Boston Red Sox. His lifetime earned run average was an impressive 2.82. In 1917 he battled pleurisy and was out of action part of the year. His mound opponent upon his return was none other than the great Walter Johnson. Ray pitched a shutout to beat Johnson 2–0 and even hit a double off "the Big Train." He missed the 1918 season due to service in World War I and was traded to the Reds before the 1919 season. He played an important role in the Reds' run to the pennant, compiling a 14–5 record and throwing five shutouts.

Ray left major league baseball under unusual circumstances that showed his feisty side. After going 10–11 (with a 2.73 ERA) for a Reds team that finished second, he became unhappy when Cincinnati tried to cut his salary. He had a young family and was looking to settle down, so during the spring he applied for the baseball coaching job at the University of Michigan. After interviewing him, Michigan offered him the position. When his salary negotiations with Reds owner Garry Herrmann reached an impasse, he picked up the phone on Herrmann's desk, called Ann Arbor, and accepted the Michigan job.

Rather than place him on the voluntary retired list, the Reds sought to have him placed on organized baseball's suspended list on the technicality that he had given the Reds only seven days' notice of his departure, not the required ten days under baseball's standard player agreement. National League President John Heydler and Commissioner Kenesaw Mountain Landis agreed with the Reds, even after a face-to-face meeting between the commissioner and Ray. For the next 60 years, Ray was on organized baseball's suspended list until commissioner Bowie Kuhn decided otherwise in 1980, two years before Ray's death.

In the meantime, Ray had a tremendous coaching career at Michigan from 1921 to 1958, winning 661 games while losing only 292 for a .694 winning percentage. Along the way, his teams won 15 Big Ten championships and the NCAA championship in 1953, when Ray was named national coach of the year. In 1970 Michigan honored Ray by renaming its baseball facility Ray Fisher Stadium.

I really enjoyed playing for Ray in Vermont those two summers. As long as you played hard, you were OK with him. During that second summer when I was pitching really well, he said to me one afternoon, "Robin, one thing I can tell you about pitching. Don't pitch anyone high and away because I could hit that pitch." Later on in my career, if I threw one high and away and a guy hit the ball nine miles, I would remember that Ray Fisher had told me way back when that he could hit that pitch.

Ray was 59 years old when I played for him, and he still liked to throw batting practice. Before the last round he would say, "OK, I'm going to throw whatever I want," and he would throw his spitball. We would all top it and hit weak ground balls. Ray would laugh and get the biggest kick out of our feeble attempts to hit his spitball.

When I reached the big leagues I would try to get up to see Ray in Ann Arbor every couple of years. In 1982 Bob Miller, my old Phillies teammate who coached baseball at the University of Detroit for many years, called me and asked me to come up and speak at a fund-raising banquet for his baseball program. I told Bob I would come if he would take me over to see Ray Fisher in Ann Arbor.

So I flew up and spoke at the banquet. I had a flight out of Detroit at about 10:30 the next morning, so I called Ray and asked, "Ray, what time do you get up?" Ray said he rose early, so I asked if I could visit him at 6:30 the next morning. Bob drove me over, and Ray was using a walker. He had lost his wife and was 94 years old. I said, "How you doing, Ray?"

He said, "Lord almighty, Robin, I think I've had it." We had a nice visit and Bob ran me back to the Detroit airport. Ray died just a few months later, soon after his 95th birthday.

* * *

Early on during the summer of 1947 I was pitching very well in a game in Montpelier and I had sense enough to ask myself, "What am I doing now? Why am I so good today?" I could feel a good hip action opening up and everything working together. From that moment on, I could throw a baseball hard, with movement, with a very comfortable, easy motion. I had found the proper mechanics that would allow me to succeed.

As proof of the change, after the Northern League season, I went home to Springfield and pitched a game for a local team, as I had the previous summer. After my first couple of pitches, my catcher from high school, Bob Cain, called time and came to the mound. "What happened to you?" he asked. "You've never thrown like that before."

That second summer I was 18–3, and we won the pennant. I won 17 consecutive starts, although I did lose a game in relief. The next to the last day of the season coach Fisher brought me in to relieve in the ninth inning against the St. Albans Giants to make sure I could set that season's league strikeout record. I was starting the season finale the next day and needed a total of seven strikeouts to beat the record of 160. I struck out two, but St. Albans scored four runs off me to come from behind and win the game 7–5. The next morning I started against the St. Johnsbury Yankees and struck out 15 to easily break the record. I lost again, however, 3–2 in 10 innings, and so finished the summer 18–3.

There were a number of good ballplayers in the Northern League that summer, including Johnny Antonelli who pitched for Rutland. Jack Mayo, my future Whiz Kid teammate, had played for Bennington the previous year. One of my teammates in Vermont the first year was a pitcher named Cliff Wise. He had pitched for Ray Fisher at Michigan and was a little older than the rest of us. He had a bad arm so he wasn't with us very long. The first day we were going to the ballpark we went by to pick Cliff up, and he asked us to come in to see his baby boy. Cliff was in Vermont with his wife and their baby was about six months old.

Years later when I was with the Phillies we flew to Portland, Oregon, to play an exhibition game. Cliff Wise had settled out there and met the plane with his son who was then 12 years old. The next time I heard about Cliff's son was in 1963 when the Phillies signed him to a large bonus contract out of high school. Cliff's son Rick pitched his first big-league game for the Phillies when he was 18 years old. Rick Wise went on to win 188 games in a stellar 18-year big-league career. In 1971 he had one of the best days a pitcher could hope for, pitching a no-hitter for the Phillies against the Cincinnati Reds and hitting two home runs to top it off. That baby boy in Vermont turned into quite a big-league pitcher.

Of course Pat Peppler was another of my teammates in Vermont and at Michigan State. We played basketball and baseball together in college, and afterward Pat went into coaching football, first at East Lansing High School in Michigan. From there Pat was hired as an assistant football coach at North Carolina State by Earl Edwards, who had been an assistant coach at Michigan State. After Edwards was fired, Pat coached at Wake Forest. All together he was in North Carolina for nine years.

Pat used to visit us during his recruiting trips to Pennsylvania. On one visit he told me this would be his last recruiting trip. When I asked why, he told me that he was going to become director of player personnel for Vince Lombardi and the Green Bay Packers. So Pat was with Green Bay during the great Packer years in the sixties. He left the Packers a couple of years after Lombardi did and took the same job with Don Shula and the Miami Dolphins. He then became general manager for the Atlanta Falcons, was let go there, and worked with Bum Phillips in Houston and New Orleans. He acquired five NFL Championship rings and two Super Bowl rings and recently celebrated his 80th birthday.

A number of big-league scouts began following me in the summer of 1947, including Chuck Ward of the Philadelphia Phillies. Chuck later told me that he had been most impressed with me on a day that I was struggling on the mound. The opposition had a runner on first, and he took off with the pitch to try to steal second base. After my delivery to the plate, I turned to watch the play at second. When I did, my catcher, George Harms, hit me right in the back of the head with the ball. The throw knocked me out, but I eventually came around and stayed in the ballgame. Although I had been in constant trouble before getting clobbered, afterward I retired 12 straight and we won the game. Ward told me, "I wanted to sign you right then. I knew anybody with that hard a head would be a whale of a pitcher."

I ended up with invitations to work out in September with the Phillies, Yankees, Red Sox, Tigers, Athletics, and Braves. After I returned to Springfield, I worked out with the Phillies first because they were playing a three-game series against the Cubs in Chicago.

I took the train to Chicago. The Phillies offered to put me up in the team hotel, but instead I stayed with Bob Silvers, a friend from my days in the air training program at Michigan State. So Bob took me to Wrigley Field each day of the three-game series. The first day, I reported to the Phillies clubhouse and went out to throw before the game. After I had loosened up and thrown a few at full speed, I overheard one of the Phillies' coaches say about me, "Don't let that kid get out of the park." I didn't know the person who said that, but it turned out to be my first exposure to Cy Perkins, who would become the most important mentor I would have in baseball.

At the end of the first workout, the Phillies offered me a $10,000 bonus to sign a professional contract. I knew that the Phillies had signed Curt Simmons for a huge bonus the previous May, but I did not have any real understanding of negotiating for large sums of money and really did not believe that I was in line for a big bonus. I was just eager to get into professional baseball and would have signed with a team for a couple of thousand dollars.

But I told the Phillies that I could not sign yet because I had promised other teams that I would work out with them. In addition, I planned to return to Michigan State in the fall to finish my degree and play my last year of basketball. The Phillies had me throw the next day and upped their offer to $15,000. I held firm, although my commitment to the other clubs was wavering. Then the Phillies brought me back a third day, the last day of their series with the Cubs. After that workout, Babe Alexander, the Phillies' traveling secretary, raised the team's offer to $25,000.

At this juncture the Phillies really had my attention. As I mentioned, my parents had sometimes fussed at me as a kid for playing sports so much and not helping my brothers more with the chores. Everywhere there was dirt, we grew something and so there was a lot of work to do around the place. One day, they were getting on me about not doing my share. Lou Gehrig was a hero of mine, and I had read about him buying his mother a house with his baseball earnings. So I said to Mom, "Well, Mom, someday I'll build you a house like Lou Gehrig did for his mother."

So when Babe Alexander offered me $25,000 to sign, I said to him, "That would buy a nice house, wouldn't it?"

"It sure would," he said.

"OK, then," I said, "let's do it."

Chuck Ward and I then took a train down to Springfield from Chicago to get my father's signature on the contract, since I was not yet 21. We went to the dining car and I ordered a steak dinner. After I finished, Chuck asked, "How was it?"

"Aw, it was great," I said.

"Do you want another?" he asked.

"That'd be nice," I said. So I ate another steak dinner.

Years later, Chuck told me that he had only been kidding when he asked if I wanted another steak. I guess he did not realize how I could eat in those days, because I did have two steak dinners.

When we got to my house in Springfield, Dad was there sitting, like he did, in his sailor's hat and old-fashioned undershirt. He signed the contract without blinking an eye, just like it was something he did every day. He had worked for $18 a week as a coal miner and then for slightly more as a night watchman, and $25,000 had to be a lot of money to him. But he acted like it was no big deal. I thought he handled it beautifully.

That is when I told Mom, "Now you can get that house I promised you." She was thrilled, but I think Dad would have liked to have put the money in the bank and continued to live in the old house. They did build a nice new house on the same lot because the old house had been set back pretty far from the street. That "new" house is still there, and one of my nephews has now lived in it for years.

I actually received $5,000 when I signed, $10,000 when I reported to spring training, and the other $10,000 at the start of the season. The house cost $19,000, and I bought myself a car and some necessities like a couple of suits and suitcases to travel with. I was flying high, but I was so inexperienced I never gave a thought to income tax liability. I ended up not having the money to pay my tax bill, which was about $5,000. Dad had saved war bonds for years, and so I had to borrow from him, although it took most of his savings. Everyone thought I had more money than I knew what to do with after I signed with the Phillies, but I ended up in debt to my father. I was not able to pay him back for about two years, until I played in the 1950 World Series. I turned my $3,300 Series check over to Dad to settle the score.

I returned to Michigan State for my senior year shortly after signing with the Phillies. I was captain of the basketball team and very much looking forward to playing my last year. Chuck Ward had assured me that my signing would not be effective until the following March so that I could play basketball. Looking back, it is hard to believe that I was so naive as to think that I could get a very large check in September from the Phillies to play professional baseball and that somehow my status as a college athlete would not be affected until the following March. But that is what Chuck Ward told me and later wrote me, and that is what I believed.

I was back at school about a week when the *Detroit Free Press* ran a big story about me signing with the Phillies. As a result, I was ineligible to play basketball because college eligibility rules then prohibited anyone who had turned professional in one sport from competing at the collegiate level in any

PHILADELPHIA NATIONAL LEAGUE CLUB

The Phillies

PACKARD BUILDING • FIFTEENTH AND CHESTNUT STREETS

PHILADELPHIA 2, PA.

R. R. M. CARPENTER, JR., PRESIDENT
HERBERT J. PENNOCK, VICE PRESIDENT-GENERAL MANAGER

September 25 1947

Dear Robin:

I received your letter relative to a statement from me respecting how good I can keep from repeating. At the time I dont contract to Wilmington my instructions was to keep everything quiet until you were able to report.

I had no intention of changing your status and told you I would do everything to keep it between the Phillies and Chuck Ward. I feel if nothing has appeared in the papers up to now you can feel you absolutely will not be questioned.

So I ask be careful this matter as your have gone further or relate.

Hope you have a leave you

Sincerely,
Chuck Ward —

The letter Chuck Ward wrote to me saying I would still be eligible as a college athlete after signing with the Phillies. I guess I was naïve . . .

sport. I was extremely disappointed, but there was nothing I could do about it but accept it.

When the story came out, I went to Ben Van Alstyne, my basketball coach, and explained to him that when I signed I thought I would still be able to play my final year of basketball at Michigan State. Coach Van Alstyne told me he was disappointed in part because he had wanted me to be his assistant coach when I was through playing basketball.

Interestingly, that was the first of three times I had an opportunity to go to work for my alma mater. In the early sixties when I was pitching for the Baltimore Orioles, Michigan State had a night for me at Tiger Stadium in Detroit. Biggie Munn, the athletic director for Michigan State, gave me a letterman's blanket at home plate before the game, and then after the game we went out to dinner. During dinner Biggie said, "I suppose you're wondering why we are doing this." I said I was curious, and Biggie said, "I want you to come and coach baseball at Michigan State."

I said, "Thanks Biggie, but I want to keep pitching. Have you talked to anyone yet?"

Biggie said, "I've talked to one guy, Danny Litwhiler."

I knew Danny well and had a very high regard for him so I said, "Well, if he is interested, you don't need to look any further. He would be a fine coach."

Biggie did hire Litwhiler, and Danny coached baseball at Michigan State for 24 years. I guess it is a good thing I'd forgiven Danny. Hank Sauer and he had hit home runs off me in the first game I won in the big leagues, a 3–2 win over the Reds in June 1948.

Then a number of years later, Jack Breslin, who had been a teammate of mine at Michigan State and was an administrator there, called me to ask if I might consider becoming the athletic director. I told Jack that I could probably learn the job if there was someone under me who really knew the ropes, but I never pursued it, nor did Jack.

I'm very proud of my association with Michigan State. I received a fine education there and got a chance to play college basketball and baseball. The university has treated me very well in the many years since I left, honoring me and having me back on campus a number of times. But my years there as a student were special.

My last winter at Michigan State I missed getting to play with Bob Brannum, who had transferred to Michigan State from the University of Kentucky after he returned from the service. In those days, returning servicemen were allowed to transfer and were immediately eligible, and Kentucky had another star at center, Alex Groza. So Bob Brannum joined us at Michigan

State and went on to a professional career with the Boston Celtics. I would have really fit in well with him because he was a great scorer and I was a good passer and assist man. We would have been a tough combination, but it was not to be.

The Chicago Stags of the National Basketball Association contacted me that winter and invited me to try out for their team. After my summer in Vermont and signing with the Phillies, I was focused on a professional baseball career, so I declined the invitation. Instead, I tried to work out my frustrations by playing basketball in the Lansing city league and going to the Michigan State games to watch my old teammates play. It was a very long winter, but I was eager to report to my first spring training.

CHAPTER 3

In the Pros

My first spring training was 1948 with the Phillies in Clearwater, Florida. I wanted to try to finish my degree at Michigan State that spring and needed permission to report to spring training a week late. Michigan State was on the quarter system, and the winter quarter ended about two weeks after spring training began. As a result, I wrote Herb Pennock, the Phillies' general manager, to ask to report late. Pennock was a well-known, highly respected baseball executive who had pitched in the big leagues for 22 years, mostly with the Red Sox and the storied Yankees teams of the twenties. He won 241 games and had a perfect 5–0 record in World Series games. He wrote me back in late January, giving me permission to report late. Unfortunately, by the time I actually received the letter, Herb had passed away. He died suddenly of a heart attack on January 30 at baseball's winter meetings in New York City. So I never got to meet Herb Pennock.

As soon as I finished my course work, I flew down to Florida to join the Phillies at spring training. After landing at the airport in Tampa, I took a cab over the causeway to Clearwater. It had been snowy and cold in Michigan, but the weather was beautiful when I arrived in Tampa. I thought I had died and gone to heaven with the beautiful weather and blue water everywhere. I checked in at the Phoenix Hotel in Clearwater and was assigned a room. Later in the day I met my first roommate, Richie Ashburn. That spring started a long association with the guy most of us called Whitey, who was also a rookie trying to break into the major leagues.

I went to the ballpark, but it was too late for me to join the team in a workout, so I just sat in the stands and watched. I was really curious to see Curt Simmons throw because he had signed for $65,000. I saw that a tall left-hander was warming up. He had a good delivery and threw pretty well but was not exceptional. I thought, "That must be Curt Simmons." Then another lefty began throwing. He threw about five pitches, and then I knew which one was Curt Simmons. (The first southpaw was Dick Koecher, who had a good career in the minor leagues but never did stick in the majors.) Curt threw the ball harder and with more movement than anyone I had ever seen. I could see why he had 15 clubs bidding for him and got a record bonus.

When I did begin working out, I immediately began having trouble with my legs. I experienced slight muscle pulls and twinges just running in the outfield and, as a result, I could not run full speed. While finishing school in the snow in Michigan, I had not worked out much, other than playing a little basketball. Once I was in Florida, my legs had trouble adjusting to the soft, sandy turf.

Of course, I wasn't a real fast runner on any surface, but I was a good base runner. I could score from second on a base hit. If you lined me up to run a race, though, I wasn't very fast. Later on, I began to think that Curt Simmons was really fast, just from running in the outfield and watching him run the bases. In fact, some of the pitchers, me included, thought that Curt might be able to outrun Richie Ashburn. Whitey could fly, but we thought Curt could, too. One day we were rained out in the Polo Grounds. Because there was no game, we thought it would be a perfect time for Curt to race Whitey. I put my five dollars on Curt, and they raced about 50 yards across the grass. Well, Whitey beat Curt easily and I forked over my five dollars. Curt was deceptive. I thought he was fast. I never bet on him again; he was a bad horse.

One day that first spring while I was still struggling with muscle pulls, I happened to be walking behind owner Bob Carpenter, unbeknownst to him. I overheard him say, "Looks like I blew another $25,000." Of course, that was the amount of my bonus, and I knew that he was talking about me. I had not yet pitched, and Bob's comment was upsetting, particularly because I thought I was there to pitch, not run.

I was so new to the club that I did not have anyone with whom I could share my troubles. Later I was sitting by my locker feeling sorry for myself and Cy Perkins, one of the Phillies' coaches, came over and said, "They're on your ass, aren't they, kid?"

I said, "Yes sir, they're all over me."

And Cy said, "Wait till you pitch; they won't be on your ass anymore."

That was the first conversation I ever had with Cy Perkins. I am not sure why Cy had such confidence in me. He had seen me throw only one time before, when I worked out for the Phillies in Wrigley Field in Chicago the previous September. Although I did not know who he was then, he was the one I had heard say, "Don't let that kid get out of the park."

Cy Perkins was a tremendous baseball man. Beginning in 1915, he had caught for Connie Mack's Philadelphia Athletics for 15 years before finishing his playing career for the Yankees in 1931. He then began his coaching

28

career for the Yankees before Mickey Cochrane brought him over to the Tigers in 1934. He loved to talk baseball with me and had a knack for telling stories about the baseball legends he had played with. He told me any number of stories about Babe Ruth, including Babe's theory of hitting. According to Cy, a bunch of the Yankees were discussing how to hit one day when Babe said, "It's not very complicated. Try to hit that white thing before it crosses home plate."

Cy said that Babe's home runs were very high and just seemed to keep going until they left the ballpark. If Babe hit a homer and sat next to Cy when he came back to the bench, Cy would say, "Nice hitting, Babe."

Babe would say, "Cy, can the Baby hit them?"

Cy had a tremendous influence on me and regularly let me know that he did not ever doubt my ability. For example, he once told me that I threw harder easier than anyone he had ever seen. He was always supportive and knew just when to say the right thing.

For example, in spring training in 1950 while I was warming up for a game Cy said, "Kid, I want to tell you something." He always called me "kid." "I've been in baseball for 35 years and the five best pitchers I've ever seen are Walter Johnson, Lefty Grove, Herb Pennock [who was of course the Phillies' general manager who died before I could meet him], Grover Cleveland Alexander, and you."

I just thanked him and chuckled to myself. My lifetime record at that time, after all of a year and a half in the major leagues, was 22 wins and 24 defeats.

He went on, "I'm not kidding. You've got the best delivery I have ever seen. You are our next 300-game winner."

Cy never tried to tell me how to pitch. He would simply tell me, "Do it your way, Kid." Cy appreciated my talent and wanted me to be in the frame of mind to get the most out of it. He knew that I was a good pitcher because of a physical gift. If I got knocked out early in a game he would say, "Don't worry about it. Those guys on the other team are getting paid, too. Some days they are going to get their hits." Or he would tell me, "Remember, it's a long career."

One time I got knocked out of a game in the first inning. We left town after the game and I was in a compartment on the train feeling really down. Cy knocked on the door and came in.

He asked, "How are you doing?"

Feeling sorry for myself, I said, "Cy, how can I be doing?"

Cy sat down and started to reminisce in a very offhand, casual manner about when he played for the Athletics. He talked about a big game Lefty

Grove was to pitch against the Yankees and how, when warming up, Grove was throwing as hard as he ever had. The A's failed to score in the top of the first, and Lefty took the mound. The Yankees proceeded to rip him for seven runs in the bottom half of the inning, finally forcing Mr. Mack to take him out of the game. Cy told me they were all astonished because no one, not even the Yankees, was supposed to hit Lefty Grove like that.

With that Cy left. And I began to feel less sorry for myself. I thought, "Lefty Grove got knocked out in the first inning, so what the hell am I worrying about?"

When I won I never saw or heard from Cy. He thought that I had the ability to win, that I should win. But if I lost he was always there. He knew that I took losing very hard. So Cy would often be there after a loss to make sure I kept things in perspective.

In the spring of 1948 I finally pitched in an exhibition game against the Cardinals' B team about a week after Cy had come over to me in the locker room. In three innings I got nine consecutive outs, struck out four, and hit a triple. Of course, that was the first time I pitched for the Phillies and afterward everybody was very excited about my outing and nobody was worried about my legs anymore. I was sitting in the clubhouse after the game feeling very good about my performance when someone tapped my arm. I looked around and Cy just gave me a wink and walked on by.

That spring was the beginning of a wonderful baseball friendship. I believed in Cy totally, and I knew that he was completely behind me. We did not socialize off the field, and our conversations were almost all between starts and after I lost a ballgame. But his quiet, low-key manner had a remarkable way of keeping me believing in myself and my God-given talent.

Once I arrived at spring training and got over my early leg miseries, I pitched well. After my first outing against the Cardinals' B squad, I pitched four shutout innings against the Washington Senators and got the win. I had several more successful appearances, including a game against Cincinnati in Clearwater that I lost in the ninth inning on a home run to Hank Sauer, after relieving Ken Heintzelman in the fourth.

Although the Phillies had a number of youngsters in camp in '48, the team was still largely an older outfit. The veterans included infielders Bert Haas, Eddie Miller, Emil Verban, and Bama Rowell, outfielder Harry Walker, catchers Al Lakeman and Don Padgett, and pitchers Schoolboy Rowe, Nick Strincevich, and Dutch Leonard, who was from Auburn, Illinois, about 10 miles south of Springfield. Dutch was a 39-year-old knuckleballer beginning his 15th season in the big leagues. He had won 20 games in

1939 for the Washington Senators and once had been on a staff with four knuckleballers. The Senators' catcher, Rick Ferrell, ended up in the Hall of Fame. He probably could have just as easily ended up in a mental institution from trying to catch all those flutterballs.

I used to follow through on my pitching motion with my glove ending up behind my back. The first time Dutch saw me warm up, he said, "Hey, kid, you can't catch them that way. You've got to hold your glove in front of you." It was funny that no one had ever mentioned that to me, but it was easy for me to correct and carry my glove in front where I could field balls hit back through the middle.

Padgett was an outstanding left-handed hitter who never really found a position. In 1948 he was 36 years old and hanging on as a pinch-hitter and occasional catcher. If someone asked him how he felt, his pet expression was, "I'm sicker than two mules." I never did figure out where he came up with that, but it sounded like he was pretty sick.

Although I did not realize it at the time, many of the veteran players like Harry Walker had sacrificed years of their baseball careers to military service in World War II. I recently read a new biography on Eddie Waitkus, who became my teammate in 1949. I was struck by, among other things, Eddie's service in the Pacific theater in World War II. His combat experience earned him 10 service awards, including four bronze stars. When we were teammates, Eddie, like most World War II veterans, never talked about his war experiences, so I wasn't even aware that he had been in the service. Bubba Church, who would join us in 1950, and Maje McDonnell, our batting practice pitcher, were also combat veterans, but you would never have known it to talk to them. Of course, I had lost my older brother Tom to the war, so I was fully aware of war's consequences. My brother John had won the Distinguished Flying Cross as a top turret gunner on B-24 bombers.

I knew something about the service records of Ted Williams and Bob Feller, but I did not really understand the sacrifices many ballplayers made to serve in the war. Jocko Thompson, a left-handed pitcher and teammate with the Phillies in the late forties and early fifties, was one of the most decorated paratroopers in World War II. But Jocko was another guy who didn't talk about the war, although he had parachuted into Germany right around D day.

I once decided that I wanted to be a paratrooper while I was in the Air Corps training program at Michigan State. I had a couple of buddies with similar aspirations, so we went to see Colonel Buford, the commanding officer, to volunteer for the paratroopers. He looked at us and said, "Forget it. Go on back to your rooms." It was probably the best advice I ever got.

It still seems remarkable to me that so many men, of whom ballplayers were just a very small part, made such supreme sacrifices to fight in the war. Then, if they were fortunate enough to come home, they resumed their lives and carried on as if their service to their country was no big deal.

Dusty Cooke was a Phillies coach that spring and had previously served as the club's trainer. Dusty and Ben Chapman had been close friends since their days on the Yankees in the early thirties, so when Ben became the Phillies manager he brought Dusty in as the trainer. Dusty had been an outstanding ballplayer until a broken collarbone and then a broken leg drastically shortened his playing career, but he had no particular experience as a trainer. The story was that all the equipment Dusty had in his training room was a whirlpool and a roll of tape and a bottle of rubbing alcohol. He wasn't very sympathetic to aches and pains, and most guys dodged him. Granny Hamner told me that one time he had some boils on his back and made the mistake of going to Dusty. After taking a look, Dusty shaved them off with a razor blade and poured rubbing alcohol over them. Ham said, "Dusty scared the hell out of those boils. It hurt like hell, but they never came back."

Babe Ruth had been teammates with Ben Chapman, Dusty Cooke, and Benny Bengough, and so he visited our training camp one day while I happened to be warming up. The Babe was talking to sportswriter Stan Baumgartner, and it occurred to me that my mother would really appreciate an autographed ball from Babe Ruth, because she was such a baseball fan. So I got a brand-new ball out of the ball bag and asked to borrow a pen from Baumgartner. I asked Babe to sign the ball, and he said, "Sure, kid," with his raspy voice. Babe's visit was in March, and he died that August of throat cancer. My mother was thrilled to get that baseball, and we still have it in the family.

I always enjoyed meeting and listening to old ballplayers. Cy Perkins once told me that when he was a young catcher he blocked the plate on Ty Cobb before he had the ball, which of course a catcher is not supposed to do. Cobb slid by and reached and tagged the plate. The next day Cobb sought out Cy and said, "Look, kid, you give me six inches of the plate or I'll cut your legs off."

Later on in 1948 the Phillies played the exhibition game at the Hall of Fame induction weekend in Cooperstown. After the game I was sitting near Ty Cobb on the veranda at the Otesaga Hotel. Cobb was with several reporters who were interviewing him. One asked him about how it felt to have accumulated more than 4,000 hits. He said, "I wish I'd had a few more friends and a few less hits." I could understand why he didn't have many friends.

Many years later, after I retired from baseball, I was at a memorabilia show in Atlantic City with Billy Herman. I had followed Billy when I was a kid, because he had played for the Cubs in the thirties. I asked him about Goose Goslin's hit with two outs in the bottom of the ninth inning of the last game of the '35 World Series. Goslin's hit off Larry French had driven in Mickey Cochrane and won the Series for the Detroit Tigers. It was the first Series that I followed on the radio as a kid, and I had always thought that Goose's hit must have been a line drive. At least it sounded like a rope on the radio. But Herman set me straight, saying, "Five of us almost ran together trying to catch that damn pop fly."

Billy was also the Cubs' second baseman in the 1932 Series against the Yankees when Babe Ruth supposedly called his shot by pointing to center field and then hitting a home run off Charlie Root. So I asked Billy if Babe really had pointed. Billy said, "Aw, he didn't point. That was just the first year they ever allowed liquor in the press box."

* * *

One day in that spring of '48 just before we broke camp in Clearwater to begin playing our way north to start the season, Ben Chapman came over to me and said, "Hey, kid."

And I said, "Yes, sir."

He told me, "You are the best pitcher that I've got."

"Well, thank you."

Chapman said, "Kid, they tell me you're too young for me to keep you up here. But I'm taking you to Philly. I don't care what they say."

So I thought I was going to start the season with the Phillies. A few days later I pitched against the Washington Senators in Charlotte, North Carolina. I was lifted for a pinch-hitter, losing 5–4 in a game we eventually lost 7 to 4.

After the game, Babe Alexander, our traveling secretary, came up to me in the hotel and said, "Hey Robin, can I buy you a milkshake?"

I thought that was a nice gesture and said, "Sure, Babe, that would be fine."

So while I'm drinking the milkshake Babe said, "Robin, we're sending you to Sumter, South Carolina, to join the Wilmington Blue Rocks club."

"No, no, no," I said, "the skipper said I was going with him to Philly."

"Well," Babe said, "Bob Carpenter says you are going to Wilmington." And Babe was correct. The owner said I was going to Wilmington, so I went to Wilmington. I was disappointed, but I was young and got over it quickly.

The next day, a Wednesday, I packed my bags and headed for the train station to join the Wilmington Blue Rocks in Sumter. While I was waiting for my train, none other than Dick Sisler got off the same train. The Phillies had just traded for him from the Cardinals, and he was reporting to his new team. It was the first time that I met Dick.

I arrived at the ballpark in Sumter on Thursday and immediately reported to Jack Sanford, the Wilmington manager. Sanford, who coincidentally was Ben Chapman's brother-in-law, asked me, "How are you feeling?"

I said, "Fine."

He said, "How about pitching tomorrow?"

"OK," I said.

So I pitched the next day, Friday, and won a great ballgame, 1 to 0 in 10 innings. On Saturday I reported to the ballpark and Sanford immediately began screaming at me, "What are you trying to do, get me fired? Carpenter is so mad at me."

I said, "Why? What is wrong?"

He said, "You didn't tell me you pitched six innings on Tuesday."

"But you didn't ask me," I said.

"Boy," he said, "I am in deep trouble for pitching you with two days' rest."

In those days, of course, I never gave any thought to how much rest I'd had. I had a good arm, and I just pitched when they told me to.

The Blue Rocks turned out to be a great team and one that I thoroughly enjoyed playing for. We had two catchers, Eddie Oswald and Jack Warner; future Whiz Kid Mike Goliat played first; Charlie Dykes (son of long-time major league player and manager Jimmy Dykes) played second; Rudy Rufer was the shortstop; Red O'Connell was at third; and in the outfield we had Barney Lutz, Jack Lorenz, and Frankie Whalen, a great defensive player.

On Opening Day I pitched and won 19 to 1 over the Harrisburg Senators with 17 strikeouts. Ed Musial, Stan's brother, drove in the only run in the ninth inning. In my next start, against the Trenton Giants, I threw a shutout and struck out 14. We continued to win, and I was having so much fun that I never thought about going up to the Phillies. I lived in a private home with my catcher Eddie Oswald, and we were all just having a great time playing ball. Eddie was a superb defensive catcher who was an absolute delight for a young pitcher like me to throw to. He quickly became a good friend. He was from St. John's University but, despite his defensive skills, never made it to the big leagues. Tragically, Eddie's life was cut short by cancer when he was in his early thirties.

I won most of my starts in Wilmington and pitched one memorable 15-inning game against the York White Roses that ended in a 2–2 tie. I struck out

16 but also struck out six times myself against opposing pitcher Joe Muir. I'm glad that Muir made it to the major leagues with the Pirates in 1951. Although Joe had a brief big-league career, I would hate to think that any pitcher who had struck me out six times in one ballgame was not a major league pitcher.

Bob Carpenter's parents lived in Wilmington and were big Blue Rock fans. They had seats right behind our dugout and were enthusiastic rooters. After I would leave the diamond with a good performance they would yell down, "Nice pitching, Robin." Curt Simmons had pitched for Wilmington in 1947; maybe the Phillies had sent us to Wilmington so that Mr. and Mrs. Carpenter could come and watch us pitch.

By mid-June the team was in first place and I was rocking along with a 9–1 record, averaging 12 strikeouts a game. We were winning, I had a great catcher in Eddie Oswald, and I really fit in with all the guys. I was enjoying myself so much that I just assumed that I would finish the year in Wilmington. Although I did not know it at the time, Bob Carpenter and Ben Chapman had come down to see me pitch in Wilmington one night.

On June 17 we were in Hagerstown, Maryland, the morning after playing a night game. I was still in bed about 10:00 in the morning when I got a call from Jack Sanford, the manager. He said, "Robin, what are you doing?"

"Well," I said, "I'm still in bed."

He said, "Come on down to the lobby. I want to see you."

So I quickly got dressed, wondering what I had done wrong, and went down to the lobby. There I found the whole club waiting for me. Sanford said, "Congratulations Robbie, you've just been called up by the Phillies." Then he gave me a pen and pencil set that was inscribed "Robin Roberts, Philadelphia Phillies."

Needless to say, I was really touched by this wonderful farewell, which was totally unexpected. I later lost that pen and pencil set, and I've never forgiven myself.

After saying good-bye and thanking everyone, I went back to Wilmington to collect my belongings. The next day I took the train to Philadelphia and checked into the Bellevue-Stratford Hotel at about 4:30 that afternoon. After checking in, I reported to Ben Chapman at the ballpark about 6:00. Chapman said, "How are you, Roberts?"

I said, "I'm fine sir."

"Can you pitch tonight?" Chapman asked.

"Yessir," I said.

"Fine," Chapman said, "You'll be pitching."

So I took my duffel bag and walked from Chapman's office into the clubhouse, and Unk Russell, the clubhouse man whom I knew from spring training, motioned to me and said, "Wait a minute, Robin." He had me stand sort of out of the way. I could see another player was in the clubhouse cleaning out his locker, obviously the guy whom I was replacing. He finished filling his duffel and started to walk out the door. Then he saw me, stopped, and walked over to me.

He said, "Are you Roberts?"

I said, "Yessir, I am."

"Well," he said, "I hope to hell you are a better pitcher than I am." Then he walked out the door.

That player was Nick Strincevich. He never returned to the major leagues. His number with the Phillies was 36, and so that became my number for my entire career with the team.

About two hours after reporting, I was on the mound for the Phillies against the Pittsburgh Pirates, who happened to be in first place at the time. It was June 18 and only a little more than two years since coach Kobs at Michigan State had asked me what position I played. When I went out to warm up for the first time, I was in awe of Shibe Park. After pitching on college fields and in small towns in Vermont and in Wilmington, I thought Shibe Park seemed like the most beautiful ballpark in the world. It was a big-league ballpark and I was the starting pitcher.

My knees were shaking, I was so nervous facing the first batter, Pirate shortstop Stan Rojek. I threw him four very wild pitches and promptly put him on first base. I was still nervous going to a 3 and 2 count on the second hitter, third baseman Frank Gustine. I threw him a high fastball, and he chased it for strike three. Fortunately, that strikeout got me over my nervousness.

In fact, I was nervous only one other time in my big-league career. In 1955 I had a no-hitter against the New York Giants with one out in the ninth. Pitching to Alvin Dark, I had the same unsettled, nervous feeling that I had experienced pitching to Stan Rojek in 1948. Dark proceeded to get a base hit, ruining my no-hitter.

I think much of the reason nerves never bothered me when I pitched, except for those two occasions, was that I was able to concentrate so well on the mound. I just stood out there in total isolation, focused on throwing the ball as well as I could. Nothing bothered me, and I was oblivious to even the batter. When I was throwing well, I would see the bat only when he swung, my concentration was so centered on the catcher. As far as I was concerned, the ball was going to the catcher, not the batter.

Of course, sometimes I was wrong. I saw a lot of full swings, mostly on home-run pitches. Those were often caused by my not finishing my delivery properly, although sometimes good hitters would just hit good pitches.

I don't think I ever suffered from what Cy Perkins called "fear of the bat." According to Cy, some pitchers worried too much about how far the hitter was going to hit the ball. Pitchers who had a fear of the bat often did not follow through properly or concentrate on throwing by the batter to the catcher. But concentration was never a problem for me.

When I first came up, Leo Durocher, like a lot of managers in those days, coached third base. He was much like Ben Chapman in that he would really get on the opposing pitchers, calling them bushers or worse to try to distract them. I could hear him when I was in the dugout watching someone else pitch, but when I was pitching I concentrated so hard that I did not ever hear him hollering at me. One day I was beating the Giants in the Polo Grounds pretty soundly, and as I was coming off the mound toward our third-base dugout, Durocher waited for me. He said, "Kid, I really bother you, don't I?"

I looked at him and just kind of smiled. From then on Leo changed tactics, and I was the greatest pitcher who ever lived. He continually tried to butter me up. Leo never gave up. If one tactic failed to work, he would just try another. But bench jockeying was never a problem for me because my concentration was such that I just did not hear it.

The Phillies played a lot of big ballgames in the early fifties, often against the Dodgers with Don Newcombe and I opposing each other. After one such game I asked my wife, Mary, "Was there a big crowd tonight?"

She said, "It was jammed, over 30,000 people in the stands."

Not once, warming up or pitching the game, would I look at the crowd. Nor did I ever hear the crowd. That is how intense my concentration was.

As strange as it sounds, I felt that I belonged in the big leagues right away, even during that first ballgame. I just knew that I could throw hard and that I could put the ball where I wanted it. And of course, I knew I had Cy Perkins in my corner.

Nevertheless, I lost that first game to the Pirates 2 to 0. Elmer Riddle pitched a five-hit shutout against us, and the Pirates scored a run in the third on two hits and a force out and another run in the seventh on a Wally Westlake home run. I pitched eight innings and gave up five hits before Harry Walker pinch hit for me.

I got my first victory in my next start on June 23 against the Reds, beating ex-Phil Tommy Hughes 3 to 2. In the second inning, Andy Seminick hit a double off the right-field wall to send Granny Hamner, who had walked, to third. I then got my first big-league RBI by sending a high bounder to second baseman Benny Zientara, who just missed getting Granny at the plate. Ashburn then singled to center to score Andy. In the fourth, Richie manufactured another run by walking, stealing second, and scoring on a single by Walker.

It was a good thing he did, because Hank Sauer connected off me in the sixth for a home run to make it 3–1, and another former Phillie, Danny Litwhiler, hit a round-tripper off me in the ninth to close it to 3–2. Ironically, I had struck both out twice before their home runs. I was already giving up the long ball but, happily, with no one on base. For the game I gave up seven hits in going the distance, striking out nine and walking two.

My next start was against the Cubs on June 27 in the second game of a doubleheader. It was a special game for me, not only because it was my first game against my boyhood team, but also because I would pitch against my favorite player from listening to Cubs games on the radio as a kid, Bill "Swish" Nicholson. Bill was a slugging outfielder for the Cubs who had led the National League in runs batted in and home runs in 1943 and 1944. He was to become my teammate after the 1948 season when the Phils traded Harry Walker for him.

We lost the first game 6 to 2 before I won the nightcap 7 to 4 in a game called after eight innings because of the Sunday curfew law then in effect. Del Ennis, who had had a baby boy born just two days before, led the way for us with a double, a home run, and four RBIs while I got my first major league hit and second RBI off Cubs pitcher Cliff Chambers.

I struggled on the mound, giving up 10 hits in eight innings while striking out five and issuing two walks. Nick, my old boyhood hero, was 2 for 4 against me.

I next pitched on the Fourth of July against the Boston Braves, again in the second game of a doubleheader. After Blix Donnelly won the opener 7 to 2, I again scattered 10 hits to win 5 to 2 and run my record to 3 wins and 1 loss. I had to pitch out of several jams because I allowed 5 walks in addition to all those hits. Richie, Harry Walker, and third baseman Bert Haas were the hitting stars while I was helped by several good catches by Ashburn and terrific defense by Andy Seminick.

Unfortunately, I did not fare so well in my next start, July 9 against the Braves in Boston. In my first outing away from Shibe Park, I could not get through the second inning, in which the Braves scored 5 runs on 4 hits. After Braves pitcher Johnny Sain, a good hitting pitcher, doubled with the bases loaded to clear the bases, manager Chapman came out to get me.

"Kid," he said, "you don't hang that curve up here." My successors did not fare any better, and we lost 13 to 2. Of course, Sain and the Braves beat a lot of teams in 1948. That was the year they, led by Sain and Warren Spahn, went on to win the pennant by 6½ games over the Cardinals, immortalizing the phrase, "Spahn and Sain and pray for rain."

There really was something to that phrase; Spahn and Sain started 74 of the Braves' 154 games. Sain in particular had a monster year with 24 wins and a 2.60 earned run average in 315 innings. He was also outstanding in the World Series against the Cleveland Indians, beating Bob Feller 1–0 on a four-hitter in Game 1 before losing 2–1 to Steve Gromek in Game 4. Sain was a workhorse and was not a smooth or slick-looking pitcher. He had a great curveball and a great fastball that year. He really stood out to me in large part because he was such a battler.

The '48 Braves were the first team that I ever saw that used a platoon system. Their manager, Billy Southworth, platooned catchers Phil Masi, who was a right-handed batter, and Bill Salkeld, a lefty swinger, depending on whether they were facing a right-handed or left-handed pitcher. He also platooned Earl Torgeson and Frank McCormick at first base and Jim Russell, Mike McCormick, Clint Conatser, and Jeff Heath in the outfield.

Jeff Heath was a guy who absolutely wore me out during my rookie year. He was a burly outfielder from Canada who was a key to the Braves' pennant, batting .319 for the year. He was a pure left-handed hitter, really a designated hitter before his time. After my call-up in June, I pitched to Heath 10 times. In those 10 at-bats, Jeff nailed me for nine hits, and every one was a rope somewhere.

Unfortunately, Heath broke his ankle in a gruesome slide at home plate against the Brooklyn Dodgers in late September and missed the World Series. He was injured after the Braves clinched the pennant and only a week before the Series opener.

Jeff had a tough time coming back from his broken ankle and appeared in only 36 games for the Braves in 1949, his last year in the big leagues. He could still hit but, with the limited mobility from his weak ankle, was a man without a position. I never had to face him again after my rookie year, which helped my earned run average considerably.

After the All-Star break we traveled to St. Louis for a series with the Cardinals. The club had not been playing well, and Ben Chapman called a meeting in his hotel suite. He said, "I'll tell you one thing. If you guys don't shake yourself, some of you aren't going to be here." Don't you know, Bob Carpenter flew out to St. Louis and fired Chapman the very next day.

At the time, the Phillies were in seventh place, although with a 37–42 record. We were only 10½ games out of first place and 2 games out of fourth. Of course, I was just a rookie and knew very little about the reasons for

Chapman's dismissal. Ben was an outspoken guy and had apparently more than once suggested that Bob Carpenter should hire a baseball man to succeed Herb Pennock as general manager. Carpenter had taken on the duties himself after Pennock died the previous winter and probably didn't appreciate Chapman's advice.

Bob Carpenter immediately named coach Dusty Cooke interim manager. Dusty had been elevated to coach once the season began when the Phillies hired a real trainer. Dusty started me in the first game of a doubleheader against the Cubs in Wrigley Field, the place I had heard so many games broadcast from as a kid and where, about nine months before, I had tried out for the Phillies.

The game turned out to be a heartbreaker. We took a 2–0 lead in the fourth on a double by Johnny Blatnik, a single by Ennis that was knocked down in the infield, a sacrifice by Dick Sisler, and a two-run single to left by Granny Hamner. The Cubs tied it in the bottom of the sixth on a single to right by future teammate Eddie Waitkus, an RBI double to left by Phil Cavarretta, and a single by Andy Pafko, driving in Cavarretta.

The game remained tied until the bottom of the ninth. With one out Cubs southpaw pitcher Johnny Schmitz singled. Andy then made a fine play in front of the plate on a ball topped by Hank Schenz to force Schmitz at second. With two outs and a runner on first it looked like I was out of trouble. But Waitkus singled to put two runners on and then for some unknown reason I got wild. I plunked Cavarretta in the midsection to load the bases and then on the very next pitch hit Pafko in the ribs to force in the winning run.

So my first start in Wrigley Field ended in disaster. As I started walking to the dugout with the game over, Pafko, who was upset because I had hit him, acted like he was going to charge the mound. The Cubs' first-base coach was a tough character called Hard Rock Johnson. He grabbed Pafko by the shirt and said, "You dumb SOB, he wasn't throwing at you, he just lost the game."

Years later Chicago newspaper columnist Mike Royko wrote a column about the dumbest things he had seen in his life. One of the things he mentioned was the time Pafko had started to charge the mound after I had hit him and lost the game.

I always had a hard time accepting defeat, even early in my career. After a loss, it really helped me to walk. I would walk back to the hotel from the ballpark or just walk around the city after the game to unwind. I replayed the game in my head over and over, thinking of what I had done wrong. But if I did not go walking, I had a tough time sleeping after a loss. After a tough loss like my first outing in Chicago, I just needed to unwind.

Maje McDonnell was a young coach on the Phillies who was always willing to hang out with me after a difficult defeat. Maje had served 40 months in the infantry in Europe in World War II and had a Bronze Star, a Purple Heart, and five battle stars to show for it. After the war he returned to Villanova University to get his degree and in 1947 pitched an exhibition game against the Phillies for Villanova, losing 7–6. He struck out seven and impressed the Phillies with his control, overhand curve, and live fastball. Maje was only 5'6" and weighed 125 pounds, but some of the players suggested to Ben Chapman that Maje would make an excellent batting practice pitcher, so the Phillies hired him. Maje joined the Phillies the day after he graduated from Villanova in 1947 and, with a couple of breaks, has been with them ever since. He still works for the team in community relations.

Maje would do anything he could to support us and help us win. Harry Walker won the batting title for the Phillies in '47 and Maje pitched extra batting practice to him every day, keeping him in a groove. He worked so hard and became so valuable that at the end of the year Harry urged Ben Chapman to make Maje a coach. So Chapman called Maje in and made him a coach, even though he was only 28 years old.

Maje and I shared an interest in sports of all kinds, and we spent a lot of time together on the road, attending boxing matches or going to movies. Once in 1955 I lost a tough game in Milwaukee when Chuck Tanner hit a home run off me in the bottom of the thirteenth inning. Afterward Maje asked, "What are you thinking of doing?" We decided to walk back to the Schroeder Hotel from County Stadium. It was about a seven-mile walk, and we sat in a city park and chewed the fat and just took our time getting back. It was one of those nights when I knew I wasn't going to get any sleep and Maje was nice enough to keep me company. We got to the hotel about 7:00 in the morning and walked straight into the coffee shop for breakfast because we were quite hungry. Mayo Smith, our manager, was in there eating breakfast and probably thought we were just up early.

I am not sure why I was such a tough loser. Although I realized that the competition was stiff (as Cy would sometimes remind me), I had confidence in my ability and thought that if I did what I was supposed to, my team should win. So when we lost, I assumed it was because I had not done my job properly and it bothered me.

Once in 1951 my wife's two sisters and their husbands had come down to Chicago from Wisconsin to see me pitch and go to dinner after the game. We were playing a doubleheader, and I pitched and lost the first game, a tough loss in a close ballgame. The second game was close also and Eddie got me up in the bullpen and brought me in to relieve in the ninth inning. The Cubs had runners on second and third, and we were clinging to a one-run lead. I walked Smoky Burgess, the first batter, intentionally to load the bases and set up a force at any base. Phil Cavarretta, the Cubs' player/manager, pinch hit and hit my first pitch for a grand-slam home run.

So after losing the first game and contributing substantially to our loss in the second game, I was supposed to go to dinner with Mary's sisters and their husbands, none of whom I knew very well. I did manage to make it through the dinner, but it certainly was not one of my better meals.

* * *

I managed to shake off my tough loss in Chicago and win my next start in Cincinnati 6–1 with the aid of a fourth-inning triple play. With Ted Kluszewski and Danny Litwhiler on base and no one out, Virgil Stallcup twice tried to sacrifice. With two strikes, he hit a torrid line drive to Putsy Caballero at third. Putsy dove to his left to make a great catch and threw to Granny at second to double off big Ted. Granny then relayed the ball to Dick Sisler at first to get both runners and allow me to escape the inning unscathed. The win would be the start of a personal three-game winning streak.

Shortly thereafter, on July 26, 10 days after he fired Ben Chapman, Bob Carpenter promoted Eddie Sawyer from our Triple A Toronto Maple Leafs franchise to manage the Phillies. I knew Eddie slightly from spring training that year and was aware that he had managed a number of my teammates with Utica in the Eastern League. Guys like Richie Ashburn, Granny Hamner, Putsy Caballero, and Stan Lopata all thought very highly of him. It turned out that they were right, although I didn't realize it for several years. July 26, 1948, would turn out to be a decisive turning point for our ballclub and for my own career.

The 1948 Phillies were a team in transition all the way around. Just as I replaced Nick Strincevich on the roster, other kids were coming up, and many of the veterans whom I had seen in spring training were being released or traded. The team's roster would look very different by the beginning of the '49 season as the future Whiz Kids would begin to take hold.

As I mentioned, by the time I was called up, the club had hired a real trainer, Frank Wiechec, from Temple University. Frank was a college-educated physical therapist but did not know too much about baseball when he joined us. But he was enthusiastic and became a very effective trainer, with an occasional glitch.

Frank would typically rub the starting pitcher's arm to loosen and stretch it. One day he was working on Curt Simmons, who was starting that day. I noticed that he was working on Curt's right arm, even though Curt was a southpaw, but thought Frank must have decided to loosen up both arms. Finally, Frank finished, patted Curt on the shoulder and said, "Good luck, Curt." Curt looked at him and said, "Doc, I'm left-handed."

In my first start after Eddie took over, I beat the Reds again 8–5 in a come-from-behind win. Two errors by Bama Rowell at third led to four runs for the Reds in the top of the second, but we came back thanks to two home runs by Andy Seminick and an inside-the-park round-tripper by Richie Ashburn.

My third consecutive victory came on August 7 in Philadelphia over St. Louis 6–2 to stop a five-game Cardinals win streak. I was shaky for the first five innings, walking six and allowing five hits and two runs. But Eddie Sawyer stayed with me and I finished strong, retiring the last 12 batters in a row.

That ballgame was particularly memorable for me. In the seventh inning I hit my first major league home run over the right-field wall by the Shibe Park scoreboard off of Gerry Staley. In fact, it was my first home run since high school. After I touched second base and headed to third, Cardinals shortstop Marty Marion said, "What the hell's going on here?"

The Cardinals were a formidable club in those days and would finish second to the Boston Braves and a game ahead of the third-place Brooklyn Dodgers. In addition to Marion, they had guys like Red Schoendienst, Enos Slaughter, Terry Moore, Whitey Kurowski, Harry Brecheen, and Howie Pollet. And they had Stan Musial. The three top players in baseball in 1948 were Stan Musial, Ted Williams, and Joe DiMaggio. Because Williams and DiMaggio were in the other league, Musial was without a doubt the best player in the National League. All he did in 1948 was lead the league in batting (.376), runs batted in (131), hits (230), doubles (46), triples (18), runs (135), slugging (.702), and total bases (429, more than 100 more than second-place Johnny Mize). He was exactly 1 home run from the triple crown, finishing with 39, behind Mize and Ralph Kiner with 40.

You could tell just by watching Musial warm up that he enjoyed playing baseball. While we took batting practice, Stan and Red Schoendienst would take turns throwing off of the warm-up mound that used to be in front of the dugout to see who could throw the most strikes. Stan always seemed to be in a good mood. When Curt Simmons was Stan's teammate with the Cardinals in the early sixties, one of the young players asked him, "Stan, how come you're happy all the time?"

Stan said, "Kid, if you knew you were going to hit .340, you'd be happy, too."

One day I was standing at the batting cage watching the Cardinals finish batting practice. As Stan finished hitting, he walked by me and asked, "Robin, do you want this bat?" I took it, figuring I was going to hit ropes all over the park, but Stan had worn it out.

Although Musial was a wonderful hitter who ended up with 3,630 base hits and a lifetime batting average of .331 over a 22-year career, people often forget that he was a fine all-round ballplayer. He was an exceptional base runner and could go from first to third as well as anyone. He was also enjoyable to compete against.

Once I was pitching and Musial hit a line drive over Granny Hamner's head at shortstop into the gap in left-center field. I went over to back up third because I knew he had at least a double. Whitey Ashburn ran the ball down but threw it over Granny's head in the cutoff position. Puddin' Head Jones hustled over to get the ball, and I ran up to cover third. Pud threw the ball to me, and I tagged Stan out trying to stretch a triple. He got up, wapped me on the butt, said, "Nice play, Robin," and ran off the field.

Stan was signed out of Donora, Pennsylvania, as a pitcher and outfielder, but he hurt his arm in the low minors and gave up pitching. For much of the forties, he was part of the best outfield in baseball along with Enos Slaughter and Terry Moore. Although Stan never fully recovered from his arm injury, he could throw adequately and was a sure-handed fielder with good range.

Musial certainly had his share of success against me. In 1950 he hit a line shot deep to right-center field off me in Sportsman's Park in St. Louis. The ball was hit so hard that it ricocheted off the outfield fence all the way back to our second baseman, Mike Goliat, who had gone out to take the relay throw from the outfield. I thought it was a double, like anything off the wall generally is, but I looked up and Bill Jankowski, the second-base umpire, was calling it a home run. Stan, of course, took his home run but was kind of chuckling as he went around the bases.

I went over to Jankowski and asked, "Bill, what do you mean, home run?"

"Well," he said, "it hit a guy in the chest in the first row of the bleachers."

There was no way that ball hit someone in the chest and bounced all the way back to Goliat. But a Polish guy hit the ball and a Polish umpire called it, so I figured that it must have been some Polish guy in the stands with a real hard chest.

One time I did have success against Stan in St. Louis after I started throwing my curveball a little more like a slider, so that it had different movement.

It was a game in which I struggled against the Cardinals but struck Musial out three times, twice with the bases loaded. That just did not happen to Stan, but I thought that maybe I had a pitch that would keep him from wearing me out.

The Cards came to Philadelphia for a series about a week later. The first time Stan came up I threw him that curveball and he hit it against the fence. It had taken him all of one game to figure out that new pitch.

* * *

After defeating the Cardinals on August 7, I was feeling pretty good about my performance. I had 6 wins against 3 losses and eight complete games in nine starts. Although I had lost a couple of tough ballgames, I had only been knocked out once. But little did I know that my rookie year was only going to get considerably more difficult.

On August 14, I lost to Sheldon Jones of the Giants 3–1 on a two-run single in the fourth by Giants rookie left fielder Don Mueller. Then on August 18 in my first start against the Brooklyn Dodgers, I lost a heart-breaker 1–0. Fireballing Rex Barney allowed only one hit, a clean single to center in the fifth by Putsy Caballero. Putsy stole second and Andy Semi-nick slammed a ball to left that looked good for at least extra bases. But Dodgers left fielder Marvin Rackley made a nice catch at the wall to end our only real threat.

I had given up a cheap run in the first when Rackley led off with a single. He moved to second on a Jackie Robinson ground-out, and I gave him third due to a bad pickoff throw to second. I fanned Snider but threw a wild pitch to Reese, allowing the run to score. Due to Rex's masterpiece, that, unfortunately, was the ballgame.

Barney was probably the hardest thrower in the league but was plagued by wildness. For the last half of the '48 season he was virtually unhittable, winning 13 games after the All-Star break. In addition to the one-hitter against the Phillies, he threw a no-hitter in September against the New York Giants. But after that stretch in '48 Rex was never able to harness his talent, and he was out of the big leagues for good after the 1950 season, washed up at 25 years of age.

I followed the Rex Barney game with a couple of no-decisions in close ballgames. One was especially memorable because I led the Pirates 3–0 at Forbes Field going into the eighth inning. The Pirates loaded the bases with one out, and I got Ralph Kiner to ground to our shortstop, Eddie Miller, for a potential double play. Eddie missed a ball about every four years, but this one went right through his legs and two runs scored. The Bucs went on to tie the game and, after I was lifted for a pinch-hitter, we lost 4–3. Then I lost to the Cardinals 4–2 and got rocked by the pennant-bound Braves 13–2. After two more no-decisions, my final victory of the year came on September 20 against the Pirates 5 to 2. I beat Pittsburgh ace Bob Chesnes thanks to a homer by Del Ennis and the first major league home run by Willie Puddin' Head Jones, who had just been called up. I had an RBI and two hits myself, one over the third-base bag and one over first base.

Late in the season Cy invited me to go with him to a party in honor of Connie Mack, who, at 86 years of age, was still managing the Philadelphia Athletics. Cy had caught for Mr. Mack for 15 years beginning back in 1915. I was thrilled just to be there and went up to the honoree and said, "Mr. Mack, I'm Robin Roberts. I pitch for the Phillies."

He looked me straight in the eye and said, "You don't have to introduce yourself to me, Mr. Roberts. I've seen you pitch." I have always wished that I could think of things to say like that.

I ended the season with two starts against the Dodgers. They beat me 5–1 on September 26 as Ralph Branca pitched a five-hitter against us. The Bums knocked me around for five runs and eight hits in five innings, including a home run by Roy Campanella. My last outing, on October 2 in Ebbets Field, was even worse. The Dodgers chased me in the first inning, thanks to three hits and three errors, including a throw at first that I dropped. Although we came back to tie the game before losing 5–4, I had all winter to think about that first inning of my last outing.

I finished my rookie season with seven wins and nine losses in 147 innings. I completed 9 of my 20 starts and ended with a 3.19 earned run average. It was not a bad beginning, but I was disappointed with how I ended the season, going from 6–3 to 7–9 and losing my last two starts to the Dodgers. Brooklyn had a powerful lineup and I had not beaten them. When I got home to Springfield, I really dwelled on that and the end of the season.

CHAPTER 4

'49

The winter after my rookie season turned out to be a very eventful off-season as I met my future wife, Mary Ann Kalnes, who was a young schoolteacher in Springfield. Mary is from McFarland, Wisconsin, and graduated from the University of Wisconsin. She studied there at the same time that I was playing basketball at Michigan State. We played basketball against Wisconsin in Madison a couple of times, and Mary remembers going to the games, but she does not remember me. I guess I didn't make much of a first impression.

After Mary graduated she applied for teaching jobs in two places: Denver, Colorado, and Springfield, because of her fascination with Abraham Lincoln. She got an offer from the Dubois School in Springfield and taught sixth-, seventh-, and eighth-grade history there.

That winter was the first time I had spent much time in Springfield since high school, occupied as I had been with the service, college, and summer ball in Vermont. My sister Nora lived next door to our parents where I was staying. One day her friend Middie Langston, who taught at the Dubois School, was visiting and I went out to say hello. Middie said, "Nora, there is a young lady from Wisconsin teaching with me and she doesn't know anyone. Why doesn't Evan call her?"

So I called Mary, and 53 years later I'm still calling her. From the time we went on our first date, she was the only girl I ever went out with. In fact, I wanted to get married that spring, but Mary was not quite ready for that, so we waited and got married the following winter. Of course, that was the winter before the Phillies won the National League pennant and I won 20 games for the first time. Mary always says that I never won 20 games without her, and she is correct.

Other than my possessing a strong right arm, Mary is the biggest reason I had a successful career in baseball. She gave me the love and stability that I needed. I think we were a perfect match, but Mary may have a different opinion. I do appreciate our life together all these years.

I was eager to get to spring training in 1949 for the start of my first full year in the big leagues. Eddie Sawyer would also spend his first full year as manager, and he had made some trades in the off-season to try to strengthen our club. I was particularly excited that we had acquired 34-year-old Bill Nicholson, my boyhood favorite, in a trade with the Cubs for Harry "the Hat" Walker.

Although Nicholson was usually "Nick" to his teammates, he was known as "Swish" to the fans. It seems that Nick had the habit of taking some very healthy practice swings each time he came to the plate before stepping into the batter's box, and so the Brooklyn fans began yelling "swish" after each cut. Pretty soon fans all over the league would holler "swish" whenever he took a cut.

I certainly was not disappointed when I got to know Nick personally. He quickly earned the respect of the entire team. Nick was the consummate professional ballplayer, willing to give advice if asked but mainly leading by example. For much of the 1949 season he started in right field until a shoulder injury hampered him later in the year. During our pennant-winning year the next season, he served mostly as a pinch-hitter, winning two games with dramatic home runs until diabetes put him into the hospital in September. Nick had played on a pennant-winner before with the 1945 Cubs and knew what it takes to win. His mere presence was a steadying influence on the young Whiz Kids.

Nick was quick with a quip. I remember in 1953 Nick was on third base in the eighth inning of a game against the Braves in which I happened to be going after my 100th career win. Our batter hit a fly ball to right field deep enough to score Nick easily, but Nick slid into home even though there was no throw. When he came into the dugout, I asked, "Nick, why did you slide home?"

He said, "That's far as I have to go." That was a great crack, but the truth is that Bill Nicholson was one of those ballplayers that played hard all the time, no matter what the score or the circumstances. He practiced hard and he played hard.

Nick was able to play through the war years because his color blindness made him 4-F. He was the leading slugger in the National League in 1943 and 1944, leading the league in home runs and RBIs both years. In 1944 Bill hit four consecutive home runs (three in one game) in a doubleheader against the Giants at the Polo Grounds. In a move befitting the present-day Barry Bonds, Giants manager Mel Ott actually ordered Nick intentionally walked late in the second game with the bases loaded and the Giants leading 9–6.

Nick was from Chestertown, a farming community on Maryland's eastern shore. It was a very isolated area, and the people there didn't know much about baseball. Nick told me that in 1943 he led the league in home runs and RBIs playing for the Cubs. He came home to Chestertown after the season and soon ran into his neighbor who asked, "Hey, Bill. Where've you been all summer?"

About 15 years ago, Chestertown honored Nick with a statue in the town square. Eddie Sawyer, Curt Simmons, Maje McDonnell, and I all traveled to the eastern shore to join in the celebration. It was a particularly nostalgic day for me. I had gone from listening to Nick playing baseball on the radio as a kid to being his teammate to watching his hometown dedicate a statue of him.

* * *

Although I did not realize it at the time, the hiring of Eddie Sawyer was a real turning point for the Phillies and for me personally. Under Eddie, the Phillies would race to the 1950 pennant and I would develop into a 20-game winner.

Eddie was an honors graduate of Ithaca College and had a master's degree in biology and physiology from Cornell, so he was not a typical baseball man. For many years he had taught at Ithaca in the off-season, and with his photographic memory, the story goes, he could call every one of the 1,500 students by his or her first name and name each one's hometown. As a player, he had been a prize prospect in the Yankees organization before a serious shoulder injury suffered with the Oakland Oaks of the Pacific Coast League halted his progress.

When Eddie's old friend Herb Pennock became the Phillies' general manager in 1943, he hired Eddie to manage the Phillies' top farm team at Utica. There Eddie managed my future teammates Richie Ashburn, Granny Hamner, Stan Lopata, and Putsy Caballero. In 1948 the Phillies established a working agreement with the Triple A team in Toronto and named Sawyer the Maple Leafs manager. When he was elevated to the Phillies job in mid-1948, he put on a big-league uniform for the first time. Because of his inexperience in the major leagues, in an unusual move he kept all three of Ben Chapman's coaches, Dusty Cooke, Benny Bengough, and, happily for me, Cy Perkins. All three had vast experience in the major leagues as both players and coaches.

Eddie had a very hands-off leadership style that I did not grow to appreciate until much later in my baseball career. We knew who was boss, but he did not flaunt his authority or force himself on us. We had very few meetings, and Eddie had very few conversations with individual players. When he did talk to a player it was in private and had a purpose, usually to correct a mistake or give a quiet confidence boost.

I personally did not have any kind of conversation with Eddie for almost a year after he became the Phillies' manager, except to say hello and good-bye each day. He never talked to me before I pitched. Most of the time I would read in the paper that I was starting so I would get a ball, warm up, and pitch the game. Sometimes I would hear from a coach that I was pitching, but I never heard from Eddie.

Finally, one day in Pittsburgh in July 1949, I walked by the coffee shop of our hotel and saw Eddie inside. He motioned me in and said, "Robin, you think you are a big-league pitcher, don't you?"

"Yes sir, I do," I said.

"Well so do I," he said.

That was it. It was the first real conversation I had with Eddie in the year he had been manager.

Unlike most managers then and all managers now, Eddie did not have pregame meetings to go over how to pitch to the opposing lineup. Eddie wanted to keep the game simple and let pitchers throw to their strengths, which, as a young pitcher, I appreciated.

Eddie also believed that pitchers should be watching the game all the time when they were not pitching because they could learn a lot that way. And I did watch the games, often with Cy, who had great insight and stories about how the game should be played. For example, Cy told me that when he was a young ballplayer for Connie Mack's Philadelphia Athletics, he came to bat late in a game with a runner on second, no outs, and the A's down by a run. With the count 2–0, Cy said that he figured he would rip the next pitch. Cy did hit a rope directly to the left fielder for an out. Because the ball was hit to left, however, the runner on second was unable to advance.

Cy said the A's lost the game and afterward he was sitting by his locker, undressing. One of the A's coaches came over and said, "Mr. Mack would like to see you on the field." Cy walked back out to the field and saw that someone was ready to throw him batting practice. Mr. Mack told him, "I want you hitting only to the grass between first and second," and so for about 30 minutes Cy practiced hitting the ball to the right side of the infield so he could move a runner over from second. He told me that he never went to left field again with a man on second and no outs.

Cy also related a conversation he had with Grover Cleveland Alexander about pitching. Alexander said, "Throw the first pitch for a strike. Throw two different curveballs. And don't go past 2–2 on the hitter." It sounds easy, but it takes big-league stuff.

A good example of carrying these rules into practice occurred when I pitched to Ted Williams in a spring training game one year in Montgomery, Alabama. I pitched to Ted four times and threw him a total of six pitches. He popped up four times, two to first base and two to right field. They were the highest pop flies I have ever seen.

The next day during our batting practice Ted gruffly said, "Roberts, come here." When I went over to him, he said, "How can you pitch me like a pitcher?"

I said, "None of those 2–0 or 3–1 counts with me, Ted."

He said, "The only guy in the American League who pitches me like that is Frank Lary of the Tigers." No one gets a good hitter out all the time, but you've got a better chance if you stay ahead in the count.

There is an old saw in baseball that a pitcher should never give up a hit on an 0–2 count. It irritated Harry Walker so much if one of his pitchers allowed a hit on a two-strike count that he imposed an automatic $25 fine on any offender. One day one of his pitchers was pitching in Wrigley Field and got ahead of a hitter 0–2. A couple of days earlier another pitcher on the staff had given up an 0–2 hit and been fined $25, so this pitcher threw the next pitch against the screen behind home plate to make sure he avoided a $25 base hit.

I never thought it was the end of the world if a batter got a hit on an 0–2 pitch. You are facing a big-league batter, and if you go 0–2 most of the time you are going to be in good shape as a pitcher. I think it bothered former infielders and outfielders like Harry Walker more than former pitchers.

In recent years, the Phillies have often asked me over to Clearwater during spring training to throw out the first pitch. Several years ago I was there in the dugout and Curt Schilling, who was with the Phillies then, came over and sat down. He said, "Robin, I've got a question. What should I do with the 0–2 pitch?"

I said, "Get 0–3." Curt kind of chuckled, but I'm not sure he considered my advice that helpful.

It was the kind of crack Eddie Sawyer might have made. Most of his communication to the players came from his coaches. Eddie, in keeping with his hands-off approach, very seldom came to the mound during a game. If he came out of the dugout, it was usually to change pitchers. Once in a while we would have a conversation on the mound, but it would be very short. At the end of the '51 season Eddie brought me in to pitch in an extra-inning game against Brooklyn with the pennant on the line for the Dodgers. I got two outs, but Brooklyn had a man on second. Jackie Robinson was the next batter, followed by Roy Campanella. Eddie ran out and asked, "Who would you rather pitch to, Robinson or Campanella?"

I said, "It doesn't matter to me, Skip."

Eddie said, "It doesn't matter to me either," and ran back to the dugout.

I got Robinson to pop up to end the inning. It probably should have mattered to me the next time Robinson came up, in the fourteenth inning. He hit a 1–1 fastball into the stands to win the game for the Dodgers, 9–8, and propel them into a playoff with the Giants.

Looking back, it is amazing how low-key Eddie was with us. He was the same when he was hired in July 1948 as he was on October 1, 1950, when we finally won the pennant. The way he acted in the clubhouse never changed, no matter what the situation.

Although I did not appreciate it at the time, Eddie was truly a ballplayers' manager, at least if you were a regular. We were able to play without any undue pressure, although we knew that Eddie expected our total effort. Without question, he was in charge, but he never did anything that would make us doubt ourselves. Cy Perkins and he instilled confidence by simply letting us play the game to the best of our abilities.

Eddie kept the game simple. He picked the lineup and by and large let those players run the ballgame. The catcher called all the pitches, and he did not complicate the game with a lot of strategy.

At the time, I was not convinced that Eddie was a great manager because he just never talked to us. When Bob Carpenter fired Eddie in June 1952 and replaced him with Steve O'Neill, I was pretty noncommittal about the transition. We were not playing very well for the second season in a row, and it was fairly obvious that Eddie was not getting along very well with Carpenter, so it was not much of a surprise when it happened.

Right after Eddie was fired, my teammate Richie Ashburn and I were discussing the change, and I told Whitey that I thought Steve O'Neill would be fine. I've never forgotten Richie's response. "Loyalty, Robin, loyalty," he said. I suppose the guys like Richie who had played for Eddie in the minor leagues had more reason to appreciate Eddie than someone like me who had encountered him only in the major leagues. Later, however, when I had experience with several managers, it became obvious to me that Eddie was a great manager to play for. I wish I could have played for him all 18 years of my career. It would have been a pleasure.

The Phillies performed well during the 1949 spring training, strengthened by Russ Meyer, Eddie Waitkus, Hank Borowy, and Bill Nicholson, all players Eddie Sawyer acquired in the off-season. My most memorable outing that spring occurred when I pitched against Ted Williams and his Red Sox at old Recreation Field in Clearwater, where the right-field fence, although fairly high, was only about 280 feet from home plate. The first time I faced Williams I ran the count to 3–2. I then threw him a slow curve, a pitch I rarely tried to throw, and he took it for strike three called. Ted glared and spit in my direction before walking back to the bench.

On his next trip to the plate, Williams hit a ball off me that not only cleared that short right-field fence but cleared the ground behind the fence and the street running outside the park before landing in the parking lot beyond. I learned that Ted could get even in a hurry. My catcher Andy Seminick told me that it was the longest home run he had ever seen. I asked Andy to keep that quiet.

Once the season began, I lived, for the second year, in a rooming house run by Richie Ashburn's parents, Neil and Toots, for some of the Phillies who were still single. Neil Ashburn had sold his machine shop back in Tilden, Nebraska, and moved to Philadelphia the year before when Richie made the ballclub. The Ashburns simply wanted to be able to watch their son play major league baseball.

The Ashburns began their boarding house right after I joined the Phillies in June 1948, and it worked out beautifully. That first year they rented a house in suburban Bala Cynwyd and Richie, Curt Simmons, Charlie Bicknell, and I lived with them. The four of us shared a ride to the ballpark. If we had a night game, we often shot pool or occasionally went swimming during the day. We also spent a lot of time just sitting around relaxing and talking.

Mrs. Ashburn was a wonderful cook and prepared great pregame meals for us. Sometimes I would feel a little sluggish working out early at the ballpark if I was not pitching because Mrs. Ashburn cooked so well and we ate so much. She would sometimes bake a cherry pie, knowing it was my favorite. In fact, I last saw Toots in Cooperstown in 1995 when her boy Richie was inducted into the Hall of Fame, and she still remembered baking me those cherry pies.

For the 1949 season, the Ashburns rented a house in Bryn Mawr, also a Philadelphia suburb, from some schoolteachers who were away for the summer. The previous summer a Philadelphia sportswriter had printed our street address, so young fans frequently rang our doorbell. The move to a new neighborhood was in part to provide us with a little more privacy.

Jack Mayo joined Richie, Charlie, Curt, and me in the rooming house that year. When Jack broke his ankle late in the year, Mike Goliat was called up from the minors and moved in while Jack recuperated back in his hometown, Youngstown, Ohio.

Several of us got married after the '49 season, but the Ashburn rooming house was, for two years, an ideal setting for a group of young ballplayers. All of our needs were taken care of, and all we had to worry about was playing baseball.

The 1949 season proved to be an eventful one for a number of reasons. We started slowly, losing 8 of our first 11 games, but began to improve when Eddie Sawyer reinserted veteran Andy Seminick as the starting catcher. Rookie Stan Lopata had won the job in spring training, but Andy was a much more seasoned backstop, and when he started hitting, Eddie started playing him. I started the season with indifferent success and by mid-May I was 2–3. On May 17 I threw three and two-thirds innings of scoreless relief at St. Louis and was the winning pitcher when we scored in the twelfth inning to beat the Cardinals 5–4. It was the first of six straight wins for me over the next month, which would bring my record to 8–3 by mid-June.

On June 2 we played the Cincinnati Reds in Shibe Park in the second game of a three-game series. Our record was 19–21 and we were in sixth place but only 4½ games behind the league-leading Boston Braves. The bad news was that we were mired in a team batting slump that had plagued us for two weeks. The slump seemed to continue as we trailed the Reds 3–2 going into the bottom of the eighth inning against lefty Ken Raffensberger. It appeared that Curt Simmons, our starter, was going to suffer another tough loss.

Del Ennis changed that on the first pitch with a screaming line drive into the left-field stands to tie the score. Andy Seminick clobbered the second pitch of the inning over the left-field roof to untie the score and finish Raffensberger. It was one of the longest home runs ever hit in Shibe Park and Andy's second round-tripper of the day. Before the Reds could get us out, "Puddin' Head" Jones and Schoolboy Rowe also slugged homers, and Seminick hit his second of the inning and third of the game. All told, we scored 10 runs and tied a major league record by hitting five home runs in one inning. Even more remarkable is that the Phils came within about 15 inches of hitting seven out of the park. Granny Hamner's double had missed going out by less than a foot, and Willie Jones' triple had come within an inch or two of being his second circuit clout of the inning.

The next day Andy hit a game-winning double, and then on June 4 he smashed his fourth homer in three games for the only run in a 1–0 win behind Kenny Heintzelman. On June 8 I pitched my first big-league shutout, beating Ernie Bonham and the Pittsburgh Pirates 2–0, thanks to Stan Hollmig's second major league home run, to run my record to 6–3. Spearheaded by Seminick's continued hot hitting, we won 12 of 17 to vault into third place.

Near the end of that streak we took the train to Chicago to begin a 15-game western road trip. Russ Meyer defeated the Cubs 9–2 in the series opener on June 14, spoiling Frankie Frisch's debut as the Cubs' manager. That evening I went to dinner with Bob Silvers, the army buddy of mine whom I had stayed with when I first worked out for the Phillies. After dinner I went to sleep in my room at the Edgewater Beach Hotel, where we stayed in Chicago.

The next morning about 10:00, Bob called me, asking, "How's Waitkus?"

I said, "What do you mean, how's Waitkus?"

He said, "Eddie Waitkus was shot last night in the hotel." That was how I learned that my teammate had been shot by a deranged female fan the previous evening.

Waitkus was a slick-fielding first baseman whom the Phils had acquired from the Cubs in the off-season. Eddie was also a bachelor and known as one of baseball's best-dressed players. It turned out that, unknown to Eddie, a 19-year-old fan named Ruth Steinhagen had become obsessed with him while he was with the Cubs. She sat behind first base in Wrigley Field to be as close as possible to him. Apparently she was distraught when the Cubs traded Eddie to the Phillies.

When Eddie came in from dinner the night after our opening win over the Cubs, he found a note from a woman purporting to be Ruth Ann Burns saying she urgently needed to see him. Eddie called her room on the phone, but the woman insisted that she talk to him in person. When Eddie went to her room, she let him in and ducked into a closet, then came out with a .22-caliber rifle and shot him. The woman was Ruth Steinhagen, who, after the shooting, immediately called the hotel switchboard and reported the incident. That call probably saved Eddie from bleeding to death.

He was seriously wounded and near death with a bullet lodged near his spine. In the weeks that followed, Eddie gradually improved, although he had to undergo four operations and his baseball future was very uncertain. He spent the winter in a vigorous rehabilitation and conditioning program in Florida under our team trainer, Frank Wiechec, and was able to come back and play a key role in our 1950 pennant-winning year.

Ruth Steinhagen was found mentally incapable of standing trial and spent three years in a mental institution.

Of course, much has been made of the Waitkus shooting serving as the inspiration for Bernard Malamud's book *The Natural*, later to be made into a movie starring Robert Redford. But for Eddie's teammates at the time, we were in shock, yet we had a baseball season to play. In fact, we had a doubleheader with the Cubs that very day. Somehow we managed to win both games, 4–1 and 3–0. Dick Sisler took over first base for Waitkus and contributed three key hits in the first game. I relieved Hank Borowy in the ninth inning of the second game with one out and runners on first and third. I walked Rube Walker to load the bases but then got Frank Gustine to hit into a double play to end the game.

The baseball schedule may have helped us deal with the Eddie Waitkus tragedy in a healthy way. We had a game to play nearly every day and did not have too much time to dwell on anything, even traumatic events. The schedule forced us right back into our normal routine.

The following day, June 16, was the last game of our series in Chicago. The Cubs led 3–0 going into the top of the eighth, when we struck for four runs with two outs to win the game 4–3 and sweep the series. Eddie Sawyer allowed Jim Konstanty, our crack relief pitcher, to bat in the eighth with the score tied and the go-ahead run on third. Jim came through with a two-strike, two-out single over second baseman Emil Verban to drive in Bill Nicholson with the winning run.

From Chicago we traveled to St. Louis for a series against the Cardinals. I was to pitch the opener, a night game that was very special for me. More than three busloads of friends and family from Springfield, including some of my high school teammates from Lanphier High, my high school baseball coach Ted Boyle, and my parents and brothers and sisters, came down to watch Evan Roberts pitch. I always knew when I heard someone holler "Evan" from the stands that someone from Springfield was rooting for me.

That night I sent them all back to Springfield happy after I threw my second major league shutout to beat Cardinal ace Harry Brecheen 8–0, putting us in third place. It was my sixth win in a row and brought my record to 8–3 for the year. Dick Sisler again slugged three hits, including his first home run of the year, to raise his average to .333. He was 8 for 18 since taking over for Waitkus.

By June 25 we were nine games above .500 and only two games behind the league-leading Dodgers. On July 3 I pitched my third career shutout, defeating Johnny Sain and the Boston Braves 7–0 on five hits in Braves Field. It was a particularly nice win because it ended a personal three-game losing streak. The wind was blowing in and I threw nothing but my rising fastball, causing the Braves to hit fly balls and pop fouls all day.

In Braves Field you had to go through the Braves' dugout to get to the visitors' clubhouse. So after I retired the Braves in the ninth, I walked to our dugout to get my jacket and then walked over to the Braves' dugout. I was taking my time and could see that the Boston dugout was completely empty except for Sain, who seemed to be sitting there waiting for me. I had never had any kind of conversation with John, but when I got to the dugout he looked up at me and said, "It ain't that easy, kid." With that he got up, shook his head, and walked to his clubhouse. End of conversation.

The team slumped, however, heading into the All-Star Game, losing 10 of 14. I was 9–6 at the break and the Philadelphia fans and press were very unhappy that neither I nor Kenny Heintzelman, who was 10–5, was named to the All-Star pitching staff by manager Billy Southworth. I was a little disappointed but, because I had never been to the All-Star Game, I really did not expect to go. I made it the next seven years, so I ended up with plenty of All-Star experiences, all of which I enjoyed very much.

We were all pleased that Andy Seminick, who was not even our starting catcher when the season began, was voted the National League's starting catcher by the fans, beating out Roy Campanella and Walker Cooper. In a nice gesture, Eddie Waitkus was named an honorary All-Star and attended the game, which was the only All-Star Game ever held in Brooklyn. The American League won 11–7 in a seesaw affair.

After the break we continued to win about as many as we lost, alternating between fourth and fifth place but effectively dropping out of the pennant race. On August 3 I lost a tough 2–0 game to the seventh-place Cincinnati Reds and Ken Raffensberger to start a four-game series at Crosley Field. Danny Litwhiler hit a home run to beat me and drop my record to 10–10. The next day we dropped below .500 for the season by losing a doubleheader to the Reds. Russ Meyer started the first game and couldn't get out of the first inning. When Eddie Sawyer came to the mound to pull him, Russ slammed the ball down in disgust. It hit the rubber and bounced almost to the first-base line.

When Russ got to the dugout, he gave the ammonia bucket a swift kick and immediately fell to the dugout floor, howling in great pain. He wasn't known as the Mad Monk for nothing. X rays taken at the hospital showed a break, and he showed up the next day with a large cast on his foot and the news that he was through for the year.

Monk stayed with us the rest of the road trip and a couple of days later in Pittsburgh mentioned to Bill Nicholson that his foot was not hurting much at all. Bill had been Russ's teammate with the Cubs and knew that Monk had broken his ankle a couple of years before, so he told Meyer, "Your old break probably showed up on the X ray. Go get it checked again. You're probably fine."

So Russ went to Temple University hospital in Philadelphia and sure enough, new X rays showed no new break. It turned out to be a lucky (non) break for Monk and the ballclub. Bob Carpenter had been so upset at Meyer's stupidity in kicking the bucket that he had threatened not to pay Monk for the balance of the year if he couldn't pitch. Furthermore, Monk, who was 8–6 when he injured himself, pitched again in a week and went 9–3 the rest of the way to end up with a 17–9 record, the best season of his career. It seemed that kind of stuff could only happen to Monk.

That first game in Pittsburgh turned out to be a 1–0 loss for Schoolboy Rowe against Bill Werle of the Pirates. The 17-year veteran Rowe had not been pitching much and had been pestering Eddie Sawyer for a chance. Finally, Eddie put him out there and he threw a great game, taking a shutout into the ninth inning. With two outs in the bottom of the ninth and Ralph Kiner on third, Pirate second baseman Danny Murtaugh slapped a 2–2 pitch on the ground to the right of shortstop Granny Hamner. Granny made a good pickup but threw low to Dick Sisler at first. Dick tried to scoop the ball but it bounced out of his glove as Kiner crossed the plate with the winning run.

Schoolie was beside himself and hurled his glove about 50 feet in the air, almost to the stands. Umpire Babe Pinelli picked it up and handed it to Schoolie, but Rowe dropped it to the ground and kicked it as hard as he could, sending it flying again.

Dick thought that Schoolie was showing him up and confronted him in the dugout. They were two large men, and we were afraid they were going to tangle, but Schoolboy made his peace with Dick.

That game turned out to be one of the last that Rowe pitched, and it was sad the way it ended with Schoolie so upset. A few weeks later the Phillies gave him his outright release. I was in the outfield shagging balls before the game when Schoolie walked out to me wearing a coat and tie. "Kid, I've just been released," he said.

"I'm sorry to hear that, Schoolie," I said.

"Just one thing," he said. "You're tipping your curveball. I can tell when it's coming."

I always thought it was funny that Schoolie waited until he was released to tell me. When we were on the same pitching staff, my performing well could affect his role on the team, but once he was released, he felt compelled to walk out to the outfield in his street clothes to tell me that I was tipping my curveball.

Schoolboy was one of the great characters in baseball history. While in high school in Eldorado, Arkansas, he pitched and won an exhibition game against the Chicago White Sox, scattering six hits. A sportswriter reported that "[a] schoolboy beat the White Sox today," giving Schoolboy his nickname forever after.

Schoolie once told me about a deal he struck as a kid while pitching in a semipro league in Arkansas. He was to be paid by the strikeout, but the problem was he did not trust the team's owner, who kept the official score book. So every time he struck someone out, he placed a rock behind the mound. By the game's end, he counted 15 rocks, so he collected for 15 strikeouts.

Rowe broke into the big leagues with Detroit in 1933 and led them to the 1934 pennant with a 24–8 won-loss record. That year he won 16 games in a row, tying the American League record. He won Game 2 of the World Series against the St. Louis Cardinals of Gashouse Gang fame 3–2 in 12 innings. Afterward he was being interviewed on radio when all of a sudden he blurted out to his sweetheart, Edna Mary Skinner, "How'm I doin', Edna?" That quickly became a catchphrase for fans all over the country.

Cy Perkins was a coach for the Tigers when Schoolie had his great years there. Cy told me that he would almost have to beg Schoolie to go to the mound to start a game. Schoolie would get so nervous before he pitched that he would throw up in the clubhouse and even in the dugout. Tigers manager Mickey Cochrane stopped telling Rowe when he was pitching until right before the game; otherwise he would look awful when he got to the ballpark. Even as a grizzled veteran with the Phillies near the end of his career, when he came into the game in relief from the bullpen, he would first go down into the dugout and throw up.

Early in his career Schoolie was an overpowering pitcher, but a serious arm injury in 1937 forced him to become a knuckleball and slider pitcher. The Phillies bought him in 1943 after the Tigers and Brooklyn Dodgers gave up on him. Although his career was interrupted by service in World War II, he went on to win 52 games for the Phillies over five seasons. He was also a fine hitter and led the league in 1943 with 15 pinch-hits. For his career he batted .263 and slugged 18 home runs.

Shortly after Schoolboy's heartbreaking loss to the Pirates, Eddie Sawyer had a rare team meeting at the Commodore Hotel in New York City. He thought some of the guys were sluggish and not always hustling because they were eating too much. Some of the guys had gone to the beach and gotten sunburned on an off day, affecting their performance. Eddie read us the riot act, telling us we were headed for the second division again if we didn't mend our ways. He imposed a curfew, barred wives from traveling with us, and stopped us from just signing for our meals at the hotel. Instead, he allotted us $6 a day meal money and required us to pick it up every morning of a road trip from our trainer, Frank Wiechec. So from then on there we were, a bunch of grown men, lining up every morning at Wiechec's room to get that day's meal money.

Although some of the guys groused about the new rules, we did play better the rest of the year. On that trip we even swept the Dodgers in Brooklyn before heading home. Our first game of the homestand was against the Giants on August 19 and was designated Eddie Waitkus Night. Eddie had endured four operations in recovering from his gunshot wound and looked very frail and gaunt when he visited the clubhouse before the game. In the pregame ceremony, he received a new car, a television, golf clubs, luggage, and a bronze four-leaf-clover plaque. Dick Sisler presented Eddie with a bronzed first baseman's glove mounted on a stand with all our signatures etched upon it. It was a very moving ceremony.

I pitched the ballgame that night against the Giants and Dave Koslo, who had a lifetime 10–0 record against the Phillies. In another sign that we were beginning to turn things around, we won 7–1 to pull into a fourth-place tie with the Braves. It came after I had a couple of bad outings and was my first career win over the Giants, bringing my record to 11–12. The following day we trailed the Giants 3–0 in the seventh inning but exploded for seven runs against Monte Kennedy and Kirby Higbe. We went on to win 9–3 behind Del Ennis' 4-for-4 day at the plate to vault into third place.

The following day, August 21, brought a doubleheader against New York and one of the most bizarre games I would ever witness. The first game was relatively uneventful with Ken Heintzelman chucking a 4–0 shutout for his 15th win of the year and our 6th in a row. But in the ninth inning of the second game, all hell broke lose. We trailed 3–2 with one out in the top half of the inning, and the Giants had first baseman Joe Lafata at bat. Willard Marshall had opened the inning with a single, stole second, and gone to third on Stan Lopata's wild throw. On the next pitch Lafata lashed a low liner to center field. Richie Ashburn raced in, caught the ball a good eight inches off the ground, rolled over, and threw the ball to second. I was out in the bullpen and could see that Whitey had caught the ball almost knee high.

Unfortunately, second-base umpire George Barr, who must have been screened on the play, ruled that Richie had trapped the ball, allowing Marshall to score from third to make the score 4–2. Ashburn immediately raced in to protest, followed in quick succession by Del Ennis, Granny Hamner, Willie Jones, and Eddie Sawyer. In the meantime, the crowd of close to twenty thousand booed and hissed and began to throw fruit, bottles, and anything else they could find onto the field. In fact the fans in the upper deck were causing harm to the fans below because some of their tosses didn't reach the field.

When Eddie and my teammates finally stopped arguing and returned to their positions, a new barrage came from the stands, again with many bottles.

After some near misses, the players all retreated to their dugouts. Our public-address announcer, Dave Zinkoff, all the while kept announcing to the crowd that the umpires would declare a forfeit if the pelting continued, but he was largely drowned out by the boos.

The groundskeepers were finally able to clear the debris from the field and the umpires ordered play to resume. Schoolboy Rowe, who had pitched the entire game, threw a few warm-up pitches and was about to pitch to the Giants' next batter, Bill Rigney, when the fans near home plate began another barrage. Home-plate umpire Al Barlick was nailed in the back by a tomato, and third-base ump Lee Ballanfant was grazed by a bottle and hit by a pear. That did it. The three umpires met at home plate and declared a forfeit.

That bizarre ballgame was the last time drinks were ever sold in bottles in Shibe Park. Shortly thereafter other teams in the league followed, and soon bottles were banned in both leagues.

We bounced back, beating the Cincinnati Reds 4–3 in 13 innings on August 23. I relieved Jim Konstanty, who had pitched three and two-thirds scoreless innings, in the thirteenth and got my 12th win in the bottom of the inning on a game-winning sacrifice fly by Ashburn.

It was not unusual for me to relieve between starts that year. In fact, Eddie Sawyer used me in relief 12 times in 1949, even though I started on three or four days' rest for most of the season. It certainly did not bother me to pitch between starts. I normally threw in the bullpen on the second day after a start anyway. My attitude was always to just take the ball when Eddie handed it to me and do the best I could. I never gave a thought to the number of pitches or innings or games I threw. My motion was fluid and smooth and I could pitch a lot without it bothering my arm. I guess it went back to Cy Perkins' comment when I first came up—I could throw harder easier than just about anybody else.

I remember early in my career I pitched an extra-inning game in Pitts-burgh on a Friday night. The next afternoon I was out in right field during batting practice, shagging fly balls with Bill Nicholson. I happened to say, "You know, Nick, my shoulder is a little stiff."

Nick just started laughing. He said, "I can't get over you. You pitched a 10-inning game last night, and you're surprised you have a little stiffness in your shoulder the next afternoon."

At the end of August, we really got hot, winning 14 out of 18 to move well ahead of the fourth-place Boston Braves. One of the losses was a tough 1–0 game I threw against Warren Spahn and the Braves. I gave up a run in the first on two-out hits by Jim Russell and Marv Rickert, and that proved to be the ballgame. In the eighth we got two runners on from hits by Sisler and Ennis, but Tommy Holmes made two great running catches on long drives by Stan Lopata and Stan Hollmig to save Spahn's shutout and the game.

I had another unfortunate experience with George Barr shortly thereafter, in a mid-September game against the Cardinals in Sportsman's Park in St. Louis. It happened to be Dick Sisler Day. Before the game, Dick, who was from St. Louis, was given a new car, television, luggage, and other gifts. It was to be the only highlight of the day for the Phillies.

I started the game against the Cardinals' George Munger and took a 2–1 lead into the bottom of the third. Red Schoendienst led off the inning with a double and scored on Marty Marion's single to tie the score. Stan Musial singled off Hamner's glove at shortstop to put runners on first and second with Enos Slaughter coming to bat. With the count to 3–2, the Cards sent the runners and I threw a fastball right down the pipe. Enos never took the bat off his shoulder, and Andy Seminick threw to third to nail Marion coming from second.

So now I had gone from no outs and two on to two outs and a man on second. Except George Barr, behind the plate, called the pitch ball four. The pitch was right down the middle, and I could not believe he had called it a ball. Eddie Sawyer raced out to argue, and, for one of only a few times, got thrown out of a ballgame. Barr also ran Russ Meyer, who was hollering from the bench, and, the next inning, Cy Perkins when Cy wouldn't stop complaining about the call.

We had a lot to complain about. Instead of being almost out of the inning, I had the bases loaded and no one out. After the rhubarb finally subsided, Ron Northey stepped into the batter's box. He hit my first pitch onto the roof in the right-field pavilion for a grand-slam home run to make the score 6–2. It was downhill from there, and we eventually lost 15–3, our most lopsided defeat of the year.

Even with those two blowouts, we finished the season strong, clinching third place on September 26 by beating the Dodgers 5–3 in Ebbets Field in a come-from-behind victory. We were down 3–1 in the eighth but rallied for four runs off of Jack Banta thanks to a two-run single by Dick Sisler and a two-run homer by Andy Seminick. The victory assured us of the highest finish by a Phillies team since 1917, a span of 32 years. It also filled us with optimism for the 1950 season. We were finishing the season as the hottest team in the league and ahead of the Boston Braves, the 1948 pennant winners. All of us believed we had a real shot to win the pennant next year.

We ended the year with a two-game series against the Dodgers in Shibe Park, with the pennant hanging in the balance for Brooklyn. Coming in, the

One of my first organized sports teams—the East Pleasant Hill School basketball team of 1940. I'm in the back row holding the ball next to our teacher and coach, C. B. Lindsay. My younger brother, George, is at the far right of the first row.

Catching a pass for Lanphier High. I wasn't as good as Billy Stone.

With my mother, Sarah Roberts, and my high school baseball coach, Ted Boyle.
Mom didn't want coach Boyle to pitch me so much.

The 1947 Montpelier-Barre Twin City Trojans, Northern League Champions of 1947.
We were almost as good as the Whiz Kids. I'm in the second row, second from the
left. My longtime friend Pat Peppler is in the back row, second from the left. Ray
Fisher, our feisty coach, is also in the back row, second from the right.

I was honored with the trophy for outstanding college basketball player in the state of Michigan for 1946–1947 from *Detroit Free Press* sports editor Marshall Bann before a Michigan State baseball game in the spring of 1947. I also went to class.

Four kids and a veteran: Walt Dubiel, Eddie Oswald, me, Charlie Bicknell, and Richie Ashburn at my first spring training, 1948, in Clearwater, Florida.

With my dad,
Tom Roberts.
I didn't break
this rake.

With my guru,
Cy Perkins.
The man was
a marvel.

Curt Simmons gives Robbie Jr. and me a push during the off-season. We didn't mind the snow when we were young. The dog was a Simmons.

Springfield, Illinois—my hometown—held a "Robin Roberts Day" for me on July 14, 1950, in St. Louis. I'm shaking hands with Illinois Governor Adlai Stevenson. In the background, starting from the left, is a young Harry Caray, Eddie Sawyer, Harry Eielson (the mayor of Springfield), and my dad, Thomas Roberts. Congratulations to me, but I lost the game, 4–2.

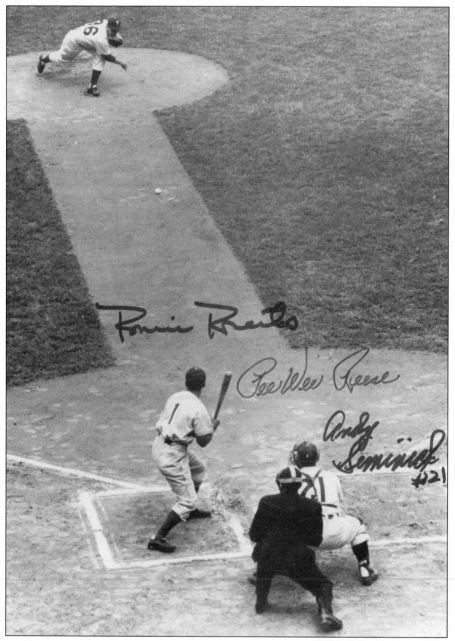

The first pitch of the 1950 season—I'm pitching to Pee Wee Reese of the Dodgers and Andy Seminick is catching. It was the start of a wonderful year. *Photo courtesy of AP/Wide World Photos.*

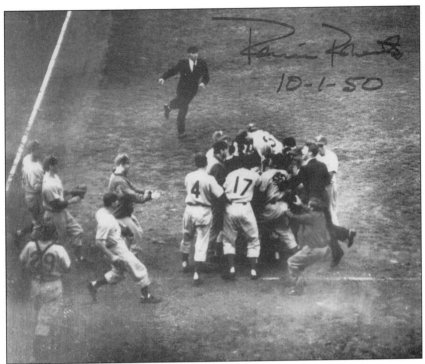

My teammates carrying me off the field after we defeated the Dodgers for the pennant on October 1, 1950. We weren't too excited. *Photo courtesy of AP/Wide World Photos.*

Two happy guys: Dick Sisler and Eddie Sawyer in the clubhouse in Brooklyn after Dick's home run propelled us to the pennant.

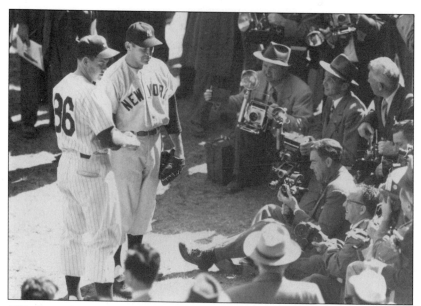

Allie Reynolds of the Yankees and I meet the press before squaring off in Game 2 of the 1950 World Series. We should have settled for a tie. *Photo courtesy of AP/Wide World Photos.*

Celebrating my 28th victory on September 28, 1952, with Bill Nicholson and Willie Jones after I beat the New York Giants at the Polo Grounds, 7–4. That was an amazing year for me. *Photo courtesy of AP/Wide World Photos.*

Dodgers were one game in front of the Cardinals, with two to play for each club. St. Louis had lost three in a row to lose their lead while Brooklyn had won two straight. As a result, the Dodgers needed just one win over us to clinch the pennant.

Eddie started Kenny Heintzelman but brought me in to relieve in the fifth inning with the bases loaded, already down 2–0. I managed to get out of the inning with only one run, a sacrifice fly to Whitey by Pee Wee Reese to score Roy Campanella. That was my only inning; Buddy Blattner pinch hit for me in the bottom of the inning as we came back to take the lead 4–3 on a triple by Dick Sisler and home runs by Del Ennis and Andy Seminick. Brooklyn tied the score in the eighth on a Carl Furillo single off Curt Simmons. Dodgers manager Burt Shotton was using his entire staff to try to win the pennant and brought in ace southpaw Preacher Roe to pitch the eighth inning. With one out rookie Eddie Sanicki worked a walk on a 3–2 count. Puddin' Head Jones then launched an 0–1 fastball into the left-field stands for a 6–4 lead that stood up after Jim Konstanty retired the Dodgers in order in the ninth.

The Cardinals lost to Chicago and Bob Chipman 3–1 for their fourth straight defeat, so Brooklyn could still win the pennant outright by beating us on Sunday, the last day of the season. The Sunday game turned out to be a classic. It would be the first of three consecutive years that we would play an extra-inning game on the last day of the season against the Dodgers with the pennant on the line for them. In 1950 the pennant would be on the line for the Phillies as well.

Sawyer started Russ Meyer, who had an eight-game winning streak, against Brooklyn's tall rookie right-hander, Don Newcombe, who had broken in with a 17–8 record. The Dodgers jumped in front again, chasing Monk with five runs in the third inning. After the first three runs scored, Eddie brought me in to try to stem the tide again. Men were on second and third, and Eddie had me intentionally walk Roy Campanella to load the bases and bring up Newcombe. Newk would end up being one of the best hitting pitchers in baseball history, and he slashed a single to left to score runs four and five before I could get us out of the inning.

The 5–0 lead seemed insurmountable, especially the way Newk was throwing. But, showing the resiliency that would characterize our pennant-winning year in 1950, we battled back to chase Don in the fourth, thanks largely to a three-run homer by Willie Jones. Stan Hollmig hit for me and doubled. By the end of the inning the lead was down to 5–4.

The Dodgers extended the lead to 7–4 in the fifth, but Bill Nicholson doubled off the scoreboard in our half to drive in Ennis and make the score

7–5. We tied it in the sixth after clutch hits by Johnny Blatnik, just up from Toronto, Hamner, Sisler, and Ennis.

Heintzelman pitched the late innings, and twice Gruber (our nickname for Kenny) worked out of tense jams to keep the score tied. Jack Banta held us in check, and the game moved into extra innings, with the pennant still on the line. Pee Wee Reese led off the tenth with a looping single in front of Del in left. Eddie Miksis sacrificed Pee Wee to second, bringing Duke Snider to the plate. Duke smashed a first-pitch single to center to score Reese with the go-ahead run. Snider took second on the throw home. We walked Jackie Robinson intentionally, but Luis Olmo sent a shot by third to score Duke. Eddie then brought Ken Trinkle in to get Carl Furillo to ground into an inning-ending double play, but the damage was done.

In the bottom half of the tenth, Mike Goliat gave us life with a sharp one-out single to left but Banta shut the door, striking out Sanicki and getting Richie to fly to Olmo in left to end the game and clinch the pennant. So we watched the Dodgers mob Banta, who had pitched four scoreless innings in relief. He had gone from goat to hero since one week before when he had blown a key game to us at Ebbets Field.

Watching the Dodgers celebrate their pennant in our ballpark was certainly bittersweet. But we felt good about our year. Our young team had improved and gained confidence as the season wore on. In fact, the last half of the season, we had the best record in the league. We had played the Dodgers very tough during the last weeks of the season when they were in a heated pennant race. We were coming on strong. In the clubhouse after that last loss to Brooklyn, Eddie Sawyer told us, "Come back next year ready to win. We are going to win it all next year."

For my second year in the big leagues, I ended with a 15–15 record and a 3.69 earned run average in 227 innings. I started 31 games, completed 11, and relieved in an additional 12 games for a total of 43 appearances. I thought that I could perform better, and I was frustrated that I had yet to defeat the powerful Brooklyn Dodgers, while losing five to them. So going into the 1950 season, I felt like I still had a lot to prove.

CHAPTER 5

The Whiz Kids Take the Pennant

The off-season was an eventful one. On December 26, 1949, Mary and I were married in her hometown of McFarland, Wisconsin. As I mentioned, we are still happily married 53 years later. Mary finished the semester in her teaching position, so we rented a little house in Springfield until the middle of January. After she finished the semester, we spent some time with her family in McFarland. It was great to be married, but I was eager for spring training to start, not only because the Phillies were now a first-division club but also because I had not pitched particularly well the last half of the previous season. At one point I had been 8–3, and at the All-Star break I was 9–6 before slumping to that final 15–15 record. Eddie had started me in only one game down the stretch after that bizarre mid-September game in St. Louis when Ron Northey hit the grand slam after our rhubarb with George Barr. That start was on September 21 against the Cubs and had not gone well. I had taken a 5–2 lead into the sixth but ended up losing 9–6.

Thereafter we had a number of days off. As a result, Eddie started Ken Heintzelman and Russ Meyer, who were both pitching very well, almost exclusively while using me in relief. But for the second season in a row the season had ended on a down note for me personally, and I was chomping at the bit to get started in 1950.

Even so, when the Phillies reported to Clearwater on February 28, Mary and I were still in McFarland. We stayed in the snow because I was unhappy with the contract Bob Carpenter had offered me. I had made $9,000 in 1949 and wanted $20,000 for 1950 because I believed that I had established myself as a big-league starting pitcher. Bob had offered me $18,500, but I didn't think it was enough.

About a week into spring training I traveled down to Clearwater to meet with Bob face-to-face. Bob finally offered me an attendance clause in addition to my base salary of $18,500, so I agreed to sign on March 7. Under our agreement I was to be paid for each fan we drew over 800,000 that season. We had drawn just under 820,000 in 1949, so it seemed like a reasonable compromise. Of course, it turned out great for me because we won the pennant and drew more than 1.2 million fans in 1950. I ended up making $22,500, more than I was asking for in spring training.

That spring Eddie Sawyer continued the tightening of the reins he began the previous August, wanting spring training to be without distractions. He forbade us from bringing wives, families, and even automobiles to camp, requiring us to live at the team hotel and walk back and forth to practice. Eddie was not very popular with the Phillies' wives, who were already unhappy about his banning them from road trips the year before. Now he was depriving them of their annual trek to Florida.

I had brought Mary with me when I came down to negotiate my contract with Bob Carpenter, only to learn that she could not stay with me in the team hotel. Mary stayed in a rooming house close by for a couple of weeks before returning to Wisconsin for the rest of spring training.

Although we had high expectations, spring training got off to a rocky start. A couple of days before I signed, highly touted rookie Steve Ridzik fractured his kneecap in an intrasquad game in a freak accident. Then we lost four of our first five spring games, including a 23–6 clobbering by the World Champion New York Yankees on March 15. Soon after, we blew ninth-inning leads on successive days to the Tigers and Red Sox.

We soon turned it around, however. As camp wore on it became clear we could hit. We won five of our last six games in Florida by scores of 13–3, 13–4, 13–8, 21–6, 10–2, and 10–3 and were hitting .318 as a team when we entrained for our two-week trip north (and west) at the end of spring training.

That spring sportswriters first began referring to us as the "Whiz Kids." Bob Carpenter had abandoned "Blue Jays" as an official team nickname over the winter. In 1943 when the Carpenters bought the team, they had sponsored a contest with the fans to rename the team. Blue Jays was the winner, but it never really caught on. In contrast, the Whiz Kids name quickly took hold because of our youth, our fast finish in 1949, and our impressive showing in the spring.

Harry Grayson, sports editor of the Newspaper Enterprise Association Service (NEA), was generally thought to have come up with the name. In covering the major league camps that spring, he had used Clearwater as his headquarters. We had apparently impressed him because he was probably the only national writer to pick us to win the pennant.

No one seemed to know whether Grayson took the name from the University of Illinois basketball team of the early forties, who were known as the

Whiz Kids because of their youth, or, as some have suggested, as a takeoff on *The Quiz Kids*, a popular radio show from the late thirties and forties that featured precocious children showing their knowledge on a variety of topics.

Whatever the origins, the 1950 Phillies have for ever after been known as the Whiz Kids, one of baseball's most enduring nicknames. It caught on very quickly so that during that summer Babe Alexander, our public relations man, arranged for the team to present Mr. Grayson with a lighter inscribed "In appreciation to Harry Grayson, the man who named us the Whiz Kids."

We really racked up the miles after we broke camp in Clearwater, playing exhibition games in Birmingham, New Orleans, Shreveport, Dallas, Ft. Worth, Little Rock, Memphis, and Louisville before heading to Philadelphia for our traditional three-game preseason city series against the Athletics. In Louisville I was pitching batting practice to my old roomie Johnny Blatnik when Eddie Sawyer hollered, "That's enough, Robin."

I said, "Just one more, Skipper," and threw a pitch that Blatnik smashed back off my calf. It was painful, but I ended up with only a bad bruise and it did not keep me from opening the season against Brooklyn a few days later. Needless to say, Eddie had a few choice words to say about "just one more."

We were brimming with optimism when we finally opened the season against Brooklyn in Shibe Park on April 18. We had followed up our fast finish in '49 with a .335 team batting average that spring. We even broke out new red pinstripe uniforms, designed by none other than Eddie Sawyer and modeled in part after the famous Yankees pinstripes. They were quite similar to the uniforms the Phillies have worn since the early nineties.

That opener was particularly significant for me not only because Sawyer named me to start my first Opening Day game but also because it was against the Dodgers. We knew we would have to beat Brooklyn, the defending champions, to win the pennant, and in my first year and a half I had yet to beat them, going 0–5. It bothered me. In fact, Bob Carpenter had brought my failure to beat the Dodgers up in our contract negotiations at the start of spring training. I had to admit that he was right.

The Dodgers had a great hitting lineup, but the only left-handed hitters were Duke Snider and sometimes George Shuba or Gene Hermanski, so most teams threw a lot of right-handers at them. I know that over the years I seldom missed Brooklyn when we played them and that I had a real rivalry with them. It seemed like so many of our games had something riding on them because the Dodgers were always in a pennant race. It was a great challenge to try to beat such an outstanding team, and over the years I relished the competition with them.

My opponent on Opening Day in 1950 was Don Newcombe, who had become the Dodgers' ace in just one year in the big leagues. A crowd of just under thirty thousand, the largest Opening Day gathering in team history, showed up on a cool, clear day. It was the kind of weather I liked because the ball always felt smaller in my hand on a cool day, which gave me a little extra pop on my fastball.

I retired the Dodgers in order in the first, and it took us only two pitches to score in the bottom half. Richie Ashburn lined Newk's first pitch to left for a single, and Granny Hamner, a notorious first-ball hitter, rifled the next offering past Duke Snider into deep right center, scoring Whitey. One batter later, Del Ennis drove in Granny with a shot off the top of the left-field wall. By the fourth inning we led 8–0 and I cruised to a 9–1 victory. We clobbered five Dodgers pitchers for 16 hits, including 4 by Mike Goliat and 3 each by Hamner and Eddie Waitkus.

When Jackie Robinson came up for the first time in the top of the second, we already led 5–0. Andy Seminick was catching and later told me that Jackie asked him, "What do you guys think you're going to do, win the pennant?"

Andy said, "Yessir, we're going to do it this year. You bet."

Mike Goliat had been my teammate at Wilmington, playing mostly first base, but he had converted to second in the spring and become our starting second baseman. In Mike's brief major league career, it was just uncanny how he could hit Newcombe. One year later, on Opening Day in 1951, Mike tagged Newk for a home run. When Mike came into the dugout after circling the bases, he asked facetiously, "What is the home-run record in this league anyway?" Unfortunately, by June that year Mike was back in the minor leagues, never to return to the majors.

In spite of our great Opening Day in '50, we struggled out of the gate and after about a week had a 2–5 won-loss record. Then I beat Brooklyn again 9–2, this time in Ebbets Field, behind Dick Sisler's four hits and Willie Jones' four RBIs. The next day at home, Curt Simmons pitched a masterful three-hitter to overpower his personal nemesis, the Boston Braves, by a 6–1 score. Curt had struggled for two years since signing his big bonus, but it now looked like he had arrived as a bona fide big-league starting pitcher.

We really got hot on our first western road trip in May, winning 11 of 14. We began the trip in sixth place and returned in first, a game in front of Brooklyn and St. Louis. Curt overpowered the Giants 7–1 on three hits in our first game at home to extend our winning streak to six games. After a loss and a suspended Sunday game, we prepared to open a three-game series against the Cincinnati Reds. I was to pitch the opener against Reds ace Ewell Blackwell.

In those days, it was common for teams to pitch their aces against each other in the first game of a series, although I am not sure I qualified just yet. Blackwell had dominated in 1947, leading the league with 22 wins (including 16 in a row) and 193 strikeouts and compiling the second-best earned run average (2.47). Known as "the Whip," he was 6'6" and, with a right-handed sidearm delivery, absolute murder on right-handed hitters. Although he had suffered from a sore arm in 1948 and 1949, he was healthy in 1950 and looked ready to dominate again.

The game turned into a classic pitching duel. We scratched out a run in the first inning on two infield hits, a walk, and a double play. That turned out to be the only score of the ballgame. Blackwell allowed only one more hit, but in the meantime I was shutting out the Reds on two hits in what was probably my best major league game to then.

For some reason, that game seemed pivotal to me. I had a feeling that we were a team to be reckoned with and had a real shot at the pennant. Defeating one of the top pitchers in the league 1–0 demonstrated for me at least that the Whiz Kids were for real.

We won 6 of 10 on that homestand and embarked on an 18-game road trip that was sure to be a test of our staying power. I opened the trip against the Giants in the Polo Grounds, and it was to be another nail-biter. We were tied 2–2 in the eighth when Jimmy Bloodworth, a veteran infielder we had just acquired from Cincinnati, hit a sacrifice fly to drive in Dick Sisler with the go-ahead run. I survived a jam in the bottom of the ninth to record my sixth win and, in the process, match my season high of 11 strikeouts.

The next afternoon we played the Giants again and I was sitting in the dugout, relaxing, enjoying the bright Saturday afternoon sunlight, and watching the game. Curt Simmons was pitching, and Andy Seminick, catching, was fussing about ball and strike calls all afternoon with home-plate umpire Artie Gore. After one inning, Andy came off the field and sat by me, still shouting at Artie. Artie walked over to the dugout and yelled, "Roberts, you're out of here." I had not said a word all day.

Artie really startled me, and I looked over to Eddie Sawyer who said, "Go ahead, Robin."

I trudged out to the visiting clubhouse, which in the Polo Grounds was located in dead center field, almost 500 feet from home plate. When I passed Artie, he said, "I had to throw somebody out, and I knew they weren't going to use you."

It was the first time I had ever been thrown out of a ballgame. While making that long walk to the clubhouse, I thought about my mother reading that I had been thrown out of a game and probably thinking that I had done something really wrong.

It was lucky for us that Artie let Andy stay in the game, because he laced three hits, including a grand-slam home run off of Sheldon Jones, to give us an 8–5 victory and a tie for the league lead with the Dodgers.

By the beginning of June we were in the thick of a five-team pennant race, although we had suffered a lot of rainouts, which would have to be made up later in the season. Ace reliever Jim Konstanty and our kid pitchers, Curt Simmons, Bob Miller, and I, along with Ken Johnson, had accounted for 22 of our 23 victories.

After dipping to 4½ games off the pace in mid-June, we quickly climbed back into the fray, beating Brooklyn three out of four in Ebbets Field. I was matched against Don Newcombe again in the second game of the series. Billy Cox led off the game with a home run, but that was all the Dodgers got. Still down 1–0 in the eighth, Richie Ashburn tied the game with a home run over the screen in right after Dick Whitman had pinch hit for me. In the ninth, we had two on and two out, and Sawyer sent Bill Nicholson up to pinch hit. The Dodgers immediately had a big conference on the mound, presumably to discuss how to pitch to Nick. Nick then smashed Newcombe's first pitch high over the scoreboard in right field for a three-run homer and a 4–1 lead. I've always wondered what was said during that meeting on the mound.

Jim Konstanty set the Dodgers down in the ninth to secure the win. It was the second time that week that Nick had beaten Brooklyn with a home run, so the Dodgers still hadn't figured out how to pitch to him.

The Dodgers beat us the next day 7–3, and so we broke for the All-Star Game on July 11 with a one-game lead and a 44–29 record. I was 10–3 at the break and was thrilled when I was selected for the National League All-Star team along with teammates Willie Jones, Dick Sisler, and Jim Konstanty. Puddin' Head had slugged 17 homers and was hitting .322, Dick was at .325, and Jim had established himself as the top reliever in the league with 36 appearances. Several more of the Whiz Kids deserved selection as well. Rookie Bob Miller was a perfect 8–0, Curt was 10–5 and often overpowering, and Del Ennis and Andy Seminick were having superb years.

Although I was excited to make the All-Star team, I was so focused on the season and the pennant race that I had not really given it much thought. But the All-Star Game experience was special and, as my career wore on, something I always looked forward to and enjoyed immensely.

The 1950 game was in Chicago's Comiskey Park, and Mary was able to come with me. My folks came up from Springfield, and so it was a special treat when manager Burt Shotton named me to be the starting pitcher, a first for the Phillies. It was the first of five All-Star Games I was lucky enough to start for the National League.

The game turned out to be a classic. In the top of the first inning Ted Williams crashed into the left-field wall to make a great catch on a long drive by Ralph Kiner. Ted continued to play until the ninth inning, although he had fractured his elbow on the play and would be lost to the Red Sox for the rest of the year.

Ted batted against me in the bottom of the first, and we employed the Boudreau shift against him, with the shortstop playing on the first-base side of second and the second baseman swung deep into the hole between first and second. Williams smashed a shot past Stan Musial that Jackie Robinson caught chest high in his exaggerated position at second. It is unbelievable that Ted could hit a ball that hard with a broken elbow, but he did.

The National League scored two runs off of American League starter Vic Raschi in the top of the second due largely to Enos Slaughter's triple off the left-center-field wall, and I gave one back in the bottom of the third off George Kell's sacrifice fly. So I left after my allotted three innings leading 2–1. After going into the clubhouse to change shirts, I returned to the dugout to watch and saw a classic ballgame. The American League came back to score two runs off Don Newcombe in the fifth inning, with a Ted Williams line single in the mix, to take the lead 3–2. There the game remained into the ninth inning, and it looked as though the National League would lose its fifth consecutive game to the American League. Ralph Kiner came through, however, and smashed the second pitch of the inning off Art Houtteman into the left-field stands for a game-tying home run.

Neither team could score until the top of the fourteenth inning when Red Schoendienst, in his first at-bat in the game, smacked a 2–2 pitch off of Ted Gray into the upper deck in left field to win the game.

Jim Konstanty, Larry Jansen, and Ewell Blackwell pitched the final nine innings of the game and held the vaunted American League sluggers to only two singles. Willie Jones played all 14 innings at third base and came to bat seven times, still an All-Star record. Dick Sisler appeared as a pinch-hitter for Newcombe in the sixth and singled off Bob Lemon, so all four Phillies contributed to the win.

Willie Jones, or Puddin' Head as we called him, is largely forgotten now, but he was one of the finest fielding third basemen of his day. He could really pick it, and I would rate him behind only Brooks Robinson and Scott Rolen as the finest third baseman I have ever seen. Eddie Sawyer used to say that the top attraction of our rivalry with Brooklyn, outside of my frequent matchups with Don Newcombe on the mound, was watching Willie Jones and Billy Cox of the Dodgers play third base.

Puddin' Head was from South Carolina and could charm a bulldog off a meat wagon, as Richie Ashburn used to say. He played a very shallow third base and had great hands and quick reflexes. He was plagued throughout his career, however, by very bad feet. Between games of a doubleheader in the heat of summer, Unk Russell, our clubhouse man, would get a bucket of ice water, and Willie would soak his feet, socks and all. When asked if his feet bothered him, Willie said, "They only hurt when they touch the ground."

Even with his chronically painful feet, Willie held down the hot corner for the Phillies for more than a decade. He led the league's third sackers in fielding five times (four consecutively) and in putouts seven times. He played every game in 1950 and slugged 25 homers, drove in 88 runs, and scored 100.

A couple of days after the All-Star break, I was honored by my hometown of Springfield, Illinois, before a night game against the Cardinals in Sportsman's Park. I was also pitching that night against southpaw Harry Brecheen, one of the top pitchers in the league. The good citizens of Springfield presented me with a savings bond and a diamond wristwatch before the game. Adlai Stevenson, the governor of Illinois, was on hand, as was Harry Eielson, the mayor of Springfield; my parents; and Ted Boyle, my high school coach. A trim young Harry Caray served as master of ceremonies.

The game was not nearly as much fun. With the score 2–2 in the bottom of the sixth, the Cards' Bill Howerton led off with a home run off the bleacher screen in right center. Although we had runners in scoring position in five different innings, we could not score, and that was the ballgame.

That game catapulted us into a five-game losing streak. At that point, Eddie Sawyer shook up our batting order, moving Eddie Waitkus into the leadoff spot, moving Whitey to second, and dropping Granny Hamner to sixth. He also gave another rookie pitcher, Emory "Bubba" Church, a start, and Bubba came through with flying colors, beating the Cubs 8–3 in the second game of a doubleheader.

Because of rainouts, we played another doubleheader the following day in Pittsburgh. The opener turned out to be a memorable extra-inning duel between Curt and Bill Werle that was deadlocked 1–1 in the top of the eleventh. With one out, Bill Nicholson lifted a high pop-up right in front of the plate for what looked like out number two. But Pirates catcher Clyde McCullough and third baseman Danny O'Connell collided, causing the ball to ricochet off Clyde's shin guard crazily toward the stands behind home plate. There was a lot of room behind the plate at Forbes Field, and by the time the Pirates could retrieve the ball Nick, running all the way, was on third with what must be the shortest triple of all time. Granny Hamner then smashed Werle's second pitch over the left-field screen to put us up 3–1. Konstanty saved Curt's 12th win in the bottom half, retiring three straight hitters with the tying run on base.

We finally returned home on July 25 after our longest road trip of the season, just two percentage points behind the Cardinals. We had survived the five-game losing streak and finished the trip with a 9–10 record. We opened our 16-game homestand with a doubleheader against the Cubs before thirty-three thousand people, our largest crowd of the season. Bubba Church threw a masterful three-hit shutout in the first game to win 7–0 and run his record to 4–0. He needed only 88 pitches to dispatch the Cubs.

I pitched the nightcap against Cubs ace Bob Rush, and we were scoreless going into the bottom of the ninth inning. Eddie let me hit in the bottom of the ninth with one out, and I managed to coax a walk, although Cubs manager Frankie Frisch disagreed so vehemently that he was ejected from the game. Putsy Caballero ran for me, went to second on a fielder's choice on a hit-and-run and scored the game-winner on a clutch single to center by Richie Ashburn.

After that second game Bubba came up to me in the clubhouse and said, "I can't believe you did that to me."

"What do you mean, Bubba?" I said.

He said, "I pitch a three-hit shutout and I can already see the headlines tomorrow, and then you come along and pitch a shutout and win 1–0 in the second game. I don't think that's fair." Of course, Bubba was kidding. At least I think he was.

That double shutout marked two years to the day since Eddie Sawyer had taken over as manager of the Phillies and vaulted us into first place, a half game ahead of St. Louis. We kept winning and stretched our lead to 2½ games going into a July 30 doubleheader with the Pirates. I coasted to a 10–0 win in the opener, my third shutout in a row. By the time I completed the game I had rolled up 28 consecutive scoreless innings. In the second game Del Ennis clubbed a grand-slam homer off Murry Dickson in the eighth inning to turn a 2–0 deficit into a 4–2 victory.

It was Del's second grand slammer of the week and concluded an incredible month in which he drove in 41 runs. He was on his way to leading the league in RBIs with 126, with 31 home runs and a fourth-place .311 batting average.

Del was from suburban Olney and would become one of the Phillies' all-time greatest sluggers. From 1949 through 1955 he drove in 100 or more runs all but one season. That year was 1951, when he was hampered by a back injury and slumped to 15 homers and 73 RBIs.

Ironically, given that he was a hometown boy and our leading slugger, Del was probably booed more in Philadelphia than was any other player in team history. It largely started during his off year in 1951 but would continue for many years. Del attributed it to South Philly fans taking shots at a North Philly kid. Through it all he remained stoic and often silenced them with dramatic, game-winning home runs. One day when the fans were on Del, Cy Perkins told me, with his typical wisdom, "You know, the only time they will appreciate him is when he is gone."

Del was very quiet and low-key but a professional ballplayer who came to the park every day ready to play. He often played hurt and never complained about anything. He was a good outfielder who played with a rather effortless style, in stark contrast to Ashburn's hell-bent-for-leather approach next door in center. To some it might have seemed that Del was a little lackadaisical, and when he did occasionally boot one, the fans would be all over him. But I never saw Del fail to run hard on a ground ball, even one back to the pitcher. I once mentioned to Del that I had never seen him coast running to first base, and he told me, "It's only 90 feet."

Over the years Del made two of the greatest outfield catches that I have ever seen. In that 1950 season, Jackie Robinson of the Dodgers smashed a shot into the right-center-field gap. Del raced over, but when he got to the ball he was off stride. So he simply reached up and caught the ball barehanded, easy as could be, and tossed the ball back in like it was a routine catch. Jackie could not believe it and ran right past first base into right field and yelled at Del, "How did you ever catch that ball?"

In 1952 in the Polo Grounds he made an even better catch against Willie Mays with the score tied in the bottom of the tenth to save the game. Mays clubbed a ball high and deep to left center that looked like it would land close to the 455-foot sign for a conceivable inside-the-park home run for the speedy Mays. Del took off with the crack off the bat and was about to reach for the ball when he tripped over our bullpen mound, which in the Polo Grounds was on the field of play. As he was going down, he reached up at the last possible moment and snared the ball barehanded.

Del treated his bats in a unique way, putting them in a barrel of linseed oil at a local gas station all winter. Then in spring training he would dry them by putting them in the same dryer that was used for the uniforms. He claimed that made the bats harder, and maybe he was right. He used the same bat for the entire 1950 season.

Although Del never said two words to anybody, he was a real practical joker, usually with coaches Benny Bengough and Cy Perkins the targets. He would put blue powder in their shoes or plant exploding cigars in Bengough's locker. Benny's number was 11, so sometimes Del would put two strips of adhesive tape over his number so that when he went out to coach it would look like he did not have a number.

After the 1956 season the Phillies traded Del to the Cardinals for Rip Repulski and Bobby Morgan. In 1957 Del had his last strong season, batting .286 with 24 home runs and 105 RBIs for the Cards. I remember one of those home runs quite well. I was pitching against the Cardinals in Connie Mack Stadium on June 12. I was down 1–0 in the sixth inning when Del came up with two on and two out. I got behind him 3–0, and he nailed a fastball into the seats to put us behind 4–0. We couldn't score against Larry Jackson, so that is how the game ended. Afterward, a sportswriter asked Del what kind of pitch he hit. He said, "I hit a knuckleball," and one of the newspapers actually printed it. It seems funnier now than it was then.

Thanks to Del's torrid July with that bat, we entered the dog days of August with a 58–39 record, three games in front of the second-place Boston Braves. We had won 13 of 18 since Eddie Sawyer shuffled the batting order.

On August 4 against the Cardinals I extended my scoreless string to 32⅔ innings, pitching shutout ball into the sixth inning until Enos Slaughter dispatched one of my infrequent curveballs over the right-field fence with Stan Musial on base to tie the score 2–2. Granny Hamner bailed me out with a two-run triple in the ninth off Howie Pollet to secure my 14th win of the year. That game was near the end of a stretch in which we won 11 of 13 and increased our lead to four games over the Braves.

By the opening of a home series against the New York Giants on August 10 we had extended our lead to six games. We had an intense rivalry with the Giants, who were managed by Leo Durocher. Earlier in the year, Eddie Sawyer had accused the Giants pitchers of intentionally throwing at our hitters, and Durocher had publicly complained about the aggressive way that Andy Seminick blocked the plate. Andy tended to wear the Giants out with his hitting, and Leo was always looking for ways to aggravate him.

We split the first two games of the series, with the Giants winning the second game 3–1 behind Sal Maglie. In that game Giants second baseman Eddie Stanky, known as "the Brat," moved over behind second base while Andy was batting and began doing jumping jacks directly in his line of vision.

Andy and Eddie Sawyer complained to umpire Al Barlick, but Al said Stanky was not breaking any rule. In addition, Maglie, who had a long history of throwing at Andy, plunked him in the elbow in the eighth inning.

I started the game the following day and, although I didn't realize it, mild-mannered Andy was really fuming over his treatment the day before. Before the game Durocher agreed to instruct Stanky to cease and desist from his jumping jacks until a ruling from league president Ford Frick could be obtained. Andy drew a walk in his first at-bat in the bottom of the second, putting runners on first and second with two outs. Giants pitcher Sheldon Jones then uncorked a beanball at Mike Goliat, our next hitter. Mike got up from the dirt, took a step toward Jones, and then thought better of it. The runners advanced to second and third on the wild pitch. Mike then laced the next pitch into left, scoring both runners.

When the play was over, Giants third baseman Hank Thompson was lying on the ground and no one knew what had happened. Andy told us that he gave him a forearm shiver to the jaw as he went by. Thompson was so woozy that he had to leave the game.

Andy next batted in the fourth inning with two outs, this time against Jack Kramer who had relieved Jones. Stanky, apparently unhappy over the havoc Andy had wreaked in the second inning, moved over behind second base behind Kramer and in Andy's sight line and, on the second pitch, wildly waved his arms over his head. Umpire Lon Warneke promptly ejected Stanky "for making a farce of the game," causing Durocher to rush out of the dugout to argue and eventually protest the game.

Bill Rigney replaced Stanky at second, and Andy again worked a walk. Mike Goliat then grounded to Alvin Dark at shortstop. Alvin tossed to Rigney covering second for the force-out to end the inning. Andy barreled into the base and bumped Rigney, who proceeded to jump on top of Andy. That was a big mistake on his part. Andy, on the bottom, grabbed Bill by his shirt with his left hand and just started popping him with his right. Rigney was still on top and bouncing up like a rag doll every time Andy would hit him.

Naturally both benches emptied. I, along with Alvin Dark, Mike Goliat, Benny Bengough, Lon Warneke, and others, tried to save Rigney. Tempers were hot on both sides, and several other skirmishes broke out. Jimmy Blood-worth got into it with Jim Hearn and Rudy Rufer and then took a swing at Durocher. The Giants' Tookie Gilbert went after Andy, only to be intercepted by Dusty Cooke, who was a big man. Bubba Church grabbed Durocher around the waist and carried him into the outfield, out of harm's way. Bubba did Leo a favor; he wasn't exactly the most popular guy among the Phillies. Finally, after about 10 minutes, the police came on to the field to help restore order. Not surprisingly, Andy and Bill Rigney were ejected.

The game resumed and went into extra innings, although I was taken out in the seventh for a pinch-hitter. Konstanty relieved me and, as he did all year, held the Giants in check until we could win it in the eleventh on Stan Lopata's booming triple and Eddie Waitkus' sacrifice fly. This was one time when Durocher's strategy of stirring the game up when he was behind backfired.

That was not the only fight we had that year, but it was certainly the longest. About a month earlier Willie Jones had slid hard into the Reds' Connie Ryan trying to break up a double play and spiked him. Connie took a swing at Puddin' Head, and the two of them wrestled on the ground, emptying both benches. No more fights broke out, although the Reds were plenty frustrated, having lost 12 of 14 to us at that point.

I, like most ballplayers, was never too eager to get into fights on a ballfield. I was always afraid that I would break my hand. Stan Musial expressed my sentiments a few years later when we got into a donnybrook with the Cardinals. Both teams raced out onto the field and Stan grabbed my arm and said, "Robin, we're making too much money to get hurt in something like this." My sentiments exactly. I wanted to pitch, not fight, in the summer.

Andy Seminick was a quiet, docile guy as well. Because he was 30 years old and had been with the Phillies since 1943, some sportswriters called him "Grandpa Whiz." But he was tough as nails and a block of granite behind the plate. He led by example and no one on the club was more respected. He got into his share of scraps, mostly because of the way he blocked the plate. You had to go through him to score, and he was rock solid back there.

Andy had a memorable encounter with Sal Maglie in 1950. We were well ahead of the Giants when Durocher brought Sal in to relieve. It was the first time I had seen Maglie pitch since he was just returning to the big leagues after his suspension for jumping to the Mexican League in 1946. He was an older-looking guy who always looked like he needed a shave, and I thought that was why they called him "the Barber." I was wrong. It was because he gave close shaves to the batters.

When Andy came up, Maglie got ahead of him in the count and then knocked him down with a high inside fastball. On the next pitch, Andy pushed a bunt down the first-base line, hoping to run Sal over when he came over to field the ball or cover first base. Maglie never moved off the mound, and Andy ran to first with a bunt single. The next day Maglie was quoted in the paper as saying, "I get paid to pitch, not to fight."

As luck would have it, we headed into the Polo Grounds just about a week after our ruckus with the Giants in Shibe Park to begin an important 17-game road trip. We were riding pretty high, having won 18 of our previous 24 games to forge a season-high seven-game lead. Curt and I had ended our long home-stand successfully, beating the Braves 9–1 and 5–1, respectively. Mine was an efficient three-hitter. I threw only 79 pitches, 54 of them strikes, and completed the game in one hour and 45 minutes.

Our opener against the Giants drew more than twenty-six thousand fans bent on booing Andy out of the park. The Giants themselves showed some good humor, waving white handkerchiefs at Andy the first time he came to bat in the second inning. That seemed to incite the fans even more, but Andy quieted them the best way he possibly could. He walloped Jim Hearn's first pitch into the upper deck in left field for a home run. By the end of the game, the fans were actually cheering Andy, appreciative of his hard play. Of course, the fact that the Giants won the game 7–4 may have helped them feel more charitable.

We continued to play well on the road, winning 11 of 14. We also had our first plane ride near the end of the trip, and it was a memorable one. By 1950 baseball teams were starting to fly sometimes on long hauls, and Bob Carpenter decided to charter a TWA Lockheed Constellation from St. Louis to Boston at the end of the trip, saving us about a 24-hour train ride. It was the first team flight in club history and the first airplane flight for some of my teammates. It was a rough indoctrination. First, our 8:00 A.M. departure was delayed about an hour and a half by mechanical problems. Then, once we got off the ground, we flew right into the middle of a severe thunder-storm. It jostled us all over the sky. Finally, Boston was rainy and fogged in, so the landing was dicey, or so it seemed to us. We actually cheered the pilot when we finally touched down, we were so happy to be back on Mother Earth. Afterward Eddie Sawyer told us that Howard Hughes, who then owned TWA, called him to check on the team right after he got to his hotel room.

We had our second team plane ride home from Boston at the end of the trip, flying a DC-6 American Airlines charter into Philadelphia. We were coming home with a 7-game lead over Brooklyn and 10½ games ahead of Boston, but we had no idea about the heroes' welcome waiting for us. About thirty thousand fans jammed the Philadelphia airport and the streets leading to it to cheer for us. Bands played and the people cheered us into our cars. Traffic was so jammed that it took those living in Center City two and a half hours to get home, an hour longer than the flight from Boston.

September proved to be a month filled with adversity for the Whiz Kids. We began the month by losing five straight at home to the Giants and Dodgers, including consecutive doubleheaders. And we lost old pro Bill Nicholson for the season. Nick had not looked well in recent weeks and appeared to be losing weight. He had uncharacteristically dropped a fly ball against the Giants on Labor Day and seemed to be swinging a tired bat.

A couple of days later, we were standing together in the outfield during batting practice and I said, "Bill, you don't look good."

Nick said, "I don't feel too good. I've lost about 15 pounds."

I said, "You need to check with the trainer to see what is wrong." Nick did talk to Frank Wiechec and ended up in the hospital that day for tests. The doctors soon found that Nick was suffering from diabetes, which required immediate treatment and ended his baseball for the year. We would really miss his clubhouse presence, not to mention his clutch hitting off the bench.

We also lost Curt Simmons for the season on September 9 when his National Guard unit was activated due to the Korean conflict. He had won 17 games with only eight losses and had been one of the most dominant pitchers in the league. It would be a long September without him.

I won a taut pitchers' duel on September 12 in the first game of a doubleheader against Max Lanier and the Cardinals in Shibe Park. I escaped a no-out jam in the first inning and prevailed 1–0 in an hour and 41 minutes due to Andy Seminick's 22nd home run of the year in the fifth. It was Grandpa Whiz's 30th birthday and my 19th victory of the year. At the time, I had no idea how tough it would be to get my 20th win.

Even with that win, our string of bad luck would continue. Almost unbelievably, we lost two more starting pitchers on consecutive days shortly thereafter, on September 15 and 16. Bubba Church started the first game of a doubleheader against the Cincinnati Reds on the 15th and was felled in the third inning by a vicious line drive off the bat of Reds slugger Ted Kluszewski. The ball hit Bubba squarely below the right eye, causing an ugly gash and sending Bubba down to his knees while the ball caromed all the way into right field. The gash below Bubba's eye was so gruesome looking that many observers actually thought his eyeball was hanging out.

Bubba was rushed to the hospital where, fortunately, he learned that nothing was broken and that his eye had no permanent damage. His first visitor in the hospital was Bill Nicholson, who was still there being treated for his diabetes and had been listening to the game on the radio. Bubba would be out for nine days and would be unable to pitch effectively for the rest of the season.

We ended up winning the game 2–1 behind six and two-thirds innings of relief from Kenny Heintzelman and Andy Seminick's 23rd home run in the fourth inning. I started the nightcap and, after two scoreless innings, faced Virgil Stallcup, the Reds' shortstop, to lead off the third. He hit my first pitch on a line right back at me. I was luckier than Bubba that night as I was able to catch the ball.

The game turned out to be a classic. I fell behind 5–0 after five innings, but we battled back in the eighth and ninth innings to tie the score. Rookie Jack Brittin pitched a scoreless eighth for us after I was taken out for a pinch-hitter, and then Sawyer brought in Jim Konstanty to pitch the ninth. Nine innings later Jim was still in there, matching goose eggs with the Reds' Herm Wehmeier. By the eighteenth inning it was after midnight and Jim finally tired, giving up two runs to put us behind 7–5. But the never-say-die Whiz Kids rallied in the bottom of the eighteenth, tying the score again on a triple by Stan Lopata.

Sawyer brought veteran Blix Donnelly in to pitch the nineteenth inning. Blix was greeted by Connie Ryan's double but got out of the inning without allowing a run. In the bottom half, we finally broke through to win the game against Ed Erautt on Del Ennis' bases-loaded drive against the left-field wall, our 23rd hit of the game. After seven hours of baseball lasting well into the wee hours, we had won a doubleheader and lost a starting pitcher.

The next afternoon both teams were bleary-eyed, but there was another ballgame to play. Bob "Bugger" Miller started for us and had to come out before the seventh inning with a sore shoulder. Bugger had had a sensational rookie year for us, starting the season 8–0 before wrenching his back in late June tripping on some steps in the 30th Street train station in Philadelphia. He had never been fully healthy since and had now developed shoulder problems. On top of that, Dick Sisler, a key to our success all year, was battling a sore wrist and had not played for more than a week.

We still had a 7½-game lead going into my next start on September 19 against the Cubs at home. I pitched a strong game, scattering only four hits and allowing a single run. Unfortunately for us, Cubs starter Frank Hiller was even better, allowing only two hits and facing only 27 batters to shut us out in an hour and 35 minutes.

The one run came in the fifth inning. When I went out to warm up for that inning, I noticed that the ball was kind of dirty. At the end of my warm-up throws, the umpire noticed also and asked Andy Seminick for the ball. Hank Sauer was the first batter, and he said, "Aw, it doesn't matter," so Andy just threw the ball back to me. I pitched with it, and Sauer hit it into the upper deck. It made me wish that I'd gotten a clean ball.

The following day we got back on track with a come-from-behind win over the Cubs led by Mike Goliat's two home runs and Jim Konstanty's three and two-thirds innings for his 16th victory of the season, all in relief. With only 11 games to go we had a 7½-game lead over both the Dodgers and the Braves, although they both had 14 games left on their schedules. We had two home games left with Brooklyn and then went on the road for our final nine games: three in Boston, four in the Polo Grounds against the Giants, and a final two in Ebbets Field with the Dodgers.

The schedule gave us a real break with two days off before the last home games with the Dodgers. That meant I could start the first game, on Saturday, on my normal three days' rest, although it would be my third start in our past six games and my second in three games. In addition, Dick Sisler, who had been out for 10 days and hampered for a month with his sore wrist, would be back in the lineup.

I was again matched against Brooklyn ace Don Newcombe, who was 18–10 for the year. The game was scoreless into the top of the third when Jackie Robinson and Carl Furillo touched me for consecutive singles. Gil Hodges was next and twice failed to sacrifice before working the count full. In those days my curveball was a big looping job that I was not too proud of. I didn't throw it much unless I was ahead in the count, but because Hodges was a pure fastball hitter, I figured I would fool him with it on a 3–2 count. I could not have been more wrong. Hodges hit my breaking ball on a line into the left-field stands for a three-run dinger that turned out to be the ballgame. We lost 3–2 because Hodges couldn't get a bunt down and I hung a curveball.

It did not get any better on Sunday. Brooklyn shellacked us 11–0 behind a two-hit shutout by Erv Palica as we committed a season-high five errors. It was quite a day for Palica who took a no-hitter into the eighth inning and blasted a grand-slam homer to boot.

Afterward we flew by charter to Boston for a Monday doubleheader with the Braves. Eddie Sawyer called a rare team meeting before the September 25 twin bill, letting us know he was unhappy with our sloppy play but telling us in a calm, quiet voice to go out and play the way we knew how to.

Eddie started Ken Heintzelman in the first game against Braves ace Warren Spahn in a battle of southpaws on a chilly day. After winning 17 games in 1949, Gruber had pitched in tough luck all year and had only two 1950 victories. Spahn, on the other hand, had already won 21 games. Eddie Sawyer knew that Gruber usually pitched well in Braves Field, and he did on this day. We knocked Spahnie from the box with four runs in the first inning, and by the third we led 8–1, on the way to a 12–4 win.

We lost the second game 5–3 as Boston struck late against Jim Konstanty but won a seesaw game the following day, 8–7, behind clutch relief pitching by veteran Blix Donnelly. It was our 90th win and 30th one-run victory of the year and officially eliminated the Braves from the pennant. Brooklyn was winning most of its games and lay five games behind with eight to play. We had six games to go, including consecutive doubleheaders against the Giants in the Polo Grounds the next two days, the result of rainouts during our previous trip to New York. Our magic number was down to three; any combination of three Phillies wins or Dodgers losses would give us the pennant.

Bob Carpenter, trying to help in any way he could, again arranged for us to fly rather than take the train to New York. I started the first game in the Polo Grounds, my fourth try to get my 20th win. I was totally unaware of that, however. I just wanted to pitch well to help us win the pennant. Unfortunately, it was not my day. I was down 5–0 after four innings, and Eddie decided to send Putsy Caballero up to pinch hit for me and save me for another day. It was 7–2 in the sixth inning but we battled back, as we did all year, with clutch hits by pinch-hitter Dick Whitman and by Eddie Waitkus to score five runs in the eighth inning to tie the score at seven. It stayed that way until the bottom of the tenth. With one out and Monte Irvin on second base, Giants shortstop Alvin Dark poked a single between first and second. Irvin, running all the way, just beat Del Ennis' strong throw to the plate and slammed into Andy Seminick to score the winning run.

Andy was knocked into the air by Irvin's slide and came down on his face. For a scary moment, he lay motionless, still clutching the ball. Andy, tough as a boot, refused to be carried off the field, even though X-rays would show that he had a separated ankle. With help, he hobbled all the way to our clubhouse in dead center field in a great deal of pain. It looked like we had lost not only a crucial ballgame but our catcher who was having a career year.

It only got worse; we lost the nightcap 5–0 as Jim Hearn threw a seven-hit shutout at us. The Dodgers split a doubleheader with the Braves, so although our lead was down to four games, our magic number was now only two with four games to play.

Somehow Andy was ready to catch again the following day, although Sal Maglie made it three losses in a row in the first game of that doubleheader, defeating us 3–1. Eddie gave me the ball for the second game, although I had pitched four innings the day before. Andy was again behind the plate and played a great game, picking a runner off first and throwing another out at second. He even caught a third-strike foul tip from Hank Thompson in his bare hand! But even Andy could not save us from our string of bad luck. With the score tied 1–1 and the bases loaded with two out in the seventh, Whitey Lockman tried to check his swing on an inside fastball and accidentally plunked the ball just beyond Granny Hamner's reach behind third for a two-run single. We threatened in the top of the ninth with runners on first and third, but Irvin at first made a great across-the-shoulder stab of Hamner's liner and beat Puddin' Head Jones back to first for an unassisted double play to take the wind out of our sails.

The 3–1 loss completed a two-day four-game sweep for the Giants and reduced our lead over Brooklyn, which had again split a twin bill with the Braves, to three games. The Dodgers loss reduced our magic number to one. If the Dodgers lost just one of their last four games or we could win one of our last two in Brooklyn, we would still win the pennant, even though we had lost five straight and seven of our past nine games.

Brooklyn did not have our injury woes, but they did have an even tougher schedule than we did with a third consecutive doubleheader with the Braves on Friday, while we had the day off before our two-game series with the Dodgers to finish the season. If Boston could win one of the Friday games against the Dodgers we would have the pennant and breathe a huge sigh of relief.

We were already in New York, and several of my teammates took the subway to Ebbets Field to watch the doubleheader, although I stayed in my hotel room and watched the games on television. I was feeling pretty confident when the Braves went ahead 5–2 in the top of the eighth inning, but the Dodgers battled back with five runs in the bottom half and won the opener 7–5. The second game kept me on the edge of my seat as well, as Boston pulled ahead 4–1 in the third inning on Bob Elliot's two-run double. Roy Campanella's two-run homer closed the gap to 4–3 in the fourth, but the Braves extended their lead to 6–3 in the fifth. Before I could get too excited, Brooklyn scrambled to tie the score in the bottom of the sixth. Then Jackie Robinson smashed Vern Bickford's first pitch in the seventh inning into the seats in left-center-field to thrust the Dodgers into the lead. Carl Erskine held the Braves at bay the rest of the way, and I knew we would have to play our way to the pennant. Our lead had shrunk to two games with two to play against the now red-hot Dodgers.

Saturday, September 30, was my 24th birthday, and I had high hopes that it would be the day we clinched the first pennant for the Phillies in 35 years. We knew it would be a struggle. The surging Dodgers had won 12 of 15 while we were mired in a deep hitting slump, beset by injuries and the loss of Curt Simmons, and had lost 7 of 9.

Eddie tabbed Bob Miller, still trying to overcome back and arm miseries, to start against Erv Palica, who six days before had thrown a two-hit shutout at us. Bugger pitched well early, scattering three hits over the first four innings, but we could still not solve Palica, so the game was scoreless into the bottom of the fifth. There Brooklyn rocked us for four two-out runs, the last two on a Duke Snider home run off Jim Konstanty in relief of Miller.

We finally got to Palica for three runs in our next at-bat, with Dick Sisler's two-run triple the big blow. We threatened in the seventh but got nothing while Roy Campanella delivered the knock-out blow in the bottom of the eighth with a three-run homer deep into the center-field bleachers. The final score was 7–3. Our lead was down to one game with one game left to play, and we were faced with the prospect of the most colossal collapse by a league leader in National League history. Just 11 days earlier, on September 19, we had held a 7½-game lead over the Boston Braves and a seemingly insurmountable nine-game lead over the Dodgers, including seven in the loss column.

If we lost again on Sunday we faced an immediate three-game playoff, with the first game in Ebbets Field and Games 2 and, if necessary, 3 in Shibe Park. A playoff, given the state of our pitching staff and Andy's injury, was not something we felt very confident about. Our best shot was to win on Sunday.

With our depleted pitching staff, it was far from clear to me who Eddie Sawyer would name to start the final game. I had started games the previous Saturday, Wednesday, and Thursday. But I had two days' rest so I thought I could pitch. The small visitors' clubhouse in Ebbets Field was very quiet and tense before the game because we all knew that we had just about blown the pennant. I was sitting in front of my locker about an hour before the game when Eddie walked over, handed me a new ball, and wished me luck. That was how I found out that I would be starting.

It turned out that the Dodgers started Don Newcombe in what would be our fifth head-to-head meeting of the year. Both Newk and I were trying for our first 20-win seasons, although 20 wins never entered my mind. When I began to warm up I really did not feel particularly good. I was having trouble getting loose and was not sure I could crank my arm up like I needed to. I was nervous and tense because so much was riding on the game. But for some reason I glanced over at Newk warming up for the Dodgers and I thought to myself, "Hell, he is just as tired as I am." I knew Newk had pitched almost as much as I had and probably was just as tired, nervous, and anxious as I was. Once I realized that, I never gave another thought to how tired or nervous I was supposed to be.

Ebbets Field was packed with a standing-room-only crowd of 35,073 on a mild, sunny afternoon. Thousands more were turned away, but a few fans from Philadelphia managed to secure tickets and get into the ballpark. Newk and I both pitched well early. I did not give up a hit until Pee Wee Reese's no-out double in the fourth. I got out of it by retiring Duke Snider, Jackie Robinson, and Carl Furillo in order to leave Pee Wee stranded. Through the first five innings we managed only three scattered singles and a walk off Newcombe, so the game remained scoreless into the sixth inning.

We broke through for the first run in the top half on consecutive two-out singles by Dick Sisler, Del Ennis, and Puddin' Head Jones. I got the first two batters in the bottom half of the inning to bring Reese to the plate again. Pee Wee hit a fly ball near the right-field foul line, which was only 297 feet from home plate. The ball hit the screen and dropped down to a six-inch ledge, where it stayed. Although the ball was in the field of play, it was beyond our reach and Reese, instead of a double or maybe only a single, had a freak inside-the-park home run. Andy Seminick was so frustrated that he yelled at Del Ennis in right field to throw his glove at the ball. The ball sat on the ledge for the rest of the afternoon, a constant reminder of why the score was tied.

The score remained that way through eight and a half innings. We had a base runner against Newk in the seventh, eighth, and ninth innings but were unable to score. I had given up only three hits, including an eighth-inning single to Roy Campanella, while we had managed eight hits against Newcombe.

As I trudged out to face Brooklyn in the bottom of the ninth, I knew that if the Dodgers scored we would very likely lose not only the ballgame but also the pennant. Mary and I had planned on taking a vacation to Florida after the season with some of my World Series money, and I remember for a brief moment thinking, "If we don't win this one, we're not going to Florida."

Cal Abrams led off the inning, and I went to a 3–2 count on him. I threw a fastball on the insider corner, but umpire Larry Goetz called it ball four. Goetz was an outstanding umpire, probably along with Al Barlick the best in the league. But I really thought that 3–2 pitch was a strike, but Goetz didn't and so Abrams led off with a walk.

Reese was next and tried to bunt Abrams over. I threw high and hard, trying to make it tougher to bunt, and Pee Wee fouled two off. With two strikes, I thought he might try to go to right field so I tried to jam him inside. Either I didn't get it far enough in or Pee Wee guessed with me, because he hit a rope to left field, his third hit of the game, to put runners on first and second with no one out. Now I was in a real pickle; a base hit would win the game for Brooklyn. Eddie had Jim Konstanty warming up in the bullpen but left me in.

Duke Snider was the next batter. Although Duke was a dangerous hitter (he had 31 homers, 107 RBIs, and a .321 batting average for 1950), I assumed that with the game on the line and no one out Duke would try to bunt the runners over. So I threw the first pitch right in there, thinking of nothing but breaking to cover the third-base line to try to force Abrams at third if Snider bunted that direction.

Well, Snider was not bunting. He ripped that first pitch right over my left shoulder into center field. The ball was a low line drive, and as I turned to watch it I could see Abrams at second hesitate a moment to make sure Mike Goliat, our second baseman, could not reach it. Richie Ashburn in center was not known to have a strong throwing arm, and the Dodgers often ran on him. Milt Stock, Brooklyn's third-base coach, decided to test Whitey and waved Abrams home, even with his late start. Richie caught the ball on the first hop and threw a beautiful one-hop strike to Stan Lopata, who was catching after Andy Seminick had been lifted for a pinch runner. Stan caught the ball and tagged Abrams out by 15 feet.

Some people believe that I missed a sign to try to pick Abrams off at second and that Richie came in shallow to back up my throw. If there was a pickoff play, it would have been the first one all year. I never even threw over to first base, much less second.

Ashburn's throw was the biggest in Phillies history, but we were still on the brink of disaster. Reese and Snider had each moved up with the throw to the plate, giving the Dodgers runners on second and third with only one out. Eddie Sawyer came to the mound to tell me to walk Jackie Robinson intentionally to set up a force at any base. That meant Carl Furillo would bat with the bases loaded. He was an excellent right-handed slugger who already had 106 RBIs to go with a .305 batting average.

When Eddie came out he also reminded me to keep the ball down on Furillo, who was a high fastball hitter. Well, my first pitch to Carl was about eye high, but it must have had something on it because he swung and popped it up to Waitkus in foul territory by first base. Another Dodgers slugger, Gil Hodges, was next. Hodges was a dangerous clutch hitter who had already driven in 113 runs. He took a strike and a ball and then lifted a soft fly ball in front of the scoreboard in right field, which was a short porch in Ebbets Field. It should have been a can of corn, but right field was the sun field in the late afternoon, especially in the fall. Del Ennis drifted back, battling the sun all the way. He stayed with it and actually caught the ball against his chest to complete my escape from the jam. After the game, Del actually had the seams of the ball imprinted on his chest, so hard did Hodges' fly ball hit him in right field.

I did not have much time to reflect on the inning because I was the leadoff hitter in the top of the tenth. Eddie told me to go ahead and hit, which was fine by me. He often let me bat in late innings of close ballgames when I was pitching. At this point, I was too charged up to feel tired, even though I'd already pitched nine innings. Getting out of that jam had revitalized me, and I did not want to come out of the game.

At bat, I was often overanxious and lunged at the ball, trying to hit it hard. But in this situation I just tried to put the ball in play. Newk was also still in the game, and his first pitch was a ball. I swung at the next pitch and hit a bouncer up the middle through the infield for a base hit.

Eddie Waitkus, our leadoff hitter, followed me. Sawyer had him bunting, but after Waitkus fouled one down the third-base line and dodged a high inside fastball, Eddie let him hit away. Waitkus responded by looping a Texas Leaguer in front of Snider in center, sending me easily into second because I could see that the ball was going to fall in safely.

We now had runners on first and second with no one out and Ashburn coming to the plate. Whitey bunted the first pitch along the third-base line, and I busted my tail to get to third, sliding headlong into the bag. But Newk made a fine play, getting to the ball quickly and firing to Brooklyn third sacker Billy Cox to just nip me. Now we had men on first and second with one out.

Dick Sisler was next. Dick was a left-handed batter with power. He had had a good year at the plate, with close to a .300 batting average, 12 homers, and 80 RBIs. He seemed pretty much fully recovered from the sore wrist that had plagued him late in the season. He had generally swung the bat well the past few days and had already touched Newk for three hits in the game.

Newcombe immediately got ahead in the count two strikes, as Sisler foul tipped the first pitch and fouled the second back to the screen. It was clear that Newk was really going after Dick, hoping to strike him out. After taking a ball high and outside, Dick hit another foul back into the press box behind home plate.

Newcombe's next pitch was another fastball out over the plate. Dick swung and really connected, driving a low line drive into deep left field. Sitting in the dugout, I knew that the ball was hit hard, but I was not sure that it was going out because a low line drive hit to the opposite field doesn't normally carry all the way out of the park. But Dick's blow did carry, landing in about the third row of the left-field stands, 350 feet from home plate. My teammates charged from the dugout to mob Dick at the plate and celebrate our 4–1 lead.

That lead felt like a real cushion, given the tension of the game and the suspense of the bottom of the ninth. The next two Phillies made outs, and before I knew it I was walking to the mound to pitch the bottom of the tenth inning, three outs from winning the pennant.

There was no real conversation as I left the dugout. Sawyer put Jack Mayo, a fleet rookie outfielder, into left field for defensive purposes, replacing Sisler. I felt good and loose and had too much adrenaline to be tired. Roy Campanella, another dangerous Brooklyn slugger with 31 homers, was up first. With the count 1–1, he drove a line drive to left that Mayo quickly moved over to nab. Dick would probably have made the play as well, but Jack had no trouble getting to it with his excellent speed.

Brooklyn manager Burt Shotton then sent Jim "Rip" Russell up to pinch hit for Billy Cox. Rip was a veteran switch-hitting outfielder with good power also; he had hit 10 home runs in little more than 200 at-bats. But I was pumped and struck him out swinging on four pitches. It was only my second strikeout of the game and my first since the third inning.

Next Shotton inserted Tommy Brown to pinch hit for Newcombe. Tommy, who would become a teammate the following year after he was traded to the Phillies, was a young utility player who hit .291 and had seven pinch-hits for the Dodgers in 1950. After fouling one back to the screen, he popped the next pitch to Waitkus at first. Eddie caught the ball, and the Whiz Kids had finally won the first pennant for the Phillies since 1915 and only the second in Phillies history.

When Eddie caught that last foul pop, I had a feeling that I never experienced before or again in athletics. It was a feeling of great relief, complete satisfaction, and exhilaration all rolled together. In addition, I was simply grateful because we had almost blown the pennant and disappointed all of Philadelphia, to say nothing of ourselves. And my vacation with Mary to Florida was back on the drawing board.

CHAPTER 6

Aftermath

The clubhouse was pure bedlam after our white-knuckle victory over the Dodgers. My teammates had carried me off the field, and when I got to the clubhouse, I just sat by my locker while the celebration went on all around me. Eddie Sawyer came over and kissed me on the cheek, certainly the only time he ever did that. Amid the hubbub, Jackie Robinson quietly came into our clubhouse and went around shaking our hands and congratulating us in a remarkable display of sportsmanship from a fierce competitor.

As we boarded the bus to the train station outside Ebbets Field, a woman kept calling Richie Ashburn by name. When he finally turned around to look at her, she spat right in his face. I had to grab Whitey and push him into the bus to keep him from going after her. Some Brooklyn fans had taken that loss personally.

We had three private cars on the train, and the celebration continued all the way back to Philadelphia. About thirty thousand people were waiting for us when we pulled into the 30th Street station. Mary; Puddin' Head's wife, Carolyn; and Stan Holmig's wife, Mary Anne, were supposed to meet us at the station, but they couldn't get close enough to even park the car. Bob Carpenter was hosting a victory party for the team at the Warwick Hotel, and the girls found out and met us there.

After we arrived at the Warwick, we called Curt Simmons at Camp Atterbury in Indiana to get him in on the celebration. It was a terrific party with a live band and all the food and drink anyone could want, but Mary and I did not stay very long. Mary was eight months pregnant with Robbie Jr., who would be born on October 20, and I was drained and exhausted. I knew Mary was in no condition to be out late, and I was eager to get home as well. Besides, we thought that the Whiz Kids would be winning lots of pennants.

The World Series opened two days later, on Wednesday, in Shibe Park. Our opponents were the vaunted New York Yankees, who had survived a tight race of their own against the Detroit Tigers and Boston Red Sox, clinching the pennant on the next-to-last day of the season. They were loaded with Joe

DiMaggio, Yogi Berra, Johnny Mize, Bobby Brown, American League MVP Phil Rizzuto, and the formidable starting pitching of 21-game winner Vic Raschi, Allie Reynolds, and Eddie Lopat. Rookie Ed "Whitey" Ford had gone 9–1 after a midseason call-up from the Kansas City Blues in the American Association.

Eddie Sawyer delayed naming his opening game starter until the day before and surprised everyone by tapping Jim Konstanty, who had not started a game all year. Of course, Jim had made a record 74 appearances and thrown 152 innings in relief and would be named the National League MVP. He pitched a terrific game, allowing only a single run and scattering four hits in eight innings before Dick Whitman pinch hit for him. Unfortunately, Yankees starter Vic Raschi was better, throwing a two-hit shutout at us for a 1–0 victory. It looked like it was going to be tough for us to get out of our hitting slump against the Yankees starters.

I started the second game. Although I had pitched a lot during the previous week, I had my normal three days' rest. Yankees manager Casey Stengel named Allie Reynolds, who had posted a 16–12 record with several one-run losses, to throw for New York. I struggled early, trying to find my good rhythm, and gave up two hits in the first inning before escaping with no damage. Then with two outs in the second I walked Jerry Coleman and gave up a single to Reynolds, moving Coleman to third. Leadoff hitter Gene Woodling then topped a high bounder to the left of Puddin' Head, just beyond his reach. Granny Hamner fielded the ball deep in the hole, and his only play was at second. He fired to Goliat to try to force Reynolds, but Allie just beat the throw. Coleman scored on the play, and we were down 1–0 before I retired the Yankees without further damage.

After missing a couple of scoring opportunities early, we finally scored our first run of the Series to tie the score in the fifth on Mike Goliat's infield single, Waitkus' bad-hop base hit over Coleman, and Ashburn's sacrifice fly.

We managed to get runners in scoring position in the seventh and ninth innings but could not break through again against Reynolds. Meanwhile, I survived a two-out jam with runners on second and third in the Yankees eighth. I then retired the Yankees in order in the ninth. In the bottom half, Hamner came through with a one-out double. Pinch-hitter Dick Whitman was intentionally walked by Stengel to bring up Goliat.

We now had runners on first and second with one out. With the count at 3–1, Goliat, who was a free swinger, took a cut at Reynold's chin-high fastball and hit a two-hopper to Rizzuto at short for the start of an inning-ending double play.

I went out to pitch the tenth inning and face the first batter, Joe DiMaggio. I had handled Joe well all day, causing him to pop up to the infield four consecutive times, once with two runners on base. I was not overconfident, however, because he was always a very dangerous hitter. This time I got behind in the count 2–1. I then threw Joe a fastball up and out over the plate a little too much, and he walloped it high into the first row of the upper deck in left for a solo home run. That is the pitch my old coach Ray Fisher said even he could hit. I recovered to retire the next three hitters in order, but we went to the bottom half of the tenth trailing 2–1.

Sawyer sent Jack Mayo up to pinch hit for me, and Jack worked Reynolds for a five-pitch walk. Waitkus laid down a nice bunt to sacrifice Mayo to second to give us the tying run on second with one out. But Allie bore down to retire Ashburn and Sisler to seal our second straight one-run defeat.

After the game, DiMaggio told the press that he had hit a slider for the game-winning home run. It actually was a fastball that tended to slide away from a right-handed hitter when I got it down and away, and it was effective in that location. If I got it up or too much over the plate, it tended to flatten out and sometimes landed in the seats.

The Series immediately moved to Yankee Stadium without the break of a travel day, which we could have used to regroup. Curt Simmons had obtained a pass to be at the World Series with us, but he was not on the active roster and so could not pitch. (He did pitch batting practice, and some of the guys complained because he threw too hard for them to get good cuts. I've often wondered how the Series might have gone if the Yankees had faced Curt out of the fall shadows a couple of times.) Eddie Sawyer decided to go with Ken Heintzelman for the third game against the Yanks' Ed Lopat, who had put together an 18–8 year.

Gruber had had a disappointing year after winning 17 games in 1949, but he was a veteran southpaw who knew how to pitch. He had thrown well in a couple of key September games and looked to be regaining his 1949 form.

Game 3 quickly became another pitchers' duel, as Heintzelman and Lopat were both at the top of their games. New York scratched out a run in the third, and going into the sixth we had scored exactly one run in 23 World Series innings. But both Del Ennis, with a double, and Dick Sisler, with a single, knocked their first base hits of the Series, and we had a run to tie the score. We finally took the lead for the first time in the Series in the seventh inning, on a Hamner single, a sacrifice bunt by Andy Seminick, and Goliat's single to center. Hamner just beat DiMaggio's throw to the plate, and the score was 2–1 Whiz Kids.

Heinz sailed along until two were out in the eighth inning when he walked Coleman on a 3–2 count. He couldn't regain his touch and followed by walking Yogi Berra and DiMaggio to load the bases. Kenny was out of gas and Eddie Sawyer brought in Konstanty to try to get out of the inning. Stengel sent Bobby Brown, who already had three hits in the Series, to pinch hit for Hank Bauer. With a two-strike count, Bobby stroked a ground ball to Hamner at short. Granny was a little overanxious to get the force-out at second and bobbled the ball. Coleman scored the tying run as all hands were safe. Konstanty then induced John Mize to pop out to Puddin' Head in foul ground for the third out of the inning.

Granny immediately redeemed himself in the top of the ninth with a ringing double to deep left center off reliever Tom Ferrick. DiMaggio made a great bare-handed stop of the ball or Ham would have had at least a triple. He made third anyway on a sacrifice bunt, and Stengel then ordered Goliat walked intentionally to put runners on the corners with one out. Dick Whitman hit for Konstanty and topped a slow bouncer to first baseman Joe Collins. Hamner took off for home on contact, and a charging Collins threw to Berra to nip Granny at the plate and effectively kill the rally. Goliat moved to second, but Waitkus flew to Cliff Mapes in right to end the inning.

Russ Meyer came in to pitch the bottom of the ninth for us. He retired the first two batters and it looked like extra innings again. But Gene Woodling got aboard on an infield hit, and Rizzuto lined a ball over second that Jimmy Bloodworth, in for Goliat, knocked down but had no play on. Jerry Coleman then hit a fly ball that fell in left-center field between Ashburn and Jack Mayo, who both seemed to hesitate slightly. Woodling scored the winning run, and we were suddenly down three games to zero. It was our third one-run loss in the Series and our second straight in the Yankees' last at-bat. We had scored exactly three runs in three games.

Time was running out for us to break out of our hitting slump and gain a win. Two rookies were tapped to start Game 4: 21-year-old Ed "Whitey" Ford for the Yankees and 24-year-old Bob Miller. Bugger, as we called Bob, had gone 11–6 for us but was still battling late-season back and arm problems. We threatened in the first with runners on second and third with one out, but the rally fizzled when Bobby Brown threw Waitkus out at the plate. The Yankees jumped ahead 2–0 in their half of the opening inning to put us immediately in the hole. We blew another great scoring chance in the fourth when we had yet another runner thrown out at home to complete a double play.

Sawyer had brought Konstanty in at the first sign of trouble, and Jim pitched well until the sixth inning, when Berra slugged a home run and Bobby

Brown smashed a run-scoring triple to trigger a three-run rally. All of a sudden it was 5–0. Meanwhile, Ford continued to keep us at bay. Eddie brought me in to pitch the bottom of the eighth after lifting Konstanty for a pinch-hitter. I held the Yankees scoreless, but we were down to our last at-bat, facing a five-run deficit.

We went down fighting, rallying for two runs to finally chase Ford and ending the game with the tying run at the plate. But still when all was said and done, the Yankees had swept us, leaving a bittersweet taste to the season.

I've often thought that maybe the Series was anticlimactic for us, because we had had such a tough time winning the pennant. Injuries and the long season had taken their toll on our young team. We had felt a real sense of relief after that final win in Ebbets Field because we had come so close to blowing the whole thing. But we were thrilled to have had the chance to play the Yankees in the World Series. And they were not exactly slouches. In fact, history reminds that those Yankees were in the middle of five consecutive World Series triumphs, the only team in history ever to accomplish such a feat. They were truly a dynasty.

Looking back, even though the Yankees swept us, three of the four games were tight. But the what-ifs in baseball will drive you batty if you dwell on them.

Of course, at the time, I fully expected that we would win several more pennants in the years ahead and have other shots at the World Series and at the Yankees. It was not to be, so over the years the Whiz Kids of 1950 have become an even more special memory for me. For that one year, under the exceptional leadership of Eddie Sawyer, we were a special team with great camaraderie, considerable talent, and the resiliency that champions must have.

The 1950 World Series was my introduction to Joe DiMaggio and was the only time I faced Joe, other than in a couple of spring training games. The Yankees trained in St. Petersburg and we were in Clearwater, which is not too far away. If we played the Yankees, Joe would always play three or four innings and would bat a couple of times. He never wanted to let the fans down. Ted Williams and Stan Musial were the same way. They would always appear in spring training games if they were physically able.

Late in his career Joe was nagged by injuries and retired from baseball after the 1951 season, although he was just 36 years old. Many years later, in the late seventies, I settled in the Tampa area. Every year for four or five years Joe would come to play in an Italian-American golf tournament that my club, the Temple Terrace Country Club, hosted. The tournament organizers always paired Joe and me together in the same golf cart. I really enjoyed playing with

Joe. Although he was in his seventies, he was still strong and could still hit the golf ball. Joe loved to play and loved the competition.

When we played, there was always another cart with security officers following us to make sure Joe was left alone. If Joe felt comfortable, he was a pleasure to be with and could be very gracious. Once Mary and I attended an Old Timers' Game in St. Louis with our young son Jimmy. We went in to have breakfast in the room the Cardinals had set aside for us and saw that there were no tables for three, only tables for two. Joe was eating by himself, noticed the predicament, and said, "Do you think the boy would like to eat with me, Robin?"

I said, "Yes, I'm sure he would, Joe," so Jimmy, who was six years old, had breakfast with Joe DiMaggio.

Of course, there was another side to Joe. One morning as I was about to go over to the club to play in the golf tournament with Joe, Mary handed me a picture of him touching home plate after he hit the home run off me in the 1950 World Series. I'm not sure why Mary kept it, but she had. It wasn't anything I was too eager to keep. Mary asked, "Would you get Joe to sign this for me?"

I said, "Nah, I don't want to ask Joe to sign that. He can be funny that way."

But Mary was somewhat insistent, and so I said that I would ask him. It turned out that Joe and I were alone in the locker room at the club before teeing off. No one else was around. I said, "Joe, Mary asked me to get you to sign this picture for her."

Joe looked up at me and said, "I'm not signing that friggin' picture." That was all he said, and of course I felt bad and was mad at Mary for putting me in the position of asking him. We went out and played golf together, never mentioned the picture, and had our normal good time. It was drizzling at the end of the round, and about 30 people were waiting, hoping to get Joe's autograph. A security guard pulled a golf cart under an overhang out of the rain, and Joe sat and signed one autograph for each person. I almost called Mary and told her to get in line.

Instead when I got home I told Mary, "Promise me that you'll never do that again. Joe said he wouldn't sign that 'friggin' thing.'"

As far as I was concerned that was the end of it. A couple of weeks later I played golf at the club and was getting a sandwich afterward. Carmen Pellecchia, who always took care of DiMaggio when he came to Tampa, came over and said, "Robin, Joe called me last night. He is so upset with himself for not signing that photo for Mary. He can't believe he did that."

I said, "Carmen, look, don't worry about it. I didn't want to ask him anyhow."

Carmen said, "Well, Joe is so upset that he is sending me a manila envelope with his return address on it for you to send the photo to him so he can sign it."

I said, "OK, that'll be fine." So when the envelope came, I sent the picture to Joe and in a few days it came back signed.

Mostly, Joe and I got along great and really enjoyed golfing together. We would usually bet the other twosome a dollar or so for the round. One day it was raining pretty hard after the front nine, and Sam Ferlita, the tournament director, said, "Joe, you don't have to play the back nine today."

Joe said, "Oh no, we're behind. We're going to play." I would just as soon have given the other guys a dollar. I can't remember whether we won or not, but we played all 18 holes.

We lockered next to each other the first time I was at an Old Timers' Game with Joe. As we were dressing, Joe looked at me and said, "Robin, I can still see that pitch you threw me."

I knew that he was referring to the home run he hit off me in the World Series to beat me 2–1 in 10 innings. I said, "Joe, you ought to see it from my angle. It's not so pretty."

That game I lost to Joe DiMaggio was my only World Series start. The 1964 Baltimore Orioles were the closest I came to another. That year we led the league in early September and finished in third place, only two games behind the first-place Yankees. None of the other clubs I was with came close to winning a pennant. I had quite of bit of individual success over the years, but looking back, it was very special to experience the team success with the Whiz Kids of 1950. I know that even now, more than 50 years later, I am associated with the Whiz Kids more than with anything else in baseball. It is an association I am proud of.

CHAPTER 7

A Different Game

In spite of our expectations, the Phillies never seriously contended for the pennant again in the years following 1950. We were often in contention for part of the year before tailing off. It was a period when I won a lot of games and pitched a lot of innings even though the overall team performance was disappointing. In fact, counting 1950, I went on to win 20 or more games six years in a row, peaking with a 28–7 record in 1952. From 1950 through 1955, I won 138 games. I pitched well over 300 innings in each of my 20-game years, leading the league five times and peaking at 347 innings pitched in 1953. I generally started every fourth day and would sometimes be used in relief on the middle day. (Before my time, Dizzy Dean, in his 30-win season in 1934, started 33 games and relieved in 17 more. I once heard Dizzy asked if he was the best pitcher of all time. He said, "I don't know about that, but I'm amongst them.") I also led the league in complete games five straight years, peaking with 30 in 1952, 33 in 1953, and 29 in 1954. In fact, I threw 28 straight complete games in 1952 and 1953.

One day I was talking to Gaylord Perry about complete games at one of the Hall of Fame functions. He ended his long and illustrious career with 303 complete games, two fewer than I had. He told me that if he had known that, he would have hung around longer so that he could throw three more.

It was not uncommon for starting pitchers in the fifties to pitch into extra innings. I probably pitched at least 15 extra-inning complete games, some of which were really long affairs. For example, in 1952 I pitched all 17 innings of a 7–6 win over the Boston Braves for my 23rd win of the year. In June 1954 I threw all 15 innings of a 3–2 win over the St. Louis Cardinals. Some of those complete games were tough to come by, but a lot of starting pitchers did that then.

Of course, today complete games are uncommon, starting pitchers typically get four or five days' rest, and relief pitchers are specialists with middle relievers, set-up men, and closers. When modern baseball fans look back on my record in the fifties, they treat me like I was Hercules. But in those days, many starting pitchers pitched a lot of innings and threw complete games. In my case, I was mentally an everyday ballplayer. I always wanted to play every day. Even as a pitcher, I wanted to play as often and as long as I could. My attitude was that the game was nine innings long, and sometimes longer, and I wanted to be out there the entire game. Eddie Sawyer and his successor Steve O'Neill both believed in pitching their top pitchers as much as possible, and that was fine with me. As a result, however, they didn't really use the whole staff like managers do today.

I'm certainly not one of those old ballplayers who insists that the way we did it was better. It was just different. For example, Roger Clemens won 20 games and the Cy Young Award in 2001 and did not throw a single complete game. But with set-up men like Ramiro Mendoza and Mike Stanton and a closer like Mariano Rivera, who can blame Yankees manager Joe Torre for pitching Clemens six or seven innings and then bringing in the bullpen? The idea is to win games, and Roger was 20 and 3 in 2001.

Even in my day, I believe that complete games were overrated. The top clubs often had topflight relievers like Joe Page of the Yankees, Joe Black of the Dodgers, and Hoyt Wilhelm of the Giants. Jim Konstanty won the National League Most Valuable Player Award as a relief pitcher for us in 1950, setting a league record with 74 appearances. But he often pitched in long relief as well as short relief and threw 152 innings for the year.

I think it is wrong to shortchange the game today by comparing statistics like complete games and innings pitched. The game has changed for the better, I believe, with pitchers having more defined roles, pitch counts (which were more unusual in my day), and more rest for the starters between starts. I would much rather be pitching today with adequate rest and knowing I was going to go to the mound with great stuff. I think it really helps pitchers like Curt Schilling, Randy Johnson, and Greg Maddux to have four days' rest and be on pitch counts. They can go six or seven innings or longer if the situation dictates, but when they do come out they have a relief specialist throwing 95 miles per hour with good control to follow.

In the off-season, I played touch football with the kids, played quite a bit of basketball with the Phillies' basketball team that Maje McDonnell organized, and in later years played some golf as well. Beginning January 15, Curt Simmons and I would go to a local gym and throw to each other for 20 to 30 minutes each. Then we would get a couple of other guys and play two-on-two basketball to really work up a sweat. I understand that today Roger Clemens and other pitchers work out year-round with personal trainers. Nolan Ryan's incredible longevity can at least partially be explained by his dedication to staying in shape. Even after pitching no-hitters late in his career, he would conduct his postgame interviews from his postgame workout on a stationary bicycle.

In 1984 baseball was an exhibition sport in the Olympic Games in Los Angeles. I worked in public relations and promotions for the White Division of General Electric, the sponsor of Olympic baseball, and watched the Olympic baseball games, which were played in Chavez Ravine. Taiwan had a fine pitcher who later played in the Japanese League. He pitched 11 shutout innings against Japan before he was taken out of the game. Afterward he jogged down to the bullpen and threw a little bit. Then he jogged back and forth in the bullpen for a few minutes. Afterward the Taiwanese coach through the interpreter told me that they called that cooling down.

I never did that after pitching, but it is a great idea. That may be what Nolan Ryan was doing on his stationary bicycle, and I expect other pitchers do it as well. It certainly beats sitting by your locker and getting stiff. Ray Fisher, my old coach in Vermont, may have been ahead of his time. He told me that after he pitched he took a swim at the New York Athletic Club where he lived.

Another big difference today is the packing of the pitcher's arm in ice immediately after he finishes pitching. Ray Fisher said that he always ran hot water over his arm for about 20 minutes after he finished pitching. Satchel Paige did the same thing, and it made sense to me because hot water would seem to keep the circulation going. So that is what I did my entire career, and my arm never got near ice. In fact, I got so I could stand really hot water. If I was in the shower running hot water over my arm, the next guy in would get scalded.

Sandy Koufax may have been the first to use ice when he was battling arm problems in the sixties. It certainly is accepted practice today, and the trainers must know what they are doing. But it sure used to feel good to run hot water over my arm after I'd pitched.

When I reported to spring training, I would be the first guy to pitch batting practice, then the first one to pitch in an intrasquad game. Most clubs did it that way, ranking their starters and then giving their top starters priority. When I wasn't pitching we would do our running in the outfield, field a hundred or so ground balls in the infield, and then shag fly balls in the outfield. I remember that Bob Gibson would always go out to shortstop to field ground balls, and Lew Burdette and Warren Spahn would field grounders and then go out into the outfield and play long toss.

During the season I would pitch batting practice to the regulars for 10 or 15 minutes on my middle day of rest between starts. And we threw batting practice from the regular distance and did not have a screen in front to protect us from line shots. As I mentioned, Johnny Blatnik nailed me right on the shin one day during batting practice in Louisville. Today, big-league pitchers rarely throw batting practice and don't field many ground balls.

Also, whether in spring training or during the regular season, we played pepper every day. In pepper several players stand in a line and toss the ball at short range to a batter who strokes, or "peppers," the ball back to them in order to develop reflexes. Early in my career I would play for quarters with Richie Ashburn, Bill Nicholson, Putsy Caballero, and others and have the best time trying to line a ball off someone's shin. It also was great hand-eye coordination exercise, but mostly it was just fun. Pepper today is a lost art and in fact most big-league ballparks have "no pepper" signs because of liability concerns.

All our training in those days involved baseball. Today, with all the money involved, the players lift weights, have special diets, and don't do some of the stuff we took for granted, like pitching batting practice or playing pepper.

When the exhibition games began, I would pitch three innings the first game, then come back four days later and pitch five innings. I would typically throw a complete game for the last start of the exhibition season. Of course, spring training was longer back then because the season typically did not open until about April 15, rather than the first of April as it does now. Not all starting pitchers threw a complete game in spring training, but I wanted the feeling of pitching in the late innings before the season started.

I felt that I was ready for the regular season with a complete game behind me. And I generally was. In 1957, for example, I pitched an extra-inning game on Opening Day against the Brooklyn Dodgers, losing when Gino Cimoli hit a home run for the Dodgers in the top of the twelfth. Although I generally liked cool weather, it was downright cold that night, and I had trouble staying loose. Still I was out there all 12 innings.

* * *

Before spring training in 1951, Bob Carpenter gave me a nice raise to $30,000 from the $22,500 I ended up with the year before with the attendance clause. I reported to our camp in Clearwater in 1951 fully expecting to be embroiled in another pennant race. We knew we would be without Curt Simmons, who was still on active duty, but we had other young pitchers in camp like Jack Brittin, Steve Ridzik, Paul Stuffel, Lou Possehl, Leo Cristante, and Andy Hansen whom we hoped were ready to take up the slack. We had virtually everyone else back from our 1950 staff, including young veterans like Bubba Church, Bob Miller, Ken Johnson, and Jocko Thompson, and we had the reigning MVP, Jim Konstanty, coming out of the bullpen. In addition, we had our entire starting lineup back, and because we had all been through a pennant race and emerged victorious, I assumed we could win again.

I had a good spring, and one night on the train heading north, I was in the dining car, sitting next to Willie Jones. One of the porters came up to Willie and asked, "Where is that Robbie Robinson? That man, he can throw the ball right by the Pope." So Puddin' Head pointed me out, and I had a nice chat with the porter.

Several years later I told that story to Maury Wills of the Los Angeles Dodgers when we were on a trip to Germany to put on baseball clinics. Still later, at the end of my career, I was with the Houston Astros; we were playing the Dodgers and I was on second base. Maury was at shortstop and snuck up behind me and said, "Are you the man who can throw the ball by the Pope?"

The 1951 season turned out to be a huge disappointment. We started the season the same place we had ended 1950—Ebbets Field in Brooklyn. I beat the Dodgers and Carl Erskine 5–2, but the season soon went sour. We actually descended to seventh place in late June before playing well in July and getting as high as third place in early August. We didn't finish well, however, and ended below .500 in fifth place with a 73–81 record, 23½ games behind the Giants. We never did overcome losing Curt Simmons to active duty for the year. Only Bubba Church and I had good seasons on the mound, with Bubba bouncing back from his frightening line-drive injury to win 15 games while losing 11. Jim Konstanty lost his magic touch, virtually everyone else had a tough year, and the rookies weren't able to step up, as had Bubba, Bob Miller, and Ken Johnson the year before.

In the field, Richie Ashburn had a wonderful year, batting .344 to finish second to Stan Musial for the batting title and leading the league in hits with 221. He also finished second in stolen bases and led all outfielders in putouts. But otherwise only Willie Jones and Dick Sisler came close to or equaled their offensive production of the year before. Del Ennis battled a bad back most of the year and fell from a league-leading 126 RBIs to 73.

Andy Seminick had a tough year as well. Early in the year we received some new helmet liners to put inside our caps while at bat. In those days, batters wore no protective covering on their heads. In the clubhouse before the game, Andy tried one on and tossed it aside, thinking that it would not offer much protection. That night Max Lanier of the Cardinals seriously beaned Andy with a high inside fastball. Andy was taken to the hospital with an irregular pulse and then tried to come back three days later. He was still very weak and was rushed back to the hospital where he this time stayed several days. Even when Andy came back, he had a tough time getting his timing down all year long.

The previous September, I had hooked up with Lanier in a pitching duel in the heat of the pennant race. It was Andy's 30th birthday, and he broke an 0-for-20 slump with what turned out to be a game-winning home run in the fifth inning in a 2–1 victory. The very next time Andy faced Lanier, he got hit in the head.

When I pitched in St. Louis, my parents would drive down to watch me pitch against the Cardinals, because Springfield was only 105 miles from St. Louis. I would then drive home with them after the game and stay overnight. They came down on September 17 when, as it happened, I was going for my 20th win of the year. The game was a tense, taut affair, but we won 2–1 in 10 innings after Tommy Brown hit a home run off Al Brazle in the top of the tenth. That win brought my season's record to 20 and 12.

Afterward I was driving my folks back to Springfield and Dad said to me, "Bud, do you mind if I don't go anymore?"

I said, "No, Dad, I don't mind if you don't go."

He said, "I can't stand it. The games drive me crazy."

Dad never saw another major league game. Instead, he stayed home and listened to the games on the radio. Mom told me that if I got a couple of men on base, Dad would turn the radio off, go outside, and take a walk. Then he would come back, turn the radio back on, and if I was still pitching, he knew I had gotten out of the jam. If I was not still in the game, he had not missed anything that he wanted to hear anyway.

In contrast, my mother enjoyed the games immensely, smiling and saying hello to everyone. I know she cared whether I won or lost, but only because she knew how much it meant to me.

Although I won 20 games for the second season in a row, the end of the 1951 season was frustrating for a couple of reasons. After my 20th win in St. Louis, I won my next start against the Dodgers in Ebbets Field, a complete-game 9–6 win over Clem Labine to run my record to 21–12. But then I lost my last three decisions—two starts and a relief appearance on the last day of the season—to finish 21–15 and take some gloss off my second 20-win season.

Two of the losses were against the Dodgers as for the third consecutive year we faced them in the last series of the season with the pennant on the line. Unfortunately for us, the race was between the Giants and Dodgers because, with Curt Simmons in the military all year, we had faded to fifth place. The Giants had come roaring back from a 13½-game deficit on August 11, and going into the last weekend of the season they trailed Brooklyn by only half a game. They were to play two games against the Boston Braves at Braves Field while we hosted the Dodgers at Shibe Park in Philadelphia for Friday, Saturday, and Sunday games to end the regular season.

With the Giants idle on Friday, the Dodgers took a 3–1 lead into the bottom of the eighth behind Carl Erskine. Andy Seminick, however, slammed a clutch two-run homer off Ersk to tie the game. Brooklyn failed to score in the top of the ninth, and Richie Ashburn led off the bottom half with a single to left. Dick Sisler sacrificed him to second, and the Dodgers walked Bill Nicholson intentionally to bring up Willie Jones. Puddin' Head slashed a sharp grounder under the glove of Billy Cox at third to send Whitey home with the winning run.

The Dodgers' once-insurmountable lead was down to zero. The Dodgers and Giants were both 94–58 with two games each on their schedules.

On Saturday afternoon in Boston, the Giants, behind Sal Maglie's five-hit shutout, beat Warren Spahn and the Braves 3–0. New York thus nosed ahead of the Dodgers by a half-game pending our Saturday night game in Philadelphia that matched Don Newcombe and me for another of our crucial matchups. This time Newk won 5–0, scattering seven hits and earning his 20th victory of the season. The big blows were Roy Campanella's second-inning double followed by Andy Pafko's home run.

So it all came down to the Sunday games with the Giants and Dodgers still in a dead heat. Both games were in the afternoon. I hadn't slept much after losing the night before but went out to the bullpen in case I might be needed to relieve our starter, Bubba Church. I watched as we jumped to a 4–0 lead in the second off of Preacher Roe, who Dodgers manager Charlie Dressen was starting on two days' rest. Preacher had a gaudy 22–3 record but did not have his stuff that day, and Ralph Branca relieved him in the second. By the end of the third inning we were on top 6–1 while in Boston the Giants had a 3–1 lead over the Braves behind 20-game winner Larry Jansen. But the Dodgers, showing their customary resilience, came back, closing to 6–5 in the top of the fifth, knocking Bubba from the game. In the bottom of the inning, Granny Hamner clubbed a triple against Dodgers reliever Clyde King to drive in two runs and extend our lead to 8–5. That was the score a little while later when the scoreboard showed that the Giants had hung on to defeat the Braves by that 3–1 score. They had won 37 of their final 44 games, 12 of their last 13, and their final 7 in a row in their incredible push for the pennant.

With their backs against the wall, Brooklyn mounted a rally in the eighth. The phone rang in the bullpen, and Ken Silvestri answered it and said, "Warm up, Robin." Of course, I was a little tired from pitching the night before, but it was the last day of the season and I wasn't saving it for anything. So Eddie Sawyer brought me to relieve Karl Drews with the score 8–7 and Don Thompson, running for Rube Walker who had doubled to drive in two runs, on second base. Carl Furillo was the first batter, and he singled to drive in Thompson with the tying run before I could get out of the inning.

Newcombe, who had pitched a shutout the night before, was by now pitching in relief for Brooklyn, and we matched goose eggs into the eleventh inning. In our eleventh, Sawyer let me bat and I led off with a hit to right field. Eddie Pellagrini was next and bunted, trying to sacrifice me to second. I guess it was a pretty good bunt. I busted my can and beat the throw to second trying to force me, giving us runners on first and second and nobody out. Ashburn then hit a two-hopper to Gil Hodges at first base, but his only play was at first, leaving me on third and Pellagrini on second with one out. Newk then intentionally walked Willie Jones, who had been tough on the Dodgers, to load the bases.

Del Ennis was next and worked the count to 2–2 but took strike three looking. That brought up Eddie Waitkus with two outs and the bases still loaded. Eddie smashed a low line drive just to the right of the pitcher's box. With two outs I ran in from third, watching the ball all the way. Jackie Robinson at second base dived for the ball, reaching across his body with his glove hand. It looked to me like he trapped the ball. As he rolled over he tossed the ball wildly over his head in the direction of second base, like he was trying in desperation to get a force-out there because he knew he had trapped the ball.

I tagged home plate and thought, "The game's over. We won." I started for our dugout to collect my gear and looked up to see my teammates running back on the field. I thought, "What is going on?" Then I realized that the umpire, Lon Warneke, had ruled that Jackie had caught Waitkus' liner for the third out. So I went out and continued to pitch, shutting the Dodgers out in the twelfth and thirteenth innings.

In the bottom of the thirteenth, Newk walked two with two out. By then Don had pitched five and two-thirds innings of relief, so Dressen replaced him with Bud Podbielan to try to get the third out of the inning. Unfortunately for us, he did, retiring Pellagrini on an easy fly ball.

I went out for the top of the fourteenth inning, my sixth in relief. I got Pee Wee Reese and Duke Snider on pop-outs to bring up Jackie Robinson.

He nailed a 1–1 fastball into the left-field stands for a home run to make the score 9–8. Ouch.

We still had some fight left in the bottom half. Ashburn led off with a single, his fourth hit of the day. Puddin' Head sacrificed him to second, but Del Ennis popped out on a full count and Eddie Waitkus flied to Andy Pafko in left to end the game and send the Dodgers into the playoff against the Giants, who were by then on the train back to New York.

We lost, but without Lon Warneke's ruling that Robinson caught Waitkus' line drive in the eleventh inning, there would have been no playoff and no "Shot Heard 'Round the World" when Bobby Thomson homered in the bottom of the ninth of the third game to win the pennant for the Giants.

That off-season, I saw Jackie at a winter banquet. I said, "Jackie, you didn't catch that ball that Waitkus hit."

Jackie just grinned at me and said, "What did the umpire say?"

In 1997 baseball honored Jackie Robinson throughout the country, commemorating 50 years since he broke baseball's color barrier. I spoke at a luncheon put on by the Philadelphia City Council and told the story of our 14-inning game against the Dodgers on the last day of the season in 1951, including how it looked to me like Jackie had clearly trapped Waitkus' drive. Richie Ashburn was there and came up to me afterward and said, "You know what, I didn't think Jackie caught that ball either."

I said, "I couldn't believe the call. But it seemed like nobody argued or anything."

Richie said, "I was in the dugout. I thought he trapped it for sure."

* * *

I really enjoyed the competition when I pitched in the big leagues, and there was no one who was a more fierce competitor than Jackie Robinson. Jackie played in the major leagues from 1947 to 1957, so his career pretty much paralleled my best years. In fact, I understand that I faced Jackie more than any other pitcher by a wide margin, because I pitched so often against the Dodgers in those years.

Of course, Jackie Robinson broke the game's color barrier in 1947, the year before I broke into the major leagues. Robinson was handpicked by Dodgers President Branch Rickey to integrate baseball, and Rickey chose well. Jackie was a very intelligent, college-educated (he had lettered in four sports at UCLA) man who had a remarkable inner spirit and drive. He had promised Rickey that he would not fight back initially at the expected racial taunts, and he did not. Jackie was able to keep his composure against bean-balls, flying spikes, and racial epithets while competing fiercely on the ball-field and earning the respect of everyone in baseball, even those heaping abuse on him.

The first time I saw Jackie Robinson play was in 1946. I was pitching in the Northern League, the summer college league in Vermont, and on a day off three of us decided to drive up to Montreal to see Jackie perform. Rickey had signed Jackie to a professional contract on October 23, 1945, and assigned him to play for the top Dodgers farm club in Montreal for the 1946 season, where the racial pressure was likely to be less severe. Although it was a long drive, we made it by game time. Jackie put on quite a show, going 3 for 4 with a home run and a steal of home while playing errorless ball at second base. It was easy to recognize that Jackie was quite a player. Of course, I did not have an inkling that we would later face each other so often in crucial situations in the major leagues.

It is well known that the Phillies, led by manager Ben Chapman from Birmingham, coach Dusty Cooke of North Carolina, and several veteran ballplayers from the South, were particularly rough on Jackie when he broke into the big leagues in 1947. It apparently just made Jackie play all the harder, because by June of 1948, when I was called up to the Phillies, the taunting of Robinson was largely in the past.

Although Chapman knew that Robinson was an outstanding ballplayer, he could not overcome his bigotry. Shortly before Chapman was fired as manager in July of 1948, Curt Simmons and I happened to be following Ben off the field into the tunnel at Ebbets Field. Robinson had had a big day against the Phillies, helping the Dodgers sweep a doubleheader with seven hits and a couple of stolen bases. In Ebbets Field the runways from the two dugouts met underneath the stands, and there was a common tunnel to the two dressing rooms. Chapman seemed to be waiting for Robinson in the tunnel, and when Jackie passed by, Chapman blurted out to him, "Robinson, you're one hell of a ballplayer, but you're still a nigger." But to Jackie's everlasting credit, he just looked at Ben and walked on by.

I remember thinking at the time that we would have had one whale of a battle if Jackie had lit into Ben. Both were big, broad, strong men who knew how to take care of themselves.

Jackie Robinson was not only a tremendous competitor but was a fine sportsman as well. I have already told of how he came into our clubhouse in Ebbets Field after we won the pennant on the last day of the 1950 season and moved from locker to locker shaking hands and congratulating us. It was an exceptional act of sportsmanship given the Phillies' inexcusable treatment of Jackie just a few years before.

Even on the golf course, Jackie liked to compete. One fall when I was still playing baseball, Jackie and I played golf together at the Greenwich Country Club in Greenwich, Connecticut. We played with the club pro and Herb Steffel, a friend of mine who also knew Jackie. Of course, Jackie was a superb all-round athlete who could really hit a golf ball a long way. On a par-4, Jackie drove all the way into a sand trap near the green. When we walked up to the trap we could see that the ball was almost completely buried. It was so buried that the pro said, "Let me just pull that out of there, Jackie," and he started to reach in to get the ball.

Jackie said, "Hey, hey. I put it there and I'll knock it out of there." So he walked up to the ball and blasted away and the ball hit the lip at the edge of the trap and rolled back down into the trap. Then he had a decent lie so he hit it out of the trap again to about three feet of the pin and made his putt for a par. I thought to myself that there was Jackie Robinson at his best. He was a competitor and did not want anyone to give him anything.

Even with all he went through, Jackie truly enjoyed playing ball. Because of baseball's no fraternization rule, which forbade players from talking to the opposition before games, I only got to know Jackie at All-Star Games during our playing careers. He was relaxed and fit in very well with the guys on those occasions. He was comfortable in the locker room, joking around, laughing, and enjoying himself. I think he thought he belonged there and so did everyone else.

I consider it a privilege to have competed against Jackie Robinson, a man I very much admired. We battled toe-to-toe many times, and I learned that sometimes the media misinterprets good hard competition. Years after I retired, I attended a banquet and Howard Cosell was at the head table. When Cosell saw me, he said to the head table, "Well, here is Robin Roberts, the man who disliked Jackie Robinson so much." Of course, Howard could not have been more wrong, but he somehow assumed that because I had competed so hard against Jackie that I had negative feelings about him. To the contrary, I had more respect for Jackie than virtually anyone I played against. He was a helluva ballplayer and an even better man.

* * *

After the 1951 season, the Phillies tried to shake things up by trading Andy Seminick, Dick Sisler, infielder Eddie Pellagrini, and southpaw Niles Jordan to the Cincinnati Reds for catcher Smoky Burgess, second baseman Connie

Ryan, and right-hander Howie Fox. Although I understand that trades are part of baseball, I hated losing Andy and Dick as teammates. Dick Sisler had joined the Phillies at the beginning of the 1948 season and was simply a big, fun-loving guy. He was, of course, the son of George Sisler, one of baseball's legendary first basemen.

At the end of the 1948 season, we came home from a road trip with only a few days left in the season. Richie Ashburn's mother had gone back to Nebraska, so I had moved out of the rooming house into the Adelphia Hotel downtown for the last homestand. Dick was staying there as well. One evening I was in the lobby thinking about getting something to eat when Dick came by and asked me if I wanted to go to dinner. I said, "Sure," and Dick said, "I'll see if I can get us a sponsor."

Off we went into the hotel bar and ordered beers. All of a sudden a well-dressed man came over and said, "Aren't you George Sisler's son?"

Dick said, "Yes, I certainly am."

The man then went on for about 20 minutes about what a great ballplayer George Sisler had been and how wonderful it was to meet his son. Finally the man asked, "Have you eaten yet?"

Dick said, "No, we haven't." So we went into the dining room and had a nice steak dinner with the guy, who was a real ball fan. Of course, when the meal was over the guy picked up the check. After we said good-bye to the man and were walking out, Dick said to me, "That's what I call a sponsor. If they want to talk about my old man, they got to pay for it."

Dick had a speech impediment that caused him to stammer quite a bit. He was not self-conscious about it, and it rarely bothered him when he was in public or being interviewed on radio or television. It did contribute to some funny incidents, however. Once, in the Polo Grounds, one of the Giants hit a high pop-up between Dick at first base and Putsy Caballero playing second. Dick moved to the ball and began trying to call for it, saying, "I ga, ga, ga," but missed it, and when the ball hit the ground he looked over to Putsy with a big grin on his face and said, "You take it."

Dick told a story on himself about driving home to St. Louis after the 1951 season. He pulled into a gas station to get gas, and when he rolled down the window, the gas attendant asked, "H-H-H-H-How many gallons do you want?"

Dick said, "F-F-F-F-Fill 'er up."

The attendant said, "What are you, a wise guy?"

Dick quickly said, "No, no, no. I'm that way, too."

We sometimes called Dick "the Big Cat" because he was known more for his hitting than his fielding. He was adequate defensively but harbored no illusions about his defensive skills. When he would occasionally make a good play in the field he would bound into the dugout saying, "Ooh, what leather!"

Dick had played winter ball in Cuba after his discharge from the service in 1945. He was then with the Cardinals, and their owner Sam Breadon wanted Dick to go to Cuba to learn to play first base, because with guys like Stan Musial, Terry Moore, and Enos Slaughter, the Cards had plenty of outfielders. Dick proceeded to become a legend in Cuba in three short months, smacking two home runs in his first game and a few weeks later hitting three round-trippers in one game. Another time, he slugged a homer over a 450-foot barrier in old Havana Stadium, the first ball hit out in that spot in 20 years. All together Dick clouted 10 home runs in 35 games and batted over .400.

He was dubbed the Babe Ruth of Cuba and was so popular that he needed police protection wherever his wife, Dot, and he went. He also managed to impress Ernest Hemingway who spent a lot of time in Cuba. Hemingway included Dick in his Pulitzer Prize–winning novel *The Old Man and the Sea*. While most readers recall the old fisherman's frequent references to "the great DiMaggio," the old man also spoke with reverence of "Dick Sisler and those great drives in the old park."

In the book, the boy who fishes with the old man says of Dick, "He hits the longest ball I have ever seen," most likely in reference to Dick's gargantuan blast in the old Havana Stadium.

The old man replies, "Do you remember when he used to come to the Terrace? I wanted to take him fishing but I was too timid to ask him. Then I asked you to ask him and you were too timid."

The boy then says, "I know. It was a great mistake. He might have gone with us. Then we would have that for all of our lives."

Dick was a tough competitor who would definitely stand up for himself, as the incident with Schoolboy Rowe illustrates. He and I even had words one time after a tough loss when Hank Sauer beat me 3–2 in Wrigley Field with a late-inning home run. It took me a long time to unwind after a defeat like that, and I would usually be the last one to leave the clubhouse. Sisler had not played well and so on this occasion we were the only two left, both feeling kind of punk and keeping to ourselves.

We ended up in the shower together, neither of us saying anything to the other. All of a sudden, Dick said, "My old man says anytime you let a home-run hitter beat you late in the game you are a bad pitcher."

That was not what I needed to hear so I said, "I'll tell you something. If you hit like your old man, I wouldn't be in so many close ballgames."

In those circumstances neither one of us was joking. Dick kind of looked at me and left the shower. I was not sure what was going to happen next because we were both a little upset. Dick was a big man, and if we started to fight no one was there to stop us except the visiting clubhouse boy.

I got out of the shower and was toweling off when Dick came around carrying two beers. He gave me one and said, "That wasn't called for. We've talked enough, haven't we?"

I said, "Yes we have, Dick." So we sat there and drank a beer together and forgot about it.

Mostly, though, Dick enjoyed life and got the most out of it. After a big win, he and Andy Seminick would often lead us in singing in the shower or on the bus. Our favorites were old standards such as "Blood on a Saddle," "Detour," or "In the Evening by the Moonlight," and Andy and Dick would often make up their own lyrics. Sometimes I would sing a verse of "Shine on Harvest Moon" and my teammates would join in on the chorus. Somehow our singing got the attention of the *Ed Sullivan Show* late in the 1950 season, and Andy, Dick, Granny Hamner, and Willie Jones were scheduled to appear on the show. Our game at the Polo Grounds ran long that day, and the foursome arrived too late at the studio to get on the air in those early days of live television. That might have been just as well. We were loud, but I'm not sure how good we were.

Dick's quirky sense of humor still survives even though he passed away a few years ago. Not too many years ago I was in Cooperstown and visiting with Jim Konstanty's son Jim Jr., who is a prominent lawyer in nearby Oneonta. Jim Sr. had died quite a few years earlier and Jim Jr. asked why his dad's teammates had called him "Yimca." I told him that Dick Sisler pinned that on his father because with his glasses and straight-arrow approach to life he reminded Dick of a YMCA instructor—hence "Yimca."

* * *

The Phillies were a better team in 1952. Karl Drews became a quality starting pitcher, and we finally got Curt Simmons back from the military in late April. Connie Ryan solidified second base, and Smoky Burgess won the first-string catching job because of his timely hitting.

We still struggled along below .500, and in June Bob Carpenter decided, after our disappointing sub-.500 fifth-place finish in 1951, that it was time to make a change. I remember that we thought something might be up. It was sad to be a part of a club that went from winning a pennant to being totally disorganized.

On June 26, Curt Simmons pitched a great game against the New York Giants and beat them 6–1. Throughout the game, Eddie Sawyer sat in the dugout sort of humming, which was out of character for him. He obviously knew this would be his last game. At the time, I was surprised, but things had gotten out of hand. Besides, Eddie gave you no reason to be close to him because he was not a guy who ever talked to players. As I've said, I mentioned to Richie Ashburn that I thought things were a little out of control and Richie said to me, "Loyalty, Robin, loyalty." Years later, after I played for several more managers, I came to appreciate what Richie meant and what a pleasure it was to play for someone like Eddie who just let you do your job.

In hindsight, I believe the Phillies would have been better off if Eddie had stayed with the organization. Eddie would have been a great general manager, for example. Of course, the main problem for the Phillies was that the organization was so slow to sign black ballplayers. Eddie wasn't a big proponent of integrating the team either and that, more than anything, really hurt us. We were competing against the Dodgers who had great black ballplayers like Jackie Robinson, Don Newcombe, and Roy Campanella; the New York Giants with Willie Mays and Monte Irvin; and a little later the Milwaukee Braves with Henry Aaron, Wes Covington, and Billy Bruton.

Steve O'Neill was named to take over for Eddie. Steve was older, about 60, and was a veteran baseball man who had caught in the big leagues for 17 years, mostly with the Cleveland Indians. He had already managed 11 years in the majors including a successful stint with the Detroit Tigers, where he led them to a pennant and World Series win in 1945. He was a nice man but, again, not someone I talked much to. He started me every fourth day and sometimes used me in relief between starts, and I was happy to take the ball. One time Steve started me near the end of the season a couple of times on two days' rest and I struggled a little. He came to me and said, "Robin, I think you need a new pitch."

I said, "No, Steve, really, all I need is a week off."

The team did play better for the rest of 1952 after Steve was hired, winning 59 and losing only 32 under him. For those three months, we were the hottest team in the league, again playing to our potential. We finished 20 games over .500 at 87–67, in fourth place, 9½ games behind the pennant-winning Dodgers and only a game out of third. Del Ennis returned to form, batting a hard .289 and driving in 107 runs, and Smoky Burgess batted .296 in 110 games. In addition, Granny Hamner had one of his best years, slugging 17 homers, driving in 87 runs, and hitting .275. On the mound, Curt Simmons contributed a 14–8 season after returning from active duty; Karl Drews became an effective starting pitcher, going 14–15 with a 2.71 earned run average; and Russ Meyer returned to form late in the year to finish 13–14.

The 1952 season was the last one in a Phillies uniform for Meyer. The club traded Monk away in a four-team deal that resulted in Boston Braves first baseman Earl Torgeson joining the Phillies. Russ ended up with the Brooklyn Dodgers and would help pitch the Bums to another pennant in 1953 with a 15–5 record.

Monk was a real character who had bizarre things happen to him both on and off the field. During one of our trips to New York in 1950, Russ had gone out to dinner and decided to walk back to the Commodore Hotel, where we were staying. On the way, he ran into some guy who sold him a "hot" two-carat diamond for $50. When Monk came in he immediately showed the diamond to several of his teammates who were sitting in the lobby, telling them what a great deal he'd made. Bill Nicholson was there and said, "Let me see that diamond. You don't mind if I scratch the floor with it, do you?"

With that he took the diamond, put it on the floor, and ground it with his heel. The "diamond" immediately disintegrated and Russ was just beside himself that he had been duped so.

Believe it or not, on our next trip to New York that season, Russ was walking down 42nd Street toward Broadway to get breakfast and actually saw the guy who had sold him the phony diamond. He grabbed the guy on the crowded sidewalk and began screaming at him, demanding his money back. The guy started yelling for help and soon attracted a cop, who got an earful from Russ. The cop eventually made the guy give Russ his $50 back plus an additional $25 for his embarrassment.

When Monk got back to the hotel with this tale, Bill Nicholson shook his head and said, "You've got to be kidding. You have to be the luckiest bastard alive."

Russ did not pitch much during our stretch run in 1950, but he was rooting so hard for us to win that he was quite emotional. On our off day in New York before our last two games against Brooklyn, Russ, Maje McDonnell, Eddie Waitkus, and a couple of other guys took the subway to Ebbets Field to watch the Dodgers-Braves doubleheader. A photographer spotted them in the stands and made a pest of himself until Russ took a swing at him and almost got himself arrested. Then, after we lost to the Dodgers on Saturday, leaving us in a must-win situation for Sunday, we came into the visiting clubhouse to find television cameras all set up in case we had clinched the pennant. Russ couldn't take it and started ripping up the television equipment, resulting in a pretty hefty bill for the club.

Russ had a temper on the playing field and would sometimes just explode. It was not for nothing that the press called him "the Mad Monk" and "Russ the Red." His most famous blowup occurred in 1953 after his trade to the Dodgers, pitching against me in Connie Mack Stadium. With the bases loaded and two men out, Russ had a 3–2 count on Richie Ashburn. Monk threw Whitey a curveball that umpire Augie Donatelli called ball four, forcing in the go-ahead run. Russ went bananas and charged off the mound to confront Donatelli. He said some magic words, and Augie quickly tossed him from the game. When that occurred, Russ returned to the mound and just refused to leave until Dodgers manager Charlie Dressen came out to get him. Finally Russ stomped off the mound. Somehow he had picked up the resin bag, and as he started off the mound he flipped it into the air in disgust. It must have gone 30 feet in the air. Wouldn't you know, the resin bag came down directly on top of Russ's head, plopping down right on the peak of his cap. White powder flew everywhere, and even Monk had to laugh a little.

Monk wasn't through yet, however. When he got to the dugout, he decided he had to give Donatelli one last shot. So he yelled at Augie and grabbed his crotch for Augie's benefit. Unfortunately, the game was the national television *Game of the Week*, and there was a camera in the dugout that caught the whole episode and displayed it to the nation. The network switchboard lit up like a Christmas tree. For about the next 10 years baseball had a Meyer Rule that forbade cameras in the dugouts.

Another time, Monk was pitching to Ashburn, again with the bases loaded but this time with a big lead. Richie fouled off seven or eight pitches, which he could do with regularity. Finally, an exasperated Monk plunked him in the back, forcing in a run and yelling, "Foul that one off, you little sonuvabitch."

Monk was a good pitcher who had some fine years in the big leagues. He really had Roy Campanella's number. Monk would throw Campy his big breaking ball, and Campy just couldn't hit it. Campy was the happiest guy in the league when Monk was traded to Brooklyn because he wouldn't have to hit off Russ anymore.

When Monk was in his sixties he got back into organized baseball as a minor league pitching coach in the Yankees chain. He coached at Oneonta in the short-season Class A New York–Penn League under a young manager named Buck Showalter. Buck was so impressed that he promised if he ever got a major league managing job, he would bring Russ along as one of his coaches. When Showalter got the Yankees' managerial job a few years later, that is exactly what he did, and Monk finished his career in a big-league uniform.

* * *

Steve O'Neill was generally pretty relaxed, but he could be a little eccentric as well. At one point in 1952 we were playing well on a road trip in New York when one of the papers ran a story quoting an unnamed Phillie as saying that our manager sometimes fell asleep on the bench during games. That was in fact a true statement. We left New York on an all-night train to Cincinnati, the next stop on our road trip. We got to our hotel in Cincinnati about 8:00 in the morning, and our traveling secretary got us together and said that Steve wanted to have a meeting. That was unusual, but I thought it would be a pep talk about how well we had been playing and urging us to keep it up.

When we gathered for the meeting, Steve said, "All right, I'm going to pass around this piece of paper. If you weren't the one who talked to the newspaper writers about me falling asleep in the dugout, I want you to sign this."

With that, he started the paper around the room and the guys are all signing it. When it got to me, I said, "Steve, I ain't signing this. I didn't talk to anybody, but I thought we were going to have a meeting about the ballclub. This is ridiculous. I'm not signing some paper."

O'Neill said, "Well, don't sign it then, but somebody talked to the press about me and I want to find out who it was." So the meeting went on and on and pretty soon I regretted not signing the paper and just going to bed. I thought, "Why the hell didn't I sign it?" but it was too late. Then my next two starts I got beat 2–1 and 1–0 and I thought I had been snakebitten because I hadn't signed that silly paper. So I signed a piece of paper and slipped it into Steve's office, just to get the hex off of me.

For me personally, 1952 was a terrific year. And I think my success had something to do with an adjustment I made right after Opening Day in 1952. We opened against the New York Giants and Sal Maglie in the Polo Grounds. Although Maglie is largely forgotten now, he was an exceptional pitcher for several years during the early fifties. From 1950 through 1952 Sal won 59 games and lost only 18. His lifetime winning percentage is .657. I lost to Sal that Opening Day 5 to 3 largely because Bob Elliot hit two home runs off me. Sal threw two curves, including one that was sharp-breaking and hard. My curve was a big looping affair that I didn't throw much when I was behind in the count. I had to stand up straighter to throw it, which gave me a different delivery and arm angle.

After losing that game, I thought to myself, "I've got to shorten my curveball like Sal does." So, without telling anyone, I started working on throwing a sharper curve. I did go watch Konstanty to see how he threw his curve, but

I added a little more wrist action than Jim used. I worked on it and could throw it with the same low motion and leg push as my fastball. Of course, that was the year I won 28 games, but if I hadn't lost to Sal Maglie on Opening Day I may have never made that adjustment. I didn't talk to Cy or anyone about it. I guess one of my pitching coaches that year was Sal Maglie, only even he didn't know it.

I came out of the gate strong in 1952, and by late May my record was 7–2. Then I failed to win for five consecutive starts, losing three, with two no-decisions. So I was 7–5 and then 9–5 when Steve O'Neill came in as manager. From then to the end of the season I won 21 games and lost 2. We were shut out in the two games that I lost, 2–0 and 1–0. Otherwise, I had a phenomenal streak. I won games 1–0, 2–1, 3–2, 4–3, and 6–5. On September 6 I defeated the Boston Braves 7–6, pitching all 17 innings, for my 23rd win. My 27th victory was a complete-game 9–7 win over Clem Labine and the Dodgers. It seemed that every time I went out there I won.

In those years, I wasn't at all concerned about my earned run average. I was just trying to win games. I can honestly say for about the first 10 years I pitched in the big leagues I never looked at my earned run average. I had no idea what it was. Wins and losses were all that were important to me. As I look back, I had some pretty good earned run averages.

At the end of the year there was certainly a possibility that I would win the Most Valuable Player Award for the National League. I finished 28–7 with a 2.59 earned run average. I was 6–0 against the pennant-winning Brooklyn Dodgers. Sal Maglie, with 18 victories, had the next most wins in the league. In fact, the 28 wins were the most in the National League since Dizzy Dean in 1935. I led the league in innings pitched with 330, in complete games with 30, and in games started with 37. But when the baseball writers' votes were counted, I lost out to Hank Sauer of the Chicago Cubs. Hank put together a big year for the Cubs, with 37 home runs and 121 runs batted in to go with his .270 batting average. Joe Black had also had a great year for the pennant-winning Brooklyn Dodgers as a relief pitcher, winning 15 games and losing only 4 while compiling a 2.15 earned run average in 56 appearances. Ultimately, the eastern writers split their votes between Black and me while the western writers almost all voted for Sauer, which gave the MVP to Hank.

Today there is a lot of discussion about whether the MVP should go to a player, like Alex Rodriguez in 2002, who has a great year on a team that is out of contention. Ernie Banks did win the award in 1958 and 1959 for Cubs teams that finished below .500 in fifth place. In 1952 my Phillies finished strong and were 87–67 for the year, ending in fourth place, nine and a half games behind the Dodgers, led by Joe Black. Sauer's Cubs ended at exactly .500, in fifth place, 19½ games out.

I can't say I was all that disappointed. Awards were really not important to me, and so I accepted the outcome without giving it too much thought. I had won 28 games and that was what I really cared about.

A couple of years later I was at a dinner that Commissioner Ford Frick always held for the player representatives during the winter baseball meetings. He was a former sportswriter and was concerned that pitchers were not getting enough recognition. During dinner Mr. Frick told me, "Robin, I'm going to start a new award for pitchers and I'm going to name it after Cy Young." So that was the beginning of the Cy Young Award, which was originally awarded to the pitcher voted the best in baseball. Don Newcombe won the inaugural award in 1956 after a 27–7 season. Later the award was changed to honor a pitcher in each league every year.

I did receive a lot of notoriety following the '52 season, appearing on the cover of a number of baseball and sports magazines. But I was mostly excited about the upcoming 1953 season. We had finished 1952 as the hottest team in the league, just as we had in 1949, and I had high hopes that we would follow with a pennant in 1953, just as we had in 1950.

My '52 season does keep cropping up. In February 2003 the New York chapter of the Baseball Writers of America Association honored me with its annual Casey Stengel "You Can Look It Up" Award for winning 28 games in 1952 and not receiving any awards. The award is for a significant but over-looked accomplishment in baseball—I guess the New York baseball writers thought I qualified. I know that I'm in good company: previous Casey Stengel Award winners include the likes of Casey himself, Ty Cobb, Joe DiMaggio, Lefty Gomez, Rogers Hornsby, Pie Traynor, Zack Wheat, and, oh yes, Richie Ashburn.

I did receive a lot of attention . . .

CHAPTER 8

The Off-Seasons: Barnstorming and Working for a Living

When I came up to the big leagues in the late forties it was common for ballplayers to barnstorm after the season, playing games to supplement their salary. After the 1949 season Harry Walker asked me to join a team he was putting together to tour the middle of the country and play exhibition games against local teams. We were to be gone 10 days and play 20 games, 2 a day. We got paid $50 a game or $1,000 for the tour. That was significant money then; my salary for 1949 had been $9,000.

We had good ballplayers like Terry Moore, Dick Sisler, Andy Seminick, Eddie Miller, Clyde McCullough, and Bert Haas. Kirby Higbe, Herm Wehmeier, and I were the three pitchers. We started in my hometown, Springfield, Illinois, and then went down into southern Illinois and over into Tennessee. We played a game near George Kell's hometown of Swifton, Arkansas, and George played with us that day. Usually Herm, Kirby, and I would each pitch three innings a game. Although we often played an afternoon and an evening game, the competition was local semipro teams, so the games were pretty relaxed. I would play the outfield for three innings or so when I wasn't pitching, so I really enjoyed the trip.

We kept this pace up for about eight days. The last stop was southeastern Missouri. We were scheduled to play an afternoon game in Holcomb and an evening game in Sikeston. Everyone was pretty whipped by now, and Wehmeier and Higbe pitched the afternoon game. Before the evening game Harry Walker came up and told me that Herm's and Kirby's arms were really bothering them. He said, "You start and throw the first three innings, and then I'll come in and relieve you for the rest of the game."

This sounded reasonable because against local competition we would generally get way ahead early. As it turned out, the locals had a southpaw pitcher named Lloyd Fischer who had been quite a prospect in the Dodgers chain but was injured in the war. He could still really throw. After three innings the score was 0 to 0 and there was no Harry. Same after six innings. Finally, after nine innings the score was still 0 to 0 and I was still out there; I hadn't seen Harry yet.

Fortunately Harry hit a home run in the top of the tenth to put us up 1 to 0. Then in the bottom half, the first batter hit a ball that nicked the chalk down the right-field line and went for a triple. I thought, "You gotta be kidding." But I had enough left to get out of the inning and finish the game, popping up one batter and striking out two others. So we won 1 to 0, but Harry never did come out to relieve me.

Whenever I would see Harry after that I'd say, "Hey, Harry. I'm still waiting for you to relieve me."

I didn't do any barnstorming after our pennant-winning year in 1950 but did go down to Wilmington, Delaware, to pitch five innings against a team of All-Stars that Jackie Robinson put together in 1951. In 1952 Mary and I went to Hawaii for a week with Pee Wee Reese and other major leaguers for a series of four games against a team of local All-Stars. We played two games in Honolulu, one in Maui, and one in Kauai. It was our first trip to Hawaii and we stayed at the beautiful Royal Hawaiian Hotel in Honolulu. Mary and I spent a nice day with Pee Wee and his wife, Dottie, touring Oahu in a rental car.

A promoter knew that we had to change planes in Los Angeles on the way back from Hawaii and asked me to stop over and pitch five innings of an exhibition game against Satchel Paige. He offered me $750, which was a significant sum of money in those days. Mary and I arrived in L.A. about 5:00 in the afternoon and had a night flight to Philadelphia leaving about 11:00 that evening. So we left our main bags at the airport and went directly to the ballpark.

I was really looking forward to watching Satchel pitch, because I had heard so much about him but had never seen him. The promoter had put together a team with ballplayers who played in the Pacific Coast League or lived in the area like Bobby Sturgeon, Ed Stevens, George Metkovich, and Lennie Merullo. I just showed up at the ballpark, said hello, put on my uniform, and pitched my five innings, and then Mary and I caught the plane back to Philly. Even with the trip from Hawaii I felt rested and had good enough stuff to strike out 12 in my little stint.

I could not wait to bat against Satchel because he was so famous. He must have been at least 50 by then. He had a big easy motion, and the first pitch he threw me just exploded by me. Then he did me a favor and threw me one of his famed blooper pitches. I got lucky, timed it, and smashed a line-drive base hit right back through the box that Satch had to duck to avoid getting hit in the forehead. They sacrificed me to second, and I scored the only run of the first five innings when a teammate knocked me in with a base hit.

When Satch came to bat against me, I decided I would throw him a blooper, too. Satch saw it coming, waggled his bat, took a mighty cut, and hit a little dribbler back to me. Then he just stood at home plate laughing.

I pitched my five innings and went to the locker room to shower. As I was dressing a man came in and said, "Robin, I'm Frank Lovejoy. I'm a great base-ball fan." Frank Lovejoy was a motion picture and television actor. At the time, he starred in a popular television detective show that Mary and I really enjoyed.

He told me, "You are the best-kept secret in baseball, and you should have an agent." How right he was. Of course, owners would not have talked to agents in those days. Of all the changes in baseball since my day, the ability to have an agent represent me is what I would most appreciate. To have someone as your advocate must be a real benefit.

Years later at a Hall of Fame induction weekend in Cooperstown, I reminded Satch of the base hit I ripped off his blooper pitch.

"Robin," he said, "I got a big black book with all the best hitters I ever faced, and you ain't in it."

I don't know how he left me out of there.

When Satch was elected to the Hall of Fame I told him, "Satchel, it is so nice that you are in the Hall of Fame."

"Well," he said, "they pushed me in the back door, but I made it."

Satchel Paige was certainly special, both as a baseball player and as a person. Of course, there are a thousand stories about him. Dizzy Dean used to tell about the time he hit a triple off of Satchel in a barnstorming game. Diz was on third base with no one out, and Satch walked over to him and said, "Mr. Diz, third is where you is and where you is going to stay."

According to Diz, Satch then proceeded to strike out the side.

Satch stories keep coming long after his passing. My daughter-in-law Christie, who is married to my youngest son, Jim, has a sister named Karen who is a flight attendant for Delta Airlines. Karen worked a flight to Seattle that carried a baseball team a few years ago. She told me that she had met

Satchel Paige on that flight. This was well after Satch's death in 1982, so I told Karen that Delta must have been flying awfully high that day.

Incidentally, I had another blooper pitch experience early in my career. I was pitching against Rip Sewell of the Pirates in Forbes Field in Pittsburgh. Rip was famous for his blooper pitch, which would literally arc about 25 feet off the ground. Ted Williams timed one in the 1946 All-Star Game and parked it in the seats. In any event, Rip threw me one during one of my at-bats. I took it, and the umpire called it a strike even though it came across the plate at about a 45-degree angle. I expressed my displeasure to the umpire, made an out on the next pitch, and went to sit in the dugout next to Eddie Miller, one of our veteran infielders.

I said, "Eddie, that can't be a strike. How can that be a strike?"

He said, "You ought to do what I did. I caught it and hit it back at him."

Eddie was a good storyteller, and that is what I thought that was, just a story.

Years later when I moved to Florida to coach baseball at the University of South Florida I ran into old Rip at a charity golf tournament. He lived in Plant City, and even though he had had parts of both legs amputated because of diabetes, he wore prostheses and could play a mean game of golf.

I said, "Rip, I've been waiting to ask you something since 1949. Eddie Miller told me . . ."

Upon hearing Miller's name Sewell immediately interrupted me and said, "You know what that little bastard did to me? He caught my blooper pitch and lined it right back at me."

I said, "Come on, Rip."

"Yep, he sure did." he said.

"What did the umpire do?" I asked.

"It was George Magerkurth," Rip replied. "He ripped off his mask and said, 'No pitch. No pitch. Now quit screwing around and play ball.'"

That has to be the only pitch in baseball history that didn't count. Nobody called time, but the ump ruled it no pitch.

Eddie Miller was quite a character. He had been an All-Star shortstop with the Braves and Reds but was near the end of the line when he played for the Phillies. I remember he had a hole cut in the palm of his glove so that he could feel the ball better. He had tough hands.

In 1949 the Phillies played an exhibition game in Schenectady. During the fifth inning Eddie Sawyer told Eddie Miller to go warm up and to go in for Granny Hamner at shortstop the next inning. Miller went down the left-field line to loosen up. Nearby was a jeep that they used to drag the infield. When it was time for Eddie to take the field, he hopped into the jeep and had the driver drop him off at shortstop.

Miller often fooled around during practice and caught pop flies behind his back. No matter how high you hit a pop fly, he could catch it behind his back. That same year we played an exhibition game against our farm club in Utica during the All-Star break. We were in a tight game in the eighth inning with two out and two runners on. The batter hit a pop-up about a mile high behind the mound. With runners tearing around the bases, Eddie came in from shortstop and caught the ball behind his back. Benny Bengough was managing because Eddie Sawyer was attending the All-Star Game, and he about had a heart attack.

Eddie came to bat the next inning, and the crowd was hooting and hollering at him for showing off. Eddie stepped out of the box, pointed to left field like Babe Ruth supposedly did in the 1932 World Series, and then proceeded to hit the very next pitch out of the ballpark for a home run. Hard to believe, but he did.

Miller was not playing much in 1949, and late in the season Eddie Sawyer sent him up to pinch hit in the Polo Grounds. The clubhouses there were out in center field. Miller grounded out to shortstop and after he was thrown out kept on running down the right-field line to the right-field fence and then across the outfield and up the stairs to the clubhouse.

I mentioned that incident to Eddie Sawyer one time, and Sawyer said, "He could have kept running all the way home. That was the last time he was ever going to play for me."

And that is what happened. The Phillies brought Miller to spring training in 1950 but released him before the season began. He caught on with the St. Louis Cardinals for the 1950 season before hanging it up after 14 years and many adventures in the big leagues.

* * *

After the 1953 season I agreed to go to Japan with the Eddie Lopat All-Stars to play 12 exhibition games against Japanese ballclubs. We also were to travel to Okinawa and the Philippines for some games. My buddy Curt Simmons came along, as did Yogi Berra, Billy Martin, Bob Lemon, Nellie Fox, Mike Garcia, Jackie Jensen, Harvey Kuenn, Eddie Mathews, Hank Sauer, Enos Slaughter, Eddie Robinson, and Gus Niarhos. We were billed as the greatest team to ever visit Japan. With six future Hall of Famers and some other fine ballplayers, we certainly were not too shabby.

The promoters paid us $1,000 plus expenses or just expenses if you took your wife. Curt, I, and many others took our wives, and we had a memorable time. We gathered for the trip in Colorado Springs, where we were to play a couple of games against military bases, although Mary did not join me until we got to the West Coast.

One of the aspects of barnstorming I most enjoyed was getting to know players from other teams. Baseball had a no-fraternizing rule then, so the only time we could visit with ballplayers from other teams was during the All-Star Game or at banquets in the off-season. So I really looked forward to getting to know some of the American Leaguers in particular on our trip.

After I arrived at the Broadmoor Hotel in Colorado Springs, I saw Bob Lemon in the hotel bar and went over to introduce myself. He was one of the guys I had always admired and looked forward to getting to know. He had come up as an outfielder and switched to pitching only after reaching the big leagues. In fact he had been in the outfield when Bob Feller pitched his second no-hitter on April 30, 1946. Lemon took to pitching very quickly and ended his career with 207 wins, a winning percentage of .618, and seven 20-win seasons. He also was one of the best hitting pitchers in baseball and was often used as a pinch-hitter. Ironically, in 1976, 23 years later, Bob and I were inducted into Cooperstown on the same day.

During our first meeting, in 1953, Bob asked me, "What do you want to drink?"

I said, "Oh, I'll have a 7-Up."

Bob didn't say anything but pulled out a pack of cigarettes and offered me one. He said, "Want a cigarette?"

I said, "No thanks, I don't smoke."

He chuckled and said, "No wonder you don't walk anyone."

We first stopped over in Honolulu for a few days and played some exhibition games against a team of Roy Campanella's All-Stars. In one game, I pitched and Yogi caught. Roy Campanella came to bat and hit a towering foul ball behind the plate. Roy had a big follow-through on his swing, and this time his bat hit Yogi's glove and knocked it flying off his hand. Yogi looked at his glove on the ground and then went back and caught the pop foul barehanded. It was the third out of the inning, so I picked Yogi's glove up and handed it to him in the dugout.

"You all right, Yogi?" I asked.

"That friggin' ball hurt like hell," Yogi said.

In all my years in and around baseball, I have never heard of that happening again. Over the years, I began to wonder whether it really did happen or whether I had somehow made it up. A few years ago I was with Yogi at an Old Timers' Game at Wrigley Field in Chicago. I said to Yogi, "I'm getting older and I want to check with you about a story I've been telling for years. You remember in Hawaii when Campy hit that pop foul and knocked your glove off?"

"That friggin' ball hurt like hell," Yogi said, which was the exact same thing he had said in 1953 after he caught the pop-up. I guess I didn't make it up after all.

Yogi had been pretty rough as a catcher when he came up to the Yankees but worked hard to improve. I had never pitched to him before the trip to Japan, and he still did not have a very good reputation as a defensive catcher. Was I ever pleasantly surprised. He was a fine catcher—quick as a cat—and he gave a real low target, which I loved. I felt so strongly that I told him near the end of the trip, "Yogi, I hadn't heard all that much about you as a catcher, but you are a fine one. I really enjoy throwing to you."

We played one game in Hawaii on what was essentially a football field with a short right-field porch and forever to left field. Billy Martin was a skinny little guy, but he was strong. He hit a home run to that distant left field that went right through the goal posts sitting out there. It should have counted for at least three runs.

When we landed in Tokyo they took us to our hotel in convertibles by motorcade. Thousands of Japanese people were along our route, waving and cheering and hanging out of buildings. It was like a New York City ticker-tape parade. Our coming over was a very big deal to the Japanese.

We played the first game in Tokyo and Mike Garcia, a big burly pitcher from the Cleveland Indians whose nickname was "the Bear," pitched for us against the Mainichi Orions, a team in the Japanese Pacific League. One of the players for the Japanese was Charlie Hood, who was stationed there in the army. Charlie was a catcher in the Phillies organization. He played some games that year for the Orions.

I sat next to Bob Lemon in the dugout during the game and told Bob about Hood, "You know, Bob, this guy is a fine hitter, a really good low-ball hitter. He was in the Phillies organization."

Garcia pitched into the ninth inning and had a 4 to 3 lead. But with two outs and two on he pulled a muscle in his calf and had to come out of the game. Lopat, who was acting as manager, said, "OK, who'll go out and pitch?"

I said, "I will," so out I went to get loose. Charlie Hood was the first batter I had to face. On the first pitch I threw him a low fastball and he ripped it down the right-field line for a game-winning double. I threw one pitch, and we lost

123

the ballgame 5–4. Bob Lemon could not believe it and would not let me forget it for the whole trip. I had been telling him what a good low-ball hitter Hood was, and then he watched Hood beat me on a low fastball.

The Japanese were very excited about beating us. After the game the Japanese press gathered all around to interview me.

"Look," I said, "It's a goodwill trip and so this was some of our goodwill. You won the first game, but you won't win anymore." And they didn't. We won 11 straight, but I'm afraid some of the Japanese still believe we let them win that first game.

A few days later I started for us, and before the game they brought the Japanese starting pitcher, Tokuji Kawasaki of the Nishitetsu Lions, over for some photographs. Kawasaki could understand some English, so I asked him, "How many games did you win this year?"

He said, "Twenty-four. One more than you, huh?"

Of course, he was correct because I had won 23 games in 1953. But I won the game that day, so I always thought that we were even after that.

One of the other Japanese pitchers whom we faced was a 17-year-old left-hander named Masaichi Kaneda. Of course, I was not familiar with the Japanese players and had no real way to follow their careers after our visit. Years later in 1989 Mary and I were at Don Drysdale's Celebrity Golf Tournament in Palm Springs, California. We attended a reception the night before the tournament and noticed a Japanese couple smiling at us. We did not know who they were, but finally an interpreter who was traveling with them came over and said, "Mr. Kaneda would like to meet you."

So they came over and Mrs. Kaneda said several times, "You Kaneda's teacher. You Kaneda's teacher." I had no idea what she was talking about. Then the interpreter told us that Kaneda had copied my delivery from the time I toured Japan in 1953. It turns out that he had gone on to a brilliant career and was the winningest pitcher in Japanese baseball history, with 400 wins in his 20-year career. He also holds Japanese records for most innings pitched (5,527), most strikeouts lifetime (4,490), most complete games (365), and consecutive scoreless innings (68⅓). He is second all-time in games for a pitcher (944) and shutouts (82).

Kaneda was at that time the manager of the Lotte Orions. The interpreter went on to tell us that Kaneda wanted me to come to Japan for part of their spring training to work with his pitchers. I agreed to go over and so in February 1990 Mary and I flew to Tokyo and then down to Kagashima in the south of Japan where the Orions were training. They treated us exceptionally well, everything first class.

Mary and I decided we would follow the Japanese spring training routine so that we would get the full experience of Japanese baseball. At 7:00 in the morning, the team would walk to a running track that was near the hotel. Then they would fast walk around the track for about 30 minutes before walking back to the hotel for breakfast, where there were two buffet lines, one Japanese-style and one American food. At 10:00 the team would report to the field, but without their gloves. For the next two and a half hours they would exercise, running and performing all kinds of calisthenics.

After a quick break for a sushi lunch, they would roll out three batting cages so that three guys could hit at once. The batters were hitting into big nets while four coaches were hitting ground balls to infielders. They would work out all afternoon until about 4:30 when they would call it a day. I couldn't believe how hard they practiced and worked their players.

After observing practice for three or four days, I said to Kaneda, "Boy, you guys really work hard over here. Don't you think you work them too hard?"

Kaneda said, "Japanese baseball is different."

I had to agree with him. The Japanese players even work out before their regular-season games.

We were there on February 21, which is Mary's birthday. Kaneda threw a dinner that night, inviting club officials and all the players. I never saw a bunch of young men drink so much sake. I guess all that work made them thirsty.

Another night we were having dinner with the Kanedas and Mary asked if they had any tape of Kaneda from his pitching days. Kaneda popped a tape into the video machine and Mary gasped, "My goodness, he looks like a left-handed you." And he did, with the same easy motion, the same leg drive and low delivery. The similarity was really remarkable. The best pitcher in Japanese baseball history threw just like I did.

When Hideo Nomo broke into the major leagues in 1995 with the Los Angeles Dodgers, I wrote Kaneda telling him how well Nomo had pitched here and asking if he thought there were any other Japanese players who could succeed in the United States. Kaneda wrote back that the only ballplayer whom he believed could make an immediate impact in the United States was a young outfielder for the Orix Blue Wave named Ichiro Suzuki. I guess Kaneda was a pretty good judge of baseball talent; his report to me was about six years before Ichiro broke in with the Seattle Mariners with such a bang in 2001.

Our 1953 trip was very successful on the field, and the Japanese treated us extremely well. Hank Sauer hit 12 home runs in 12 games and won a motorcycle. I have always wondered if he ever got that motorcycle home. Their ballparks were smaller, and I even hit a home run off of a southpaw in one of our games in Tokyo. Many years later when I was coaching baseball at the University of South Florida, I told my players about my home run in Tokyo. I told them that when I ran around the bases I yelled, "That's for Pearl Harbor!" Of course, I did no such thing, but the players got a big kick out of the story.

We left Japan and flew first to Okinawa and then to the Philippines, playing a couple of games against our military personnel in both locations before heading home. Billy Martin was a character even in those days, as he displayed on the trip home. We also had Jackie Jensen along, a fine outfielder who had played for the Washington Senators in 1953. Billy and he had been teammates on the Yankees for a couple of years before Jackie was traded to the Senators during the 1952 season.

Jackie just hated to fly. In fact, his fear of flying ultimately led to his early retirement from baseball. On the trip back to the States we were flying in one of those huge Pan American Clippers. Jackie had managed to go sound asleep, which prompted Martin put on an oxygen mask and captain's hat. He walked down the aisle and shook Jensen, yelling, "Jackie, put on your Mae West, we are going down!"

Poor Jackie startled awake and just about had a heart attack. That was a tough thing to do to someone who was scared to death anyway.

* * *

Today's ballplayers work out year-round and make enough money that they don't have to worry about an off-season job. That certainly wasn't the case for me, at least in my early years in the big leagues. Most ballplayers in my era needed a job in the winter to help make ends meet.

After my rookie year I went home to Springfield, stayed with my parents, and got a job at the Roberts Brothers' Clothing Store, no relation. I can still wrap a tie around my finger to show how it will look on a shirt.

The following winter I got married and so didn't work. Mary and I spent time in Springfield and in her hometown, McFarland, Wisconsin. I didn't work after the pennant-winning 1950 season either. After Christmas Mary and I went to Florida and relaxed and got ready for spring training.

I hooked up with the Regal Corrugated Box Company of Philadelphia after the 1951 season. I traveled all around the Philly area calling on businesses and trying to sell corrugated boxes for Regal. Jerry Epstein and George

Laycow were running the company, and they were good people. I worked for them for two winters. I was never really a success as a salesman, but I enjoyed working there. I'm not sure how many orders I got, but I could sure talk baseball on my calls.

Later on Jack Sanford, my teammate with the Phillies in the late fifties, and Chuck Bednarik, the Philadelphia Eagles' star linebacker, worked for Regal.

Sometime in 1953 I received a call from Savannah, Georgia, from a man named Bill Mullis. He asked me to work in public relations for his seafood company named Tradewinds. Bill was partners with Henry Ambrose, and they sold frozen packaged shrimp to grocery chains. I worked with them for a couple of winters and traveled all over for the company. Then Bill split off and formed his own seafood business, and I did public relations for the new company for two years. After that I got tired of the off-season travel and was making good money playing baseball, so I never again had a full-time job in the winter.

* * *

For two winters in the middle fifties I hosted the *Robin Roberts Sports Club* on WCAU-TV in Philadelphia. Bill Campbell, one of the announcers for the Phillies, had the idea for the program and was one of the show's announcers. The first winter the show was an hour long every Saturday morning; it was half an hour the second year.

A number of people associated with the show went on to bigger and better things. The producer was a young guy named Frank Chirkinian who went on to produce golf tournaments like the Masters for CBS Television for many years. One of the announcers was Jack Whitaker, who became a famous network sports commentator. The show's director was Jack Dolph, who later became commissioner of the American Basketball Association, although he died a very young man. Ed McMahon also sometimes announced for the show. He was just back from the Korean War, lived in Philadelphia, and was just getting back into television. Ed was a military pilot and, like Ted Williams, served in both World War II and the Korean conflict.

It was a talented group of people, and all I had to do was show up. I later did some radio and television game announcing and, frankly, was never that comfortable doing it. But I enjoyed the *Robin Roberts Sports Club*. We normally had some kids on the program. In later years I have often run into people who tell me they were on the show with me when they were kids.

I stopped doing the show after a couple of years because I stopped pitching so well and began to not feel all that comfortable having my own television show in the winter. From that point on, I didn't work in the off-season. I was making very good money for the time, and it just didn't seem necessary.

In 1953 I was approached outside Connie Mack Stadium by a man named Don McClanen who wanted me to get involved with a new organization he was establishing called the Fellowship of Christian Athletes (FCA). I agreed to go to an organizational meeting after the season at the Duquesne Club in Pittsburgh. Other attendees included Branch Rickey; Deacon Dan Towler, the great running back for the Los Angeles Rams; Carl Erskine; and Otto Graham, among others. We agreed to speak to young people at functions around the country about effectively combining the Christian faith with athletics.

I did make several appearances around the country for the newly formed FCA. Then one day my dad called and said, "Robin, I don't think your involvement in that new organization is fair to Mary."

I have to admit that I had not really thought about the impact on Mary. I was already gone so much, leaving her home alone with our young sons, that I quickly decided that Dad was right. From then on I limited my FCA involvement, although it appears that the organization has done all right without me. It is getting close to celebrating its 50th year.

In the days when I played, the best-paid baseball players lived very comfortably and maintained a good standard of living. We owned a nice house in Meadowbrook, and I drove a Cadillac and sent my boys to private school. But I certainly was not set for life financially, as today's players are. As a result, when I finally retired from baseball, I needed to find work quickly to maintain that standard of living for the family. And, as surprising as it sounds, I had done nothing to prepare myself for life after baseball. I was so focused on pitching for a living and thought that I would be able to pitch successfully well into my forties, that I had not tried to develop a career in the off-season. I was literally clueless. But that is getting ahead of the story.

CHAPTER 9

Innings, Innings, and More Innings

The Phillies stood pretty much pat in the winter before the 1953 season, with the Russ Meyer–for–Earl Torgeson trade the only significant deal. Early in the '52 campaign, Eddie Sawyer had traded Bubba Church to the Cincinnati Reds for outfielder Johnny Wyrostek and pitcher Kent Peterson. Wyrostek had become the regular right fielder, moving Del Ennis to left, until Steve O'Neill decided to play rookie Mel Clark late in the season. Mel had come through, hitting .335 in 47 games and putting together a 17-game hitting streak. It looked like our everyday lineup would be strong with Torgeson challenging Eddie Waitkus for playing time at first.

We needed a starting pitcher to replace Monk and join Curt, Karl Drews, and me in the regular rotation. Curt had shown in 1952 that he could again be a dominant pitcher, once he got into shape after his return from the military. He had posted a 14–8 record for the year with a league-leading six shutouts and had started the All-Star Game for the National League. Bob Miller seemed to be coming back from arm miseries, young Steve Ridzik had a very strong spring, and there were other possibilities such as rookie Thornton Kipper and outfielder-turned-knuckleballer Johnny Lindell.

With our strong finish in 1952, I had high hopes that we would sweep to another pennant, just as we had in 1950. I lost the season opener 4–1 to the New York Giants and their ace Larry Jansen at home, but we won 9 out of the next 10 to break in front and confirm our optimism. We were not able to keep up that pace, however, and struggled in late May, losing five games in a row. A week later Curt Simmons had his famous lawn mower accident.

Curt's and my families lived next door to each other on Robin Hood Lane in suburban Meadowbrook beginning in 1952. I went to the drugstore about 9:00 on the morning of June 4, 1953. When I got home I noticed that Curt's power mower was out on his lawn. I thought that was strange because Curt was very meticulous and never left anything out. I went into my house, and Mary was white as a ghost.

"What's wrong?" I asked.

Mary said, "Curt cut his toe badly mowing the lawn and is in the hospital."

Curt really cut off only a little of the tip of his big toe, and it put him out of action for a month. It was bad timing; just a couple of weeks before, he had pitched the best game of his career against the Milwaukee Braves. Bill Bruton led off with a single and was promptly erased on a double play. Curt retired the next 25 batters in a row and faced only the minimum 27 to win 3–0 on a one-hitter. He struck out 10, including Bruton the next three times he faced him.

After our slump in late May, we came back and played pretty well. Our main problem was that the Dodgers ran off and left everyone behind, winning 105 games and the pennant by 13 games over the Milwaukee Braves. We tied the Cardinals for third, finishing 12 games over .500 at 83–71, 22 games in back of Brooklyn. Whitey hit .330; Del batted a hard .285 with 29 home runs and 125 runs batted in. Granny Hamner played well enough to be named the starting shortstop in the All-Star Game but shortly thereafter was moved to second base to allow bonus baby Ted Kazanski a shot at playing shortstop.

Curt bounced back from his toe injury to put together a 16–13 record; Steve Ridzik showed real promise as a spot starter, going 9–6; and Steve O'Neill started Jim Konstanty 19 times in addition to bringing him out of the bullpen. Jim came through with 14 wins, losing 10.

I had another strong year, winning 23 again to tie Warren Spahn for the league lead, while losing 16. I again led the league in innings pitched with 347, games started with 41, and complete games with 33, all career highs. In fact, I pitched complete games in my first 20 starts, which, counting my 8 straight complete games at the end of 1952, made for 28 straight complete games, dating from August 28, 1952, to July 9, 1953. My complete-game streak ended when Bob Miller came in to relieve me in the eighth inning of a game against the Dodgers in Connie Mack Stadium. We were down 5–4, but my teammates came back with two runs in the bottom of the eighth to take me off the hook and win the game for Bugger. My record stayed at 13–6.

Still, the end of the year was frustrating. I won my 20th game for the fourth consecutive year by defeating the Pirates 8–4 on August 13 in Forbes Field. That brought my record to 20–8, but for the last six weeks of the season I lost eight games while winning only three more. We played the Dodgers and Giants a lot near the end of the season, and they were tough.

We were still a solid first-division club heading into 1954 and thought with a few breaks we could be in the hunt for the pennant. The big change was that over the winter Bob Carpenter hired veteran front-office executive Roy Hamey to serve as the Phillies' general manager. As surprising as it sounds today, Hamey was the first general manager of the Phillies since Herb Pennock died in 1948.

Hamey did not immediately make many changes, but he did trade pitcher Andy Hansen and infielder Jack Lohrke to the Pirates for veteran starting pitcher Murry Dickson. He also sold Eddie Waitkus to the Baltimore Orioles, allowing Earl Torgeson to take over at first, and brought Bobby Morgan over from the Dodgers to play shortstop, allowing Hamner to stay at second.

As it developed, 1954 became our most disappointing season since '51. It was the year the New York Giants, behind the sensational Willie Mays, Alvin Dark, Don Mueller, Johnny Antonelli, Sal Maglie, and Ruben Gomez, raced to the pennant, defeating the Dodgers by five games. We were in the race early but slumped heading into summer. In mid-July, Hamey made his presence felt by suddenly firing Steve O'Neill even though we were above .500 at 40–37. Hamey replaced Steve with Terry Moore, the fine St. Louis Cardinals center fielder from the forties. Under Moore, we limped home with a 35–42 record to finish below .500, although we did manage to stay in the first division by one game over the Cincinnati Reds.

For the third year in a row, I won 23 games to lead the league, this time losing 15. Along the way I threw some games that really bring back pleasant memories, as well as some that aren't quite so nice to remember. On April 29, I pitched a one-hitter to defeat Warren Spahn and the Milwaukee Braves 4–0 at County Stadium, allowing only a third-inning double to Del Crandall. Then, about two weeks later I pitched against the Cincinnati Reds in Connie Mack Stadium. Bobby Adams was the Reds' leadoff hitter, and he homered into the left-field stands. After that I retired 27 Reds in a row to complete my second one-hitter, winning 8–1 over Corky Valentine. I guess I'm one of the few guys to ever pitch a complete game without throwing a pitch from the stretch. After Adams' homer, I relaxed and, with my good stuff, just reached back and fired.

Years later Ted Kluszewski asked me if I remembered that game. I said, "Sure, Ted, how could I forget that one?"

He said, "I remember it for another reason. That was the only time I struck out three times in one game in the big leagues."

Even with those sterling games, I carried only a 7–6 record into a June 12 start against the Milwaukee Braves at County Stadium. The veteran Jim Wilson, my mound opponent, was making only his second start of the year after spending the first two months of the season coming out of the bullpen. In his first start, he had tossed a shutout at the Pirates six days before, but he topped even that by tossing a no-hitter against us. I pitched well but surrendered two solo home runs, in the first to Johnny Logan and in the fifth to Del Crandall, to lose 2–0 and even my record at 7–7.

We didn't go down without a fight. With two outs in the eighth, Johnny Wyrostek grounded a ball sharply up the middle right through Wilson's legs. But Logan at shortstop raced behind second to grab the ball and made a strong throw to Joe Adcock at first to just nip Johnny. Then in the ninth with one out Mel Clark, pinch hitting for me, looped a 2–2 pitch over Adcock's head, but the ball landed just foul as the home crowd of almost thirty thousand breathed a sigh of relief. Clark struck out on the next pitch to bring Willie Jones to the plate. Puddin' Head worked the count to 3–2 and laced a drive down the left-field line that landed foul by inches. After fouling another pitch off, Willie grounded to Danny O'Connell at second, and Wilson had his no-hitter.

On my next start, June 17 against the Cardinals' Joe Presko, I got back above .500, but it took a rain delay and 15 innings to do it. I could not get my good rhythm at the start and, as often happened, I was overthrowing. The first two batters singled, and then Stan Musial tripled to drive in two runs. At that point, the skies opened up and we had about a 45-minute rain delay. I went into the clubhouse, relaxed, and came back out throwing nice and easy. I retired the Cardinals in the first without letting Stan score and continued to get them out. Bobby Morgan hit a home run in the bottom of the ninth to tie the score at 2–2 and send the game into extra innings. The game eventually went 15 innings, and I held the Cardinals scoreless the final 14. I finally scored the winning run myself in the bottom of the fifteenth inning to win 3–2. If it hadn't been for the rain, I might not have made it through the first inning.

I have noticed that some pitchers today, such as Tom Glavine, have the same problem getting in the groove the first couple of innings. Yogi Berra once told me that Vic Raschi, who was a fine, hard-throwing right-hander for the Yankees in the early fifties, developed a big, slow curve to help him get through the start of the game when he couldn't get his rhythm for his fastball. Once he got going, he would throw about 90 percent fastballs and pretty much ignore his curveball.

Cy Perkins used to say that the delivery is 75 percent of pitching. He believed that a pitcher needed some way to deceive the batter. If a pitcher could throw hard, with good wrist action that makes the ball move, from a nice easy motion, he would be effective. Guys like Sandy Koufax, Bob Gibson, Tom Seaver, and Steve Carlton all had that ability and threw with a good rhythm to their delivery and explosive wrist action that made their ball really jump.

Throwing a good, live fastball is similar to throwing a ball from the outfield on one hop to the catcher. Warren Spahn used to say that when he threw his fastball it was like he was throwing someone out from right field but the catcher got in the way.

On July 9 I threw seven innings against the Dodgers in Ebbets Field on a Friday night, and was behind 2–0 when our manager, Steve O'Neill, pulled me for a pinch-hitter in the top of the eighth. We went on to score four runs to take the lead 4–2. Unfortunately, Brooklyn tied the score and then won in the bottom of the tenth inning on a home run by Gil Hodges.

On Sunday, I was in the bullpen watching Herm Wehmeier pitch a fine game against the Dodgers. We were ahead 3–1 in the eighth inning when I began loosening up to get my between-starts throwing in, as was my habit. I really did not have any pop at all; I just was not throwing well. I threw for about 10 minutes and was about as loose as I could get. The Dodgers had gotten runners on first and second with one out. All of a sudden I looked up and Steve O'Neill was motioning me in from the bullpen to face Jackie Robinson. As I walked in from the bullpen I thought to myself, "Man, I really don't have it. I better throw it with the seams to try to make the ball sink." I very rarely did that, but I thought it was my only chance because I just did not have any pop on my fastball.

Jackie Robinson stepped in and took the first two sinkers, both of which broke down out of the strike zone. The count was 2 and 0, but I thought that I had to stick with it because I'd come this far. I threw it again, and Jackie hit a two-hopper to Ted Kazanski at short for a double play. I walked off thinking someone was on my side. At least I had the good sense not to throw him my fastball that day.

I won my 20th game for the fifth year in a row on September 6 in another extra-inning game, this one 11 innings, against the New York Giants in Connie Mack Stadium by a 5–4 score. The win brought my record to 20–13. Ironically, on September 26 I lost my last game of the year 3–2 to the same pennant-winning Giants in another 11-inning ballgame. The Giants had already clinched the pennant, but Willie Mays and his teammate Don Mueller were in a virtual dead heat for the batting title. I guess I contributed to Willie's first and only batting title because he went 3 for 4 to finish at .345 while Don ended 2 for 6 at .342.

The 1954 season was Willie's first complete season in the big leagues, and he had quite a year. In addition to winning the batting title, he also led the league in slugging percentage (.667) and triples (13), and he finished in the top three in home runs, total bases, hits, and runs.

Willie actually made his major league debut against the Phillies in late May 1951. I had learned from reading the newspaper that morning that the Giants were calling him up. The paper reported that the Giants had just called up a young outfielder from their top farm club, the Minneapolis Millers of the American Association, and that he was hitting .477 with the Millers. It made me think to myself, "My goodness, how can a guy be hitting .477?"

It happened that the Giants had come into Shibe Park to begin a series against us that day. We took batting practice first, and instead of going back to the clubhouse to relax and change my shirt, I decided to sit in our dugout and watch the kid hitting .477 take batting practice.

I sat down, and the Giants let Mays hit first. Willie stepped into the batter's box with his cap on the back of his head and hit five straight pitches into the upper deck. Then he ran around the bases, and it looked like he could run like the wind. After that he trotted out to the outfield and shagged fly balls effortlessly. I sat there and thought, "Wow, what a ballplayer."

Willie's debut against us caused quite a stir. He faced Karl Drews, Curt Simmons, and me in the three games and went 0–12. In his first game he even ran into right fielder Monte Irvin on a fly ball into the gap, turning an out into a double. But the Giants swept the series from us, seemingly inspired by Willie's obvious raw talent.

Even with Willie's rough start, Giants manager Leo Durocher was effusive. As the Giants boarded the train at North Philadelphia Station to return to New York, it was reported that Leo told veteran writer Tom Meany, "This kid can take us all the way!"

Meany replied, "Yeah, someday he may even get a hit."

He did the next series in New York against Warren Spahn. His first big-league hit went over the roof of the Polo Grounds.

I would face Mays and watch him play many times over the next decade. Was he the best I ever saw? That is always a difficult question to answer. I once heard a fan ask Eddie Sawyer, "Eddie, if you had your choice would you take Mantle or Mays?"

Eddie said, "I'll tell you what. I'll give you first choice and we are both in good shape."

Willie did everything well. He could run, he could hit for average and for power, he could go get the baseball, and he could throw. On top of having the five tools, Willie had such great instincts and played with such flair that I have to say he was the best ballplayer I ever saw, as hard as it is to make that kind of subjective judgment.

At the plate, if you could crowd him with the fastball you could get him out. Of course, you could get anyone out by crowding him with the fastball. But if you got the ball out over the plate he could ricochet the ball the other way with a flick of his wrists. He was so quick at the plate that if you were trying to pitch him inside and the ball got away, you couldn't hit him. He could get out of the way quicker than anybody I ever saw.

One time someone asked Willie about getting knocked down, and Willie said, "Shoot, man, the first thing you got to learn is to get out of the way."

Willie had great instincts on the bases and tried to steal only when it meant something. When I pitched I usually didn't worry much about holding a base runner on, even if it was Willie. I preferred to concentrate on the hitter, figuring that the base runner couldn't score if I got the batter out.

Once in 1957 I was walking from the clubhouse to warm up for a game against the Giants when our manager, Mayo Smith, asked me to come into his office for a minute. Mayo said, "Let's just imagine a game situation. You've got a one-run lead in the ninth inning and Willie Mays is on first base. Now what are you thinking about?"

I said, "Well, I'm pitching a helluva game, Mayo, if I got a one-run lead in the ninth inning."

Mayo did not think my crack was particularly funny. He was trying to make a point. He said, "Now you've got to hold Mays on because he'll steal second if you don't."

I said, "Mayo, if he steals second, it means they still need a base hit to score. I'd rather just concentrate on the batter."

Mayo said, "Well, I think you need to try to hold Mays close in that situation."

So I said, "OK, all right, Mayo, I will."

I went out and did pitch a whale of a game. Going into the top of the ninth inning I was ahead 1–0 and had allowed only two hits. Mays led off the inning and I jammed him, but he hit a little dribbler down the third-base line and beat it out. Ray Jablonski, the Giants' cleanup hitter, was the next batter, and I now had the exact situation Mayo had described before the game. So for the first time in my life, I paid attention to the runner on first. I looked at Mays and then delivered a pitch to Jablonski. He hit the ball to the top of the Coca-Cola sign on the roof of Connie Mack Stadium for a two-run homer, and I got beat 2–1.

I don't remember ever losing a game when I had stuff as good as I had that day. I wish Mays had stolen second *and* third and I hadn't worried about him.

* * *

In 1954 I led the league for the fifth consecutive year in games started (38), for the fourth straight year in innings pitched (336), and for the third year in a row in wins (23) and complete games (29). Even with our disappointing record, we had some other bright spots. Smoky Burgess batted a resounding .368 but with 345 at-bats lacked enough official trips to qualify for the batting title. Stan Lopata hit .290 with 14 home runs, so we had a lot of offense from our catchers. Whitey Ashburn hit .313 and had a 730-consecutive-game playing streak by the end of the year. Del Ennis polled 25 homers and drove in 119 runs in another workmanlike year for him, and Granny Hamner hit .299 and drove in 89 runs, great numbers for a second baseman. Curt Simmons pitched in hard luck and finished 14–15 in 253 innings, but his 2.81 earned run average was third in the league.

The 1954 season was personally disappointing to me, despite my good year on the mound. One day in September I went out to help Cy Perkins put the balls in the bucket behind the screen behind second base during batting practice. It was one of Cy's jobs, but he didn't like to do it and I often would go and help him. Cy always said that he wasn't a sweatin' coach. That day Cy said to me, "Kid, they're getting rid of me." I first thought he was kidding, but he was serious.

I knew that Bob Carpenter had no idea of Cy's importance to the team, so the next day I went up to see him. "Bob," I said, "Cy tells me that you are letting him go."

"Well, he's getting old."

"Hey Bob, I don't think you have any idea how important he is to us. Ask Richie; ask Ham. He has really helped me personally. Don't get rid of him," I said.

"Aw c'mon, you're kidding," Carpenter said.

I asked, "How much do you pay him?"

"About $7,500. Why?"

"I'll pay his salary," I said. "That is how much he means to me." But no matter how hard I talked, they didn't bring Cy back.

It may sound silly, but baseball was never quite the same for me after Cy was let go. I was a professional and should have been able to adjust better, but Cy's belief in me had spoiled me. He never talked to me about the mechanics of pitching, but he had so much confidence in me and had such a quiet way of reinforcing what I was trying to do. I really missed that daily relationship.

136

The following year, 1955, Mayo Smith became our manager, and he brought in Whitlow Wyatt as his pitching coach. Whitlow had been a fine pitcher with the Brooklyn Dodgers and had pitched for 16 years in the big leagues, so he knew something about the art. I kept rolling along that year, winning my 20th game on August 18 against the Dodgers by a 3–2 score. After the game, Whitlow came up to me in the clubhouse and said, "Congratulations, Robin. I have to admit, I don't know how you do it."

I realized pretty quickly that I had gone from a coach who thought I should win 300 games to one who didn't know how I did it. In the previous seven years I had won 137 games, and the guy who did know how I did it was out of a job.

Because of the way Eddie Sawyer and Cy Perkins handled me, I always wonder if there is too much emphasis on teaching young pitchers how to pitch. The advice Curt Simmons used to give to young pitchers was to remember the best game they ever pitched, and then to go pitch that way. Curt himself struggled in the big leagues as a young bonus baby out of Egypt, Pennsylvania. George Earnshaw, one of the Phillies' coaches who had been an outstanding pitcher for Connie Mack, kept trying to alter Curt's delivery because it was so herky-jerky and looked so awkward. Finally Eddie Sawyer told all of the coaches to leave Curt alone and then told Curt to just pitch the way he had in high school, where, after all, he had been a phenom. Although Curt was not immediately transformed into a successful major league pitcher, that was the beginning of his turnaround.

If a pitcher is successful at one level, that must mean he knows how to do something right to get batters out. He will learn as he progresses to higher levels, but I'm not sure anyone really has to tell him anything. I remember when Roger Clemens signed out of the University of Texas, he was sent to Winter Haven in the Florida State League, where he won. Then he went to Double A, where he won, and then to Pawtucket in Triple A, where he also won. He always won and no one had to tell him how to pitch, although I am sure he made adjustments, just like I did early in 1952 when I adopted Sal Maglie's curveball.

Roy Hamey brought Mayo Smith to manage during the winter before the '55 season. Mayo had managed in the Yankees farm system, where he had gotten to know Hamey, and had played in 73 games for the 1945 Philadelphia Athletics. Of course, he was a totally unknown quantity to us, but we were getting used to change. Mayo was our fourth manager in three years.

In those days, teams broke camp in Florida a couple of weeks before the beginning of the season and traveled to the north by train, playing exhibition games along the way. We did just that in 1955 and were supposed to play an exhibition game in a small city in North Carolina. It started raining pretty hard in the morning, and so Del Ennis, Richie Ashburn, Earl Torgeson, and I decided to shoot some pool in a local pool hall. We did not know if the game had been called or not, so we asked Jack Meyer, a rookie pitcher, to let us know if they called the game so that we could catch the team bus to the train station.

We were enjoying ourselves shooting pool when all of a sudden one of us looked up and realized that Jack was no longer there. We stepped outside and found that the bus was gone, too. We soon discovered that the team had left town on the train heading north while we were still shooting pool.

We quickly decided to call a local air charter service to see if we could fly to the next town and meet the train. The guy on the phone said he could take four small guys. When we arrived at the airstrip the pilot took one look at Del, Torgy, Whitey, and me and said, "I can't take you guys. You're too big."

We finally talked him into taking us even though it was still a cloudy, rainy day. He charged us $20 apiece. We took off and followed the train tracks and pretty soon we could see the train. We landed at the first town after we passed the train and asked the pilot to wait for us in case we could not get to the train station in time to get on the train. We all piled in a taxi and, sure enough, the train was at the station when we pulled in.

We all jumped on the train and sat down. In a few minutes our traveling secretary, Johnny Wise, walked by and asked, "Where have you been?"

I said, "What do you mean? I've been right here."

Wise said, "I know you weren't on this train. I've been looking all over for you because Mayo wanted to see you. Where were you?" But we all just sat there quietly and no one on the club ever did figure out what had happened to us.

A lot of the guys played cards on the train trips going north to pass the time. Some of the nongamblers played hearts and fan-tan, but there always was a poker game where money changed hands. Some of the guys played poker all season long, but on the trip north they played every day because we traveled virtually every day. I generally donated when I played, but never too much. One spring going north I had a lucky streak you could not believe. We didn't get paid until Opening Day, and on this occasion I was doing so well at cards that after three days of the ten-day trip, I had everyone's money. I was probably the highest-paid player on the team, and the poker players were all borrowing money from me to continue the game. My luck continued, and after a couple more days everybody but Whitey owed me money. I finally said, "I'm canceling all debts, and I'll never play poker again." And I never did.

One of the canceled debts was Earl Torgeson's $400. Later that season Torgy was traded to the Detroit Tigers. We were in Milwaukee to play the Braves, and when I came into the clubhouse, Del Ennis came up to me. He said that he had bet on a horse for me that day and it had come in and paid $400. I knew that was not true, but I didn't understand why Del was forking over $400. Then he told me that Torgy had been traded to Detroit and wanted to square his debt from the spring training card game. I took the money and did not charge Torgy interest.

* * *

I started on Opening Day against the New York Giants and Johnny Antonelli, my sixth consecutive opener and my most memorable. I had a no-hitter and a 4–0 lead after eight innings. I usually gave up hits early and got stronger as the game went on, but I was aware that I had a no-hitter going as I went out to pitch the ninth. For the first time since I pitched to Stan Rojek in 1948 in my first game in the majors, I was nervous. In fact, it was the only other time I was ever nervous on a big-league pitching mound. I managed to retire the first batter, but then Whitey Lockman hit a ground ball to shortstop and Granny Hamner threw it away for an error. I got 0–2 on Alvin Dark, and he fouled off five straight fastballs. He hit the sixth fastball, which was low and away, to right field for a base hit. I surrendered a couple more hits and two runs before closing out the 4–2 victory. It was the closest I ever came to a no-hitter in the majors.

My next start was yet another 11-inning affair against Antonelli and the Giants, which we won 4–2 due to Bobby Morgan's pinch-hit two-run homer. The club got off to a mediocre start, playing about .500 ball for the first couple of weeks of the season. Then on April 30, GM Haney decided to shake things up a little and traded Smoky Burgess, Steve Ridzik, and reserve outfielder Stan Palys to the Cincinnati Reds for outfielders Jim Greengrass, Glen Gorbous, and Andy Seminick. It was great to have Andy back, but on the day of the trade we lost the first game of what would become a 13-game losing streak, effectively knocking us out of the pennant race by mid-May. I finally ended the streak on May 15, beating the Milwaukee Braves and Chet Nichols 9–1 in County Stadium. Billy Bruton led off the game with a home run, and I shut them out after that.

Jim Greengrass was a big right-handed-hitting outfielder with a lot of power. Billy Loes happened to pitch the first time we played Brooklyn after Jim joined us. Loes really had our number; the previous year we had failed to score at all against him. Jim, however, hit a curveball into the upper deck in left in his first at-bat against Loes in a Phillies uniform. After he circled the bases and came to the dugout, I said, "Jim, that's the first run we've scored against Loes in two years."

Jim said, "He gives his pitches away. I can tell when he's throwing his curve." And Jim could hit some curves.

Later we were playing the Cubs in Wrigley Field and Sad Sam Jones was pitching for Chicago. Sad Sam had a curveball that was awesome and no right-hander could touch. Mayo Smith didn't start Greengrass, but in the ninth inning we were losing and Mayo sent Jim up to pinch hit. The first pitch was a wicked curve that broke over the plate for strike one as Jim sat down at the plate. The second was the same kind of curve for strike two as Jim again sat in the dirt. The third pitch was a fastball right down the pipe that Jim took for strike three with the bat on his shoulder. Jim walked back to the dugout, put his bat in the bat rack, walked over to Mayo Smith, pointed his finger right at Mayo's nose, and said, "Don't ever do that to me again."

We came back with an 11-game winning streak in July, and by the All-Star break I was 13–7 and was selected to represent the National League in the All-Star Game, which was held on July 12 in County Stadium in Milwaukee, for the sixth straight year. The '55 game was one of the most memorable in All-Star history, but not because of my performance.

Before the game National League manager Leo Durocher held a meeting to go over the American League hitters. I was not used to having meetings to go over hitters, and so I guess I wasn't taking it too seriously, even though I was the starting pitcher and the American League had a formidable lineup with Mickey Mantle, Ted Williams, Harvey Kuenn, Yogi Berra, and Al Kaline. At one point Leo asked, "Does anyone know anything about Yogi Berra?" Of course, Leo meant, "Does anyone know how to pitch to Yogi?" but I cracked, "No, but I'll tell you one thing. He sure has a beautiful wife, and I don't know how he did it."

Jackie Robinson fell off his stool and said, "What did you say?"

I said, "Did you ever see his wife, Jackie?"

Once the game began, Harvey Kuenn led off with a single to left. Nellie Fox followed with a single to right-center to send Kuenn to third. I then threw a wild pitch to Ted Williams, allowing Kuenn to score and Fox to take second. I ended up walking Williams to bring Mickey Mantle to the plate with two on and a run in.

Mickey was always up on the plate when I pitched to him in spring training, so I would throw him my fastball in. He couldn't get around on it and would pop it a mile high, but in the ballpark. This time when I looked up, Mantle was way back in the corner of the batter's box like Musial. I decided that presented a different problem and that I better throw my fastball low and away. It was not a good idea. Mickey hit it on top of a tree way over the center-field fence in County Stadium. It was one of the longest home runs I've seen, and it put the National League and me down 4–0. Maybe I should have paid better attention to Leo's pregame meeting.

I settled down to retire Yogi, Al Kaline, and Mickey Vernon to get out of the inning without any further damage. In fact, I retired the American League in the second and third innings as well, with only Jim Finigan reaching on an error in the second and Ted Williams on a single in the third. I have always appreciated the fact that after my rocky start Leo Durocher allowed me to stay in to finish the standard three innings that starters pitched.

We were still down after my three innings 4–0. I really enjoyed the whole experience surrounding All-Star Games, including the game itself. After my stint on the mound I went into the clubhouse to change my sweatshirt and then came back to sit on the bench and watch the rest of the game. The American League stretched their lead to 5–0 by nicking Harvey Haddix for a run in the top of the sixth and in the seventh Willie Mays made a great leaping grab well above the fence in right-center field to deprive Ted Williams of a two-run homer. The National League finally came back with two runs in the seventh and a two-out, three-run rally in the eighth to tie the game and take me off the hook. The American League threatened in their ninth on a single by Chico Carrasquel and an Al Smith walk, but Joe Nuxhall bore down with one out and induced Mantle to fly to Willie Mays in center and Yogi Berra to pop to Johnny Logan at shortstop to escape the inning unscathed.

The game went into the bottom of the twelfth inning with neither side offering much of a threat. Then Stan Musial led off against Frank Sullivan of the Red Sox and smashed a dramatic drive far into the bleachers in right field to complete our comeback and win the game 6–5. I joined my teammates con-gratulating Stan as he touched home plate.

Bill Giles, the son of National League president Warren Giles who was later president of the Phillies, once told me that the photo of the National Lea-guers congratulating Musial at home plate in the 1955 All-Star Game was one of his father's favorite pictures because it showed me out there still in uniform with my warm-up jacket on even though I had pitched early in the game and had not done all that well but had stayed around for the finish.

I suppose the 2002 All-Star Game shows that the leagues approach the All-Star Game differently from the way we did, when winning the game was very important because of the rivalry between the leagues. For example, although there were a number of substitutions in the games that I played in, it was not at all unusual for key players to play the entire game. In the '55 game Yogi Berra caught all 12 innings and Mickey Mantle, Al Kaline, and Mickey Vernon played the entire game for the American League while Ted Kluszewski and Red Schoendienst were in there all the way for the National League. In my first All-Star Game in 1950 seven players played all 14 innings: Phil Rizzuto, Larry Doby, and George Kell for the American League and Willie Jones, Ralph Kiner, Stan Musial, and Roy Campanella for the National League. The rivalry between leagues seems to have lessened in recent years because of interleague play and free agency.

I can't remember seeing a better game than the 2002 All-Star Game, but it was a shame it had to end in a tie after all the great plays and dramatic hits. I hope in the future the managers will do a better job of holding pitchers back in case of extra innings because I believe there should be a winner and loser unless it rains.

With the exception of the 1952 game, I started every All-Star Game for the National League from 1950 through 1955. I've already described the great 14-inning win in Comiskey Park in 1950 when Schoendienst homered off of Ted Gray. Eddie Sawyer was the National League manager in 1951 due to the Whiz Kids' pennant the year before, and he named me to start the '51 game in Detroit on two days' rest. I pitched the first two innings, allowing a second-inning run on a single by Yogi Berra and a triple by Ferris Fain. When I left the score was 1–1, but the National League went on to win 8–3 thanks to a record-setting four home runs, one each by Stan Musial, Gil Hodges, Bob Elliot, and Ralph Kiner.

The 1952 game was at Shibe Park, right there in Philadelphia. The game was on Tuesday, and I had pitched on Sunday, losing 2–0 to Max Lanier and the Giants. Leo Durocher was the manager that year, and before the game he told me, "I'm going to start your buddy and then you can come in and pitch the last three innings." That meant Curt Simmons was the starting pitcher for the National League. I thought it was a nice gesture for Leo to tell me his plan. Curt did start after a 20-minute rain delay and gave up only a first-inning walk and third-inning double to Dom DiMaggio in three innings of shutout pitching.

After five innings the National League led 3–2 with a monstrous two-run homer over the roof in left by Hank Sauer the key blow. Minnie Minoso was leading off the top of the sixth against Bob Rush when the drizzle turned to a downpour and caused play to stop. Fifty-six minutes later the umpires called the game, resulting in a 3–2 National League victory. Because of the rain, I didn't get a chance to finish, but we were happy to have the win.

In 1953 Charlie Dressen named me to again start the All-Star Game, which was held in Crosley Field in Cincinnati on a Tuesday, even though I had pitched nine innings against the Pirates on Sunday, winning 6–4. I had also pitched against the Dodgers a few days before and struck Roy Campanella out three times. Campy was the starting All-Star catcher, and warming up I was really having trouble getting loose and getting a good pop on the ball. Roy threw the ball to second base after my warm-up pitches before the first inning, and he came out to the mound and asked, "What's wrong, Meat? You didn't throw like this the other night."

I said, "That's why I can't throw so good now, Campy. Just stay down low and we'll be all right."

That is what we did, and I ended up with my best All-Star performance, allowing only a first-inning walk to Billy Goodman and a two-out second-inning single to Gus Zernial in three shutout innings. Crosley Field was one of the smallest ballparks in baseball, and with the wind blowing out, balls could really fly out of there. Mickey Mantle led off the third inning and tried to drag a bunt for a base hit. He didn't get it by me, and I threw him out at first. He probably could have hit a home run with his forearm with that wind.

We won the '53 game 5–1 as Warren Spahn, Curt Simmons, and Murry Dickson allowed the American Leaguers only a single run the rest of the way. Led by two hits apiece by Pee Wee Reese, Enos Slaughter, and Stan Musial, we scored runs in the fifth, seventh, and eighth innings. Forty-plus-year-old Satchel Paige of the St. Louis Browns threw the eighth inning for the American League in his only All-Star appearance.

I wasn't quite so fortunate in the 1954 All-Star Game, which was held in Municipal Stadium in Cleveland. I started against Whitey Ford and threw a scoreless first two innings, allowing only a single to Bobby Avila in the first and to Hank Bauer in the second. In my third and last inning, I began by walking Minnie Minoso and giving up a second single to Avila to put men on first and second with no one out. I bore down and struck out Mickey Mantle and got Berra on a grounder to Kluszewski at first. One more out and I could go sit down, but Al Rosen clobbered a long homer to left-center field to drive in three runs. Ray Boone, Bret and Aaron Boone's grandfather and Bob Boone's father, then followed with another homer in about the same place, and we were quickly behind 4–0. I finally struck Hank Bauer out to complete my three-inning stint.

My National League teammates got me off the hook in the top of the fourth, scoring five runs off Sandy Consuegra of the White Sox. The day

143

belonged to the hitters, and the American League eventually won the seesaw affair 11–9, scoring three runs in the bottom of the eighth to take the lead for good. The '54 game was the only game that I started that the National League lost, although my teammates had to bail me out a couple of times.

The 1955 game was my fifth All-Star start and third in a row. I would just show up and not talk to anyone and someone would tell me that I was starting. Of course, I was thrilled to do so. As I mentioned, the '55 game was one of the most exciting games in All-Star history, although not because of my contribution. I was selected for the 1956 All-Star Game, even though I had only an 8–10 record going into the break. The game was held at Griffith Stadium in Washington, D.C., and is remembered chiefly because of the ballot stuffing in Cincinnati that resulted in five of the eight National League starters coming from the Reds, who were leading the league at the break. The National League won 7–3 behind home runs by Willie Mays and Stan Musial and two doubles by Ted Kluszewski. National League manager Walter Alston used only three pitchers, Bob Friend, Warren Spahn, and Johnny Antonelli, and so I did not make an appearance.

Before the game, Stan Musial was telling me a story in the dugout when we were called out to the first-base line to stand for the playing of the National Anthem. Stan finished telling the story before the music began and it made me laugh. So I guess I was laughing during the playing of the National Anthem. A couple of weeks later I got a letter from a fan who thought it was awful that I was cutting up while the "Star-Spangled Banner" played. I really did feel bad about it.

One of my pitching coaches, Whitlow Wyatt, told me that he always gave a prayer of thanks during the playing of the National Anthem. During an Old Timers' Game while I was pitching for Baltimore a few years later, Hall of Famer Joe Medwick came to our dugout to visit at the end of their game. As we were talking they announced the playing of the National Anthem. Joe asked if he could stand in our dugout while it was played. I said, "Sure," so we stood together and at the end of the anthem tears were rolling down Joe's cheeks.

As I mentioned, I enjoyed participating in All-Star Games tremendously. In fact, I enjoyed them so much that I am at least partially responsible for Major League Baseball's experiment with a second All-Star Game from 1959 through 1962. In 1958 I was involved as the Phillies' player representative in a meeting with the owners about the players' pension fund. At that time, 60 percent of the television revenue from the All-Star Game went to the players' pension. I was of course heavily involved in the pension fund, and because I was such an advocate of the All-Star Game, I suggested to Walter O'Malley, the owner of the Dodgers, that we consider a second All-Star Game. Mr. O'Malley thought about it and said, "You know, I think that is a good idea, Robin. Let's do that."

Mr. O'Malley was quite an influential owner, and when he got behind something, it generally got done. So the owners eventually voted to have a second All-Star Game every year, beginning in 1959. The games were played about a month apart in Forbes Field in Pittsburgh and the Coliseum in Los Angeles, where the Dodgers were making their temporary home. After those games I heard some grumbling from the players about the logistics and interruption of the schedule to play two games. When I saw Mr. O'Malley, I said, "That second All-Star Game is a terrible idea, and I'm sorry I ever suggested it. Let's stop playing it because it is not working."

"No," he said, "let's give it a chance." So they kept it for three more years, although there was a lack of interest from the players and the fans. I think that some of the games were not even sellouts. But eventually the owners dropped the second game, and I'm still sorry I ever brought it up. I had good intentions, because I was really looking for ways to bolster the pension fund and I loved All-Star Games, but it was a bad idea.

* * *

We won 40 of our final 70 games in 1955 to climb back to .500 and finish in fourth place again, 21½ games behind the pennant-winning Brooklyn Dodgers. Much attention during the year focused on Richie Ashburn who hit .338 and won his first batting title. Del Ennis was rock solid again, batting .296 with 29 homers and 120 RBIs. Stan Lopata split time behind the plate with Andy and slugged 22 home runs, and Bob Miller and rookie Jack Meyer had good years out of the bullpen. Curt was plagued with arm trouble and finished 8–8.

I was 5–2 for the month after the '55 All-Star Game, which gave me a record of 18–9 heading into an August 14 Ebbets Field matchup against Don Newcombe, who also had 18 wins. Jim Greengrass smacked a two-run double for us in the top of the second, but I gave the runs back on a two-run homer to Don Zimmer in the bottom half. Then we both got stingy and went to the tenth inning still tied at two. Willie Jones drove in Ashburn with the go-ahead run in the top of the tenth and I got the Dodgers out in the bottom of the inning to secure the win.

That was on Sunday, and five days later on Friday night, August 19, Newk and I were matched again, this time in Connie Mack Stadium. We tied up in

145

another duel, and I was down 2–1 heading into the bottom of the ninth. With one out we had Bobby Morgan on third and Hamner on first. Del Ennis hit a come-backer to Newk, who hesitated a little when Morgan broke for home. Then he rushed his throw to second and threw a one-hopper to Snider in center field, as wild a throw as you'll ever see. Morgan scored to tie the game, and Hamner went all the way to third. Puddin' Head was next, and for the second consecutive game against Newk knocked a base hit to drive in the winning run. The score was 3–2 again, and I had my 20 win for the sixth straight season.

After the game Mayo Smith, who was in his first year as manager, called me into his office and said, "Nice going, big guy. I'm happy for you. Say, I might have to use you in relief. I'd really like to finish at .500."

I said, "That's fine, Mayo."

The next evening we played Brooklyn again, and I went to the bullpen to watch what turned out to be another pitchers' duel, this one between Murry Dickson and the Dodgers' Johnny Podres. We were down 2–0 in the bottom of the eighth when Stan Lopata hit a two-run homer, followed by an Andy Seminick double and a Glen Gorbous single to drive in Andy and give another 3–2 lead. At that point, Mayo had me start loosening up. The Dodgers then got two on with two out in the ninth, and I looked up and Mayo was waving me into the game to face Newcombe, who was pinch hitting for Clem Labine. Newk was a fine hitter, but I popped him up to end the game.

The next day, Sunday, I was in the bullpen again. Jack Meyer was ahead in a one-run game and loaded the bases in the ninth inning. Mayo got me up again, and up came Newcombe to pinch hit again, and I thought, "Here we go again." But this time Mayo left Meyer in to finish the game. Then my next start was August 25 against St. Louis in Philly. The Cardinals nailed me for four runs in the first, we got three back in the bottom half, and I gave up five more runs in the fourth inning, making the score 9–3, St. Louis. We scored two runs in both the fifth and sixth innings to close to 9–7, and I was still pitching. Mayo pinch hit Stan Lopata for me in the midst of our four-run rally in the bottom of the eighth, Jack Meyer got them out in the ninth, and I had a highly improbable 11–9 victory. I had thrown eight innings and given up 12 hits and nine runs, all earned.

After the game, I showered and came back to my locker and noticed that my arm would not straighten out. It didn't hurt, but it would not straighten out. Whitlow Wyatt, the pitching coach, came by and asked, "What's wrong?"

I said, "My arm won't straighten out."

He said, "Oh, you've got a tired arm. I'll talk to Mayo about it."

Well, I never heard back from Mayo or anyone. Because I never really talked to anyone except Cy and he wasn't there anymore, I just kept pitching. My arm didn't hurt, but I couldn't pop my wrist like before and just did not have that little extra. I went 2–5 the rest of the year to finish 23–14.

Overall, it was another good year; I led the league in wins, games started (38), complete games (26), and innings pitched (305). I also hit .252 for the year with two of my five lifetime home runs, so I helped myself a little at the plate.

After the end of the season, I called Bob Carpenter and said, "Bob, something is wrong with my arm. It doesn't hurt, but it won't straighten out."

Bob said, "Well, let's send you down to Johns Hopkins to check it out."

I did go down to the Johns Hopkins Medical Center in Baltimore, and they kept me two full days, giving me a complete physical. At the end of the two days, they told me that they could not find anything wrong with my arm. So I went home and never said anything about my arm to anyone again. I just assumed that I was going to have to pitch with my arm the way it was, and so I did.

CHAPTER 10

The Downhill Slide

For the 1956 season, the Phillies changed their roster, adding players such as Elmer Valo, Frankie Baumholtz, and Solly Hemus and pitchers Saul Rogovin, Harvey Haddix, and Stu Miller.

But the season quickly went south after we lost 15 of our first 20 games. From that point on we played 2 games above .500, but we finished the season in fifth place with a 71–83 record, 22 games behind the first-place Dodgers. The bright spots were Curt's comeback from arm trouble to post a 15–10 record and Stan Lopata's career year of 32 homers and 95 RBIs. Ashburn hit .303, and Del Ennis hit 26 dingers and tied Stan for the club lead in RBIs.

I struggled along with the club. After beating Newcombe and the Dodgers on Opening Day 8–6, I won two head-to-head matchups with Johnny Antonelli of the Giants, 3–1 and 6–2, to begin the season 3–0. But a June 13 8–6 loss to Ray Crone of the Milwaukee Braves dropped my record to 5–8.

Then I defeated the Cubs, the Cardinals, and the Braves in succession to even my record to 8–8 going into a June 30 start against Carl Erskine and the Dodgers at Ebbets Field. Carl and I both struggled early in the game. I batted in the top of the fifth, took a healthy cut at a fastball, and fouled it straight back. Ersk was known for having an outstanding curveball and after I just missed the fastball, Rube Walker, the Dodger catcher, said, "No more of those for you."

I thought to myself, "I'll bet Carl throws me another fastball," and, sure enough, he did. I didn't miss that one and sent it over the right-field wall for a home run. As I crossed home plate after circling the bases, Rube said, "You lucky SOB." Rube was probably right. It was the fifth and last home run I hit in the big leagues.

My five home runs put me up there in the rarified company of Mickey Mantle because I accomplished something that not even Babe Ruth, Jimmie Foxx, Willie Mays, or Hank Aaron could: I hit a home run from each side of the plate. My one right-handed homer was of the wind-blown variety, off of

Paul Minner at Wrigley Field. He still can't believe it. Folks make a lot of noise about the home runs I allowed but they probably don't know about the five I hit. So anytime I sign a bat for anyone, I put a "5" right by my signature so they will know.

I probably should mention that I lost that game to Erskine to put me under .500 again at 8–9. I would have gladly traded my home run for a win. I pitched better the next two months, however, and won four straight in late July and early August to give me a shot at 20 wins.

The Dodgers were in a tight pennant race with the Milwaukee Braves and trailed the Braves late in the year. I was to pitch against the Dodgers in Ebbets Field, and before the game I was sitting by my locker when I had a telegram delivered to me. I opened it and it said, "If you throw one pitch against the Dodgers today you will be shot."

Granny Hamner lockered next to me, so I showed him the telegram. Ham read it and just laughed. I guess he didn't care if I got shot. But I didn't think it was any big deal either, and I just tossed the telegram away and didn't tell anyone else about it. I didn't give much more thought to it and went out to warm up. After I finished warming up, I walked into the dugout to towel off. Hamner came over and said, "There he is," pointing to a guy standing on a roof of an apartment building beyond the right-field fence.

When I went out to start my warm-up pitches before facing the Dodgers in the bottom of the first, I don't know why, but I started thinking about that guy on the roof. Junior Gilliam was the Dodgers' leadoff batter. When Junior stepped in, I threw him my first pitch and dived straight forward on the mound. I decided I'd give the sniper a moving target if he was going to shoot at me. I got up and turned around to look at Hamner and he was rolling on the ground, laughing.

Gilliam ended up tripling, and they scored a couple of runs in the first inning. As I was walking off the field at the end of the inning, Hamner ran by and said, "You don't have to worry. You ain't got shit. He ain't gonna shoot you today."

I guess that is a funny story in retrospect. I lost the ballgame, however, and that wasn't funny.

I was 17–16 going into a September 13 showdown against Warren Spahn of the Braves. Spahnie was going against me for his 200th career win in the first game of a doubleheader in Connie Mack Stadium.

We both were on and went into the bottom of the ninth inning tied 1–1. With two outs and Richie Ashburn on second, Del Ennis hit a line-shot base hit to left field. I thought we had just won the ballgame, but Bobby Thomson in left field for the Braves threw a strike to nail Whitey at the plate for the third out to send the game to extra innings.

Neither team could score in the tenth. In the top of the eleventh, however, Henry Aaron led off and smashed a line drive over my head and into the lower deck over the 434-foot sign in dead center field. It was one of the hardest-hit balls I've ever seen and of course put Spahn ahead 2–1 heading into the bottom of the eleventh. But second baseman Ted Kazanski matched Aaron and hit a home run to tie the score again, 2 to 2. Mayo Smith pinch hit for me in that inning and, unfortunately, Curt Simmons could not hold the Braves in the top of the twelfth. They scored twice, and Spahnie got us out in the bottom half to secure his hard-earned 200th career victory.

Spahnie won 202 games in the fifties (1950–59), more than anyone else, and I was second with 199, so people often speak of us as the dominant pitchers of that era. Teams generally pitched their aces in the opening game of a four-game series, which meant that I threw a lot of games against the opposing teams' best pitcher, guys like Don Newcombe, Sal Maglie, and John Antonelli. But surprisingly the record reveals that Spahnie and I pitched against each other only 11 times while we were both in the National League, from mid-1948 through the 1961 season.

Spahnie and I actually go back to 1941 when I saw him pitch as a teenager in my hometown, Springfield, Illinois. Springfield had a team, called the Browns because they were a St. Louis Browns farm team, in the Class B Three-I League (Illinois, Iowa, and Indiana). The club sponsored a knothole gang that let kids in for free, and I attended quite a few games. I saw future big leaguers like Pat Seerey, my future teammate Eddie Waitkus, Lou Novikoff, Floyd Baker, Max Sukont, Al Unser, Floyd Giebell, Emil Bildilli, and Eddie Lake. Warren Spahn pitched for the Evansville Bees in 1941 and was hard to miss: he already had that high leg kick and was the best pitcher in the league, compiling a 19–6 record and a league-leading 1.83 earned run average.

Spahn ended up losing three years to World War II, where he won a Bronze Star, and did not win a major league game until he was 25 years old. He ended up with 363, the most ever by a left-hander.

When I came up in 1948 Spahnie was in just his third big-league season but was already one of the top hurlers in the league. He had gone 21–10 in 1947 for his first 20-game season and was in the midst of leading the Braves to the pennant as part of the "Spahn and Sain and pray for rain" tandem. My first game against him took place on September 11 and is one I would just as soon forget. I was wild and got knocked around pretty hard before Eddie

Sawyer took me out in the sixth inning behind 8–1 in an eventual 13–2 loss. Spahnie even hit his first career home run off Charlie Bicknell in relief. Charlie shouldn't feel too bad about it, however. Spahn was a fine hitting pitcher and wound up with 35 career home runs, second all-time for a pitcher behind Wes Ferrell, who slugged 38.

Spahnie struggled in 1952, and our guys didn't mind hitting against him too much. The Braves were mired in seventh place, and Spahn had 19 losses with about a week left in the season. At that point, Braves manager Charlie Grimm refused to start Spahn for the rest of the season. Warren later told me that Jolly Cholly, as Grimm was known, told him, "No pitcher as good as you is going to lose 20 games for me."

Spahn's earned run average that year was under 3.00, so he probably suffered from lack of run support as much as anything. But about then he came up with his screwball, and the next off year he had was when he was about 45 years old.

Before the 1953 season we picked up Earl Torgeson from the Braves in a four-team trade. Torgy was a left-handed-hitting first baseman who had been Spahn's teammate for a number of years. He was quite a character and had the talent to become an outstanding ballplayer. Although he was a solid major league performer, he never reached his potential, maybe because he was so intense on the ballfield that he almost tried too hard.

Left-handed batters did have some success against Spahn. His delivery was right over the top, directly overhand, and was a little easier for lefty hitters to pick up than from some southpaws. In any event, shortly after Torgy joined us he hit a couple of line drives against Spahn that were caught for outs. After the second one, Torgy, visibly frustrated, came back to the dugout and hollered at Spahn, "You lucky hook-nosed bastard; how do you ever get anyone out with that stuff?" Of course, Spahn must have had something on the ball. Thirteen 20-plus-win seasons don't lie.

In the early fifties the Phillies had a catcher named Del Wilber who was very artistic and who would, when we won, decorate a game ball with the highlights of the game and give it to the winning pitcher. When Del was traded, Stan Lopata took over the task. When Spahnie won his 300th game, I asked Stan to do a ball for him and put "You lucky hook-nosed bastard" on it. Then I gave it to Spahnie, and I'll bet he still has it.

Two days after my 11-inning no-decision against Spahn in 1956, I made a brief relief appearance against the Braves and saved a 6–5 win for Curt Simmons. I then won my 18th game of the year in my next start, September 18, against Art Fowler and the Reds by the score of 7–4. At that point I was

18–16 with three starts left to try to win 20 games for the seventh consecutive year. On September 22 I pitched against the Giants in the Polo Grounds and lost to Al Worthington 2–1 when I gave up a seventh-inning home run to Willie Mays.

The loss brought my record to 18–17 with two starts left. It also put me into yet another matchup four days later against Don Newcombe in Ebbets Field. I beat Newk 7–3 for my 19th win. I threw more curveballs than normal that day and struck out 10, including Jackie Robinson three times. I think Jackie was expecting fastballs, and I continued to feed him curves. Jackie was nothing if not observant. I read in the papers the next day that he said, "I know he struck me out three times, but there is something wrong. He's not throwing like he used to."

Although Jackie understood, I don't think Mayo Smith and Whitlow Wyatt had been around me enough to realize that I wasn't really my old self. Of course, I never talked to anyone, especially after Cy left, which was my shortcoming. I just took the ball and pitched whenever they asked me to. Today that sort of thing probably would not happen. With speed guns, pitch counts, and other advancements, the managers and coaches know almost immediately when a pitcher has something bothering him or is not quite right and would give him extra rest or limit his pitches more strictly.

My arm had actually been feeling OK, but I did not have the pop on my fastball that I had when I could straighten my arm. I had one more start to try to get 20 wins, on Sunday, September 30, at home against the New York Giants. It was my 30th birthday.

I used to sometimes get a catch in the back of my shoulder that kept me from throwing as hard as when my shoulder was good and loose. It hadn't been there, but before the game with the Giants I was taking batting practice and swung at and missed a knuckleball. When I did, I felt that catch come back in my shoulder. I went out and pitched and struggled, although I pitched the complete game. Ozzie Virgil and opposing pitcher Al Worthington hit home runs, and I lost 8–3 to finish the season 19–18, ending my run of 20-win years.

I led the league in complete games (22) for the fifth year in a row and threw 297 innings, second to Bob Friend, and gave up just 40 walks. But I got hit around more than I was used to, and my earned run average rose to an unsightly 4.45. It was the first time I was really even aware of my ERA.

When Cy was still with us, he mentioned that it was often beneficial for a team and star player to part ways if the team and individual success had waned. Late during the '56 season some discussion took place about a Stan Musial–for–Robin Roberts trade. I knew nothing about it, but I later learned that Stan refused to leave the Cardinals. I never gave a thought to being traded. I was a Phillie.

* * *

With today's inflated salaries in baseball, people often ask me how much I think I would make if I was pitching today and winning like I did in the fifties. I don't know the answer to that question, and I certainly do not begrudge the present-day players the salaries they are able to command. I made a very good living playing baseball and was able to provide a nice life for my wife and four boys. But I certainly did not become independently wealthy playing baseball and, as soon as I retired from the game, needed to quickly start another career to continue to support the family.

In my day, of course, there were no player agents, and ballplayers were subject to the reserve clause, which meant either we played for the team that held our rights or we did not play. As a result, the owners had significant bargaining power because it was not possible to play out a contract and become a free agent. During most of the years I won 20 or more games, the Phillies did not have a general manager, so I always negotiated my contract with the team owner, Bob Carpenter.

Beginning in 1951, Mary and I lived in Philadelphia year-round. After the 1952 season, in which I had won 28 games, Bob Carpenter called and asked me to come down to the stadium to talk about my salary for 1953. When I went down, Bob asked, "Well, what do you want?"

I had made $30,000 in 1952 and I said, "I don't have any idea, Bob. All I know is I'm doing something I really enjoy and I had a good year. I know you've only got so much you can pay the team. You figure out how much you can pay me and that'll be fine with me."

Bob said, "I'll do that and call you."

In about three weeks, Bob called and told me, "Come on down and have lunch. I've got a figure for you."

So I went to see Bob and he said, "I figure $38,500."

I said, "Fine. Give me the contract and I'll sign it."

Bob said, "Well, what do you think?"

I replied, "Eh, I think it's a little light. But I said I would sign and I will."

In 1953 I won 23 and lost 16 as we tied with the Cardinals for third, 22 games behind the red-hot Dodgers, who won 105 games to run away with the pennant. I led the league in innings pitched (347), strikeouts (198), games started (41), and complete games (33) and tied for the most wins with Warren

Spahn. After the season, I received a proposed contract in the mail from Carpenter, cutting my salary to $33,500. I immediately called Carpenter and said, "Bob, I got the contract in the mail."

"Yeah, what do you think?" Bob said.

I said, "I hope you're kidding."

He said, "Oh no, I'm serious."

I replied, "Then we've got a problem."

He said, "Well, come on down and we'll talk about it."

So we made a date, and I went down to his office and he asked, "What do you think?"

I said, "Hey, I want 50 grand. I can't believe you would try to cut me."

"Well," he said, "you only won 23 games."

"Well, I want 50 grand."

He said, "I can't do that. My payroll will be over three-quarters of a million if I pay you 50 grand."

I said, "Well, you figure it out. I want 50 grand."

With that we parted. Since I was so agreeable after winning 28 games, I really thought I was being taken advantage of and wanted to get what I was worth this time around.

Finally he called again and said, "C'mon down."

When I did, he said, "I'll give you $45,000 and I'll give you $500 expense money for every road trip."

That expense money amounted to $5,500, so that got me just past $50,000 and I accepted.

During our negotiations, I told Bob Carpenter that if I did not win 25 games in 1954, I would not ask for a raise. Well, I won 23 again, losing 15, and again led the league in innings (337), strikeouts (185), games started (38), complete games (29), and wins. But I did not ask for a raise and got the same salary for 1955. Then for the third year in a row I won 23 in 1955, losing 14 and again leading the league in innings pitched (305), games started (38), complete games (26), and wins.

By now Roy Hamey was the general manager, so I went in to talk salary with him. Roy was a nice man but gruff-talking. He said, "Well, whadya' want?"

I said, "I looked it up and I got Stan [Musial] out this year, so I want the same kind of money he's getting."

Hamey said, "Aw, that's too much for me; you'll have to talk to the boss." So I was back talking to Bob Carpenter about my salary and never talked contract with Hamey again. In fact, even when John Quinn became the general manager in 1959, it was just assumed that I would talk to Carpenter about salary.

I may not have been correct about getting Stan Musial out, but Bob agreed to raise me to $57,500 for 1956. And to his credit, he kept me at $57,500 for 1957 even though I won only 19 in 1956 and did not have the year I'd grown accustomed to.

* * *

The Phillies went with a youth movement for 1957, not unlike that of the late forties. From the minor league system came pitchers Dick Farrell, Jack Sanford, and Don Cardwell; first baseman Ed Bouchee; and outfielders Harry Anderson and Bob Bowman. The club even brought in its first black player, John Kennedy, although he appeared in only five games. We also acquired shortstop Chico Fernandez in a trade with the Dodgers and veteran pitcher Jim Hearn in a trade with the Giants. The big shocker, however, was the off-season trade of Del Ennis, after 11 years as the Phils' top run-producer, to the Cardinals for Rip Repulski.

I lost the opener to Brooklyn, 7–6 in 12 innings. It was a precursor of my season to come. The influx of youth, however, provided a real spark as Sanford, Farrell, and Cardwell got off to good starts on the mound. We were among the leaders in the first months of the season. In early July we won 12 of 14 games and swept into first place after Jack Sanford beat the Cardinals 6–2. We stayed there just two days, losing three in a row to the Braves. We hung in there for July but slumped to a 9–19 record in the dog days of August to drop from contention. We finished right at .500, in fifth place, 18 games behind the pennant-winning Braves.

I tried and did the best I could but really had a rough year, finishing 10–22. I did have a great night against the Cubs on May 2, defeating Dick Drott 4–2 for my first win of the year. I threw only 98 pitches and struck out 13 Cubs to tie the club record. But my record at the break was 6–11 so, needless to say, I did not make the All-Star team for the first time since 1949. My buddy Curt did, however, and was named the starting pitcher by National League manager Walter Alston. It was the seventh All-Star start in eight years for either Curt or me.

My worst stretch was from June 8 to July 25, when I lost seven in a row and had ten starts without a win, falling from 6–6 to 6–13. One of my no-decisions came in Connie Mack Stadium against Milwaukee on July 17 when I was told to leave the premises by umpire Jocko Conlan after only one inning. I had pitched a scoreless first inning and was in the dugout watching us bat. With Granny Hamner on second, Rip Repulski hit a low line drive to Johnny Logan at shortstop that he appeared to trap. He then threw to Red Schoendienst at second to double Hamner off the bag and end the inning.

As I went out to the mound to throw my warm-ups before the second inning, I heard the public-address announcer tell the crowd the ruling: that Logan caught the ball and doubled Hamner off second. There was no way that Logan caught the ball and, because I was going so badly, it really got to me. I started toward Conlan and said, "C'mon Jocko, what are you talking about? Logan trapped that ball."

Of course, there was nothing anyone could do about it, but I kept after Jocko and lost my temper. I ended up calling Jocko "a little Irish prick," which, naturally, he took offense to, telling me, "Get outa here." I really lost it then and made a real ass of myself. It was a good thing Mayo Smith was there. He grabbed me from behind and pulled me away from Jocko. For my trouble, I ended up with a three-day suspension and a $50 fine. On top of that we lost the ballgame, 10–3.

I saw Jocko a little while after that incident and he told me, "Robin, you know what? I wouldn't have thrown you out but when you called me a little Irish prick I could tell that you meant it."

Altogether, I got thrown out of games by umpires four times in my 18-year big-league career, if you count the first time in 1950 when Artie Gore threw me out when I was sitting next to Andy Seminick in the dugout because he knew I wasn't going to pitch that day. But I guess you have to count it. The first one that should count was in Chicago in 1951. With Tommy Brown on first base and two out, we hit a low line drive to center field that Frankie Baumholtz trapped. There were two outs, and Tommy scurried all the way around to third. Al Barlick was the second-base umpire, and he ran out toward center to make the trap call. Baumholtz threw the ball to second base, and Barlick called Brown out for missing second.

I was in the dugout, not even pitching that day, and I couldn't believe Al could make that call when he was out in center field watching the line drive as Brown raced around second. Barlick was from Springfield, about three miles from where I grew up, but I hollered enough from the top step of the dugout that he threw his hometown boy out of the game. Boy, he threw me out quickly; I think he was a little embarrassed by his call.

The other time also occurred in Wrigley Field. The Cubs had the bases loaded with two outs. I fielded a ball along the first-base line, turned and threw to first, and hit the runner in the shoulder. He was running inside the base line and should have been out, which would have been the third out of the inning. Instead, the ball rolled down the right-field line, and two runs scored.

I had a perfect view of the play and turned right away to Hal Dixon, the home-plate umpire and said, "He's out. He was inside the base line."

He said, "No. No. He was OK."

I said, "You've gotta be lying. He was way inside the base line."

Well, Dixon took exception to that comment and threw me out of the game.

I generally had great respect for umpires, and the only time I had trouble with them was when I was going badly, like with my run-in with Jocko Conlan in 1957. I understood that they were in charge of the game and, in fact, needed to be in charge of the game. You hope that they have good judgment, but they need to be in charge. I learned that in one of my first games my rookie year. Larry Goetz was the umpire, and I threw the first pitch of the game knee-high right down the pike. Goetz called it ball one. I didn't say anything but looked in at him, wondering why that was a ball. I threw another pitch in the same place, and Goetz ripped off his mask and said, "Ball two, you SOB."

Andy Seminick, my catcher, called time and came out to the mound and said, "I forgot to tell you. This guy is the best umpire in the league, but he wants you to know that he is in charge. He really doesn't like it if you question his ball-and-strike calls."

Goetz was the best umpire in the league along with Al Barlick, and I never questioned him again, because I knew he was in charge. In fact, Goetz was so respected as a ball-and-strike umpire that National League President Ford Frick instructed the umpiring crew to have Goetz behind the plate for the last game of the 1950 season when we played the Dodgers for the pennant, even though he had been the home-plate umpire the day before. I've never checked, but I suspect that is the only time that has ever happened. Augie Donatelli was part of that umpiring crew, and he once told me that the rest of the crew was happy that Larry was back there for that final game.

The Phillies had a loudmouthed fan named Pete Adelis who really got on opposing players and umpires. Adelis had a booming voice, and one day he decided to ride Larry. Goetz took it for an inning or two and then walked over to the public-address announcer and said, "The game will not continue until that loudmouthed fan leaves the ballpark." And Phillies security escorted Adelis from the ballpark so the game could continue. As I said, Goetz was in charge.

He was reputed to have a great sense of humor off the field, although I never saw him except on the playing field. Frank Slocum, who worked for many years in the commissioner's office, told me a story involving Goetz and another umpire, Augie Guglielmo, who was of very small stature. Then

Curt Simmons and I sign our contracts for 1953 with Phillies owner Bob Carpenter looking on. Bob said that we were breaking him. *Photo courtesy of AP/Wide World Photos.*

Sliding into second base against Pee Wee Reese of the Dodgers in 1956. Pee Wee must have missed me.

Preparing to take on a Japanese team in Tokyo on the Eddie Lopat All-Stars tour of Japan after the 1953 season. I'm the first one in line, next to Eddie Robinson. Next to Eddie are Bob Lemon, Billy Martin, Mike Garcia, Curt Simmons, Gus Niarhos, and Yogi Berra. We were a great team.

Me and Mary with Pee Wee Reese and his wife, Dottie, in Hawaii.

Masaichi Kaneda, the winningest pitcher in Japanese baseball history. Maybe I copied him.

After being elected National League player representative in 1954. Congratulating me (or giving me condolences) from left to right are Gil Hodges, Stan Musial, Ralph Kiner, and Whitey Lockman. It was definitely a nonpaying job.

Me with Al Lopez and Leo Durocher before the 1955 All-Star Game at County Stadium in Milwaukee. The National League won, no thanks to me.

Celebrating a 5–0 shutout of the Yankees on May 2, 1965, with Orioles manager Hank Bauer. I'd just beaten Hank's old team.

Taking a breather with the Houston Astros in 1966. We can go home soon, Mary.

In spring training with the Reading Phillies in 1967. I must have had a good workout.

Relaxing in Cooperstown with Bob Lemon (far left), Sandy Koufax (second from right), and Al Kaline (far right). Sandy threw harder than Lem and I. I was inducted into the Baseball Hall of Fame in 1976.

Me (on the far right), Joe DiMaggio, and Al Lopez at an Italian-American golf tournament in Tampa. Sam Ferlita, one of the tournament organizers, is on the far left. The little guy in front is Johnny Roventini, the famous Phillip Morris bellhop from the fifties.

National League President Warren Giles had decided to terminate Guglielmo after just a couple of years in the league, and Goetz asked him why. Giles said something about his small size, and Goetz said, "He didn't shrink after you hired him, did he?"

In those days there were only 18 umpires in each league, and you got to know them well. If you disagreed with a call, you could argue and make your point, but if you went too far or hung around too long, they would boot you from the game. Today it seems that umpires are much more aggressive, arguing back or sometimes confronting the offending player or manager. Some of them seem to think that they are part of the show. Umpires don't have to argue back or be aggressive because they have the power to eject. All an umpire has to do when he has heard enough is to tell the manager, "That's enough or you're out of the game." Sometimes I think the umpires forget that they are in charge and do not have to put on an act or argue with players or managers.

Of course, occasionally human emotions do take over and both sides can lose their cool in the heat of the moment. And today, umpires have more pressure because of television and instant replays. If they miss a call it is likely to be shown on *SportsCenter* that evening for everyone in the country to see. But if umpires are ever not in charge, then baseball is in real trouble.

I think it is positive that the umpires are combined and no longer are assigned to one league or the other. When I went to the American League later in my career, I had heard that the umpires there called the high strike more than the low strike. I was a low-ball pitcher, and I could see that it was true because the American League umpires used the balloon chest protector outside of their uniform. As a result, they stood up straighter behind the catcher than did the National League umpires, who were down lower and to the side of the catcher and thus had a different angle on the height of pitches. It did not really bother me too much, but it is certainly an improvement to eliminate those differences between the leagues.

* * *

The 1957 season ended much as it began for me. I got knocked around some, then when I threw well it seemed I pitched in quite a bit of tough luck. I defeated Spahn 5–3 on July 25 and shut out the Cubs on four hits July 29, beating Don Elston 6–0 to bring my record to 8–13, and then lost five straight. The toughest of those was that August 16 game against the New York Giants in Connie Mack Stadium when Ray Jablonski hit a home run in the top of the ninth to beat me 2–1.

I won my 10th and final game of the long season on September 14, shutting out the Reds at Crosley Field 5–0 in a game that was scoreless until the seventh inning. Two more losses and I finished at 10–22. I started 32 games, completed 14, and in 250 innings gave up 246 hits. My earned run average was 4.07.

Although the team tailed off at the end of the year, there were some very bright signs. Jack Sanford was an outstanding 19–8 and won Rookie of the Year honors from the baseball writers. Another rookie hurler, Dick Farrell finished 10–2 with a 2.39 ERA in 52 games out of the bullpen. Ed Bouchee took over first base, hit .293 in 154 games, and was named Rookie of the Year by *The Sporting News*.

It has always bothered me that some sportswriters reviewing my career have often lamented that I was a very good pitcher who was stuck pitching for bad teams or that I would have won 350 games pitching for a good team. Those observations simply are not accurate and unfairly denigrate the Phillies teams of the early and mid-fifties. Although we did not come close to another pennant after 1950, we had good clubs and were always in or very near the first division. In the late fifties the Phillies were not very good, but then I wasn't either and contributed to that mediocrity. And in 1957 we had a promising club that was very much in the pennant race for the first half of the year although I really struggled. So it just is not accurate to say that the Phillies ballclubs that I pitched for somehow were a drag on my own performance or record.

The 1958 season turned out to be a very strange one that no one could have predicted. Led by another rookie pitcher, Ray Semproch; Dick Farrell; and outfielders Harry Anderson and Richie Ashburn, who was having a banner season, we were in the thick of the pennant race the first half. Immediately before the All-Star break we reeled off seven consecutive wins to move within 2½ games of first place. But shortly after the break, we lost seven in a row, the first four by one run, and by July 21 we were 8½ games behind and effectively out of the race.

Our slump prompted Bob Carpenter to fire Mayo Smith and bring Eddie Sawyer back as manager. Eddie's first game back was the completion of a game that had been suspended in June against the San Francisco Giants in Philadelphia. At the time the game was suspended, I was losing 1–0 and we were batting in the bottom of the sixth with runners on first and third and two out. Harry Anderson, a left-handed batter, was up against Giants southpaw Johnny Antonelli. Mayo Smith had platooned Harry against left-handers but Eddie let him hit against Antonelli. He promptly hit a three-run homer to put us into the lead, 3 to 1. I gave up a run in the eighth but otherwise held them, and we won 3–2.

After the game, Eddie came by my locker and said, "You can still pitch, can't you?"

I said, "Yessir, I can."

I was glad to have Sawyer back because it was so easy to play for him and he did not confuse things. If he had good players, his team would be in the hunt. He had a knack for handling pitchers, knowing when to take one out and when to put in a certain reliever. Shortly after Eddie came back, he brought in Farrell to relieve in the ninth inning. Dick got beat and after the game, Richie Ashburn, who was really a Sawyer man, said, "Well, at least we got beat with the right guy pitching."

But even Eddie could not get us turned around. Ray Semproch had 11 wins by July 12 but won only two more the rest of the year. Dick Farrell was 6–2 with nine saves and a 1.13 earned run average at the All-Star break but finished the year at 8–9 with only two more saves. (He made the All-Star team and struck out four of seven American League batters in two scoreless innings in a 4–3 loss for the National League.) Curt Simmons had a recurrence of arm trouble, Jack Sanford slipped to 10–13, and slugging outfielder Wally Post, whom we had acquired in a preseason trade with the Reds for Harvey Haddix, disappointed with only 12 home runs.

We won only 30 of 71 games under Eddie and slipped into the cellar with a 69–85 record, 23 games behind the pennant-winning Milwaukee Braves. We were only three games out of a tie for fifth place, and our 69 victories were the most ever for a last-place team, but it was still the cellar.

On the bright side, Ashburn had a great year, winning his second batting title with a .350 average and also leading the league in hits (215), triples (13), walks (97), and putouts (495). The batting title race went down to the wire, and going into our last game of the season against the Pirates in Forbes Field, Whitey had just a couple of points lead over Willie Mays. Before the game Richie mentioned to me that if he got one hit Mays would have to go five for five to even tie him. During his first at-bat, Ashburn topped a ball off the plate that bounced about 50 feet in the air. I can still see Whitey laughing as he crossed first base far ahead of the throw. He knew he had just wrapped up the batting championship.

Harry Anderson also had a fine year in '58, hitting .301, with 23 home runs and 97 RBIs in just his second year. Veteran Dave Philley, whom we acquired from the Detroit Tigers, led the league with 18 pinch-hits in 44 tries and set a major league record with eight consecutive pinch-hits, including one on the last day of the season.

Dave Philley was a big Texan who had a miserable temper. He showed it one day when we were playing the Reds at Crosley Field. Our trainer Doc Wiechec was in the visitors' training room when a friend came in and wanted to get a baseball signed. The club was out taking batting practice and Doc couldn't find a baseball so he took one out of Dave Philley's locker. When we came in from batting practice, Dave immediately noticed the ball was gone from his locker. He asked in a very loud voice, "Who took the ball out of my locker?"

Someone said, "Wiechec did."

So Dave stomped into the training room and said, "Did you take that ball out of my locker?"

Frank said, "Yes" and was just starting to explain when Philley took a swing and hit him. So a bunch of us jumped on Philley, and some others held Wiechec, who by the way was a big guy, and nobody got hurt.

A few minutes later we were headed out to the field again and I happened to be walking beside Philley. I wasn't going very well and so, me and my big mouth, I couldn't help saying, "Dave, that was a horseshit thing to do."

He said, "You want part of me?"

I thought to myself, what the hell, I might as well. So we went at it for a little bit until our teammates broke it up. It was a typical baseball fight, no one got hurt.

I had only two other almost fights in baseball. As I mentioned, I generally wasn't too eager to fight because I was afraid I would hurt my pitching hand. But once in 1957 I was hitting in the bottom of the eighth inning with two out against Don McMahon of the Milwaukee Braves. I topped a ball down the first-base line, close to the bag. As I ran to first, McMahon fielded the ball and I tried to slide around him. He tagged me out with a hard punch to the chest. I got up to go get my glove to start the ninth inning when I thought, "That was really uncalled for." I started for McMahon, and Eddie Mathews grabbed me and said, "He ain't worth it." I quickly decided Eddie was right.

Another time in Cincinnati in 1960 Raul Sanchez knocked our pitcher Gene Conley, who was batting, on his butt. Gene rushed the mound and started hurting people. He was 6'8". I was in the bullpen and ran toward the mound with all the other players. As I ran by first base, I called Frank Robinson a black so and so. After they got control of Conley, Frank came to over to me and said, "I'll get you some night, Roberts."

I said, "None of that night shit," and I went after him and he went after me. His head hit me right in my right eye socket, and I ended up with a black eye. It was not one of my proudest moments.

* * *

The Milwaukee Braves won their second pennant in a row in 1958, beating the Pirates to the wire by eight games. Spahn was still the ace of the Braves' staff, but Lew Burdette was a very close second. In fact, Lew was one of the best pitchers of the decade and is probably best remembered for two things: his three complete-game wins over the powerful New York Yankees in the 1957 World Series and his spitball.

Burdette's spitball was legendary, but for a long time I didn't believe that he actually threw one—even though my Phillies teammates were always complaining about Lew throwing wet ones. I should have known better. The 1948 Braves had a veteran pitcher named Nelson Potter on their staff. Potter had led the 1944 St. Louis Browns to their only pennant with 19 wins and was still an effective spot starter in '48. He was frequently accused of throwing spitballs, and in a game he pitched against us in Shibe Park I saw an umpire throw him out of the game for doing just that. The league subsequently suspended him for 30 days.

In any event, Richie Ashburn used to get just furious at Burdette for throwing him spitters. He would make an out on a weak ground ball and come back to the dugout and say, "He's throwing me that crappin' spitball again." That was just the way Whitey talked.

Burdette would hear him and yell, "You keep complaining and I'll keep throwin' it to you."

Lew was a wonderful competitor and a real character, but I still really never believed that he threw a spitball. I thought he just had a really good sinker. Then one day I was pitching against Lew and came up to bat in the eighth inning of a close game with the bases loaded. I batted lefty, and I'd had some success hitting sidearm stuff. But on this occasion Burdette threw me three pitches the likes of which I'd never seen before. The bottom just dropped out of them and I struck out swinging. That was the first time I knew that Lew threw the spitball.

I quickly had real verification. My strikeout ended the inning, and Del Crandall, the Braves' catcher, rolled the ball out to the mound to try to get the spit off instead of just flipping me the ball at the plate. So I walked out to get the ball and found a big wet spot still on it.

Later that season I was beating the Braves 10–3 when Crandall came up with two outs in the ninth inning. I thought that since he had been calling all those spitballs maybe I'd just throw one to him. So I loaded one up and threw it. Crandall swung and just dribbled the ball back to me on the mound. Del knew right away that it was a spitball, but he didn't say a word; he just kind of looked at me funny.

To be honest, that is the only spitball I ever threw. But Whitey and my teammates were right about Burdette, even if I didn't believe it for a long time.

There has been some recent discussion of legalizing the spitball because of the tremendous upsurge in hitting in recent years. It was a legal pitch until it was outlawed in 1920. The rule, however, grandfathered 17 pitchers for whom the spitball was their main pitch. Ray Fisher, my coach in Vermont, was one of the grandfathered pitchers. Three made the Hall of Fame: Stanley Coveleski, Red Faber, and Burleigh Grimes. Of course, there have been a number of pitchers who have thrown the spitball in recent years, even though it remains illegal.

* * *

After 11 years with the Phillies, my importance to the team and the team's importance to me were more significant than just taking the ball every fourth day. A good illustration of my relationship to the Phillies organization involved Ed Bouchee. After Ed's great rookie year in 1957, he got himself into trouble during the off-season by exposing himself to some young girls. He was arrested and sent to a psychiatric hospital in New England to work out his problem.

We started the season without Bouchee, who was still under treatment. One day during the season Bob Carpenter called me and asked me to come to his office before the game that day. When I arrived, Bob said, "Would you like to have Ed Bouchee back?"

I said, "Sure, Bob. Ed's a good ballplayer. I hope he can work out his problems and come back."

Bob said, "Well, we can get him back. But you've got to room with him."

I said, "Who did he room with before?"

Bob said, "He roomed with Kazanski."

"Well," I said, "why doesn't he room with Ted like before?"

"No, Ford Frick's wife said the only way he can come back is to room with you."

So that is what happened. Ed joined us in midseason and we roomed together on the road the rest of the year. He was our regular first baseman until early in the 1960 season when we traded him to the Cubs along with Don Cardwell for Tony Taylor and Cal Neeman.

Eddie Sawyer generally believed in rooming a regular player with a reserve. In the late fifties and early sixties the Phillies had a number of young pitchers who had great potential but were better known for their fast-living and off-field exploits. They were dubbed the Dalton Gang by the press and included Dick Farrell, Jack Meyer, Jim Owens, Seth Morehead, and catcher Clay Dalrymple. I was asked to room with a couple of them, I suppose to try to settle them down.

I thought Jimmy Owens was going to be a good big-league pitcher and roomed with him for a while. Of course, I was struggling myself at that time, but I let Jimmy know that I thought he had great ability. My advice to him was throw it hard and mix in some sleep, but it didn't seem to take.

Dick Farrell had a good big-league career, and Dalrymple was a fine defensive catcher, but the others pretty much squandered their talent. Jack Meyer had Nolan Ryan–type stuff with a sharp curveball to go with a blazing fastball. I remember Willie Mays wanted no part of him. But Jack was very emotional on the mound and never looked like he thought he belonged. It was really a shame that that group didn't appreciate the game more and take better care of themselves.

I pitched much better in '58 after my miserable '57 season and had some nice moments along with a good deal of frustration. On May 13 I broke Grover Cleveland Alexander's team record for most wins by a pitcher by beating Bob Buhl of the Braves in County Stadium 5–2. It was my 191st win as a Phillie and made me think back to the time in Springfield when Alexander had so briefly addressed our school banquet. By July 15 I was 7–9, and then I reeled off five wins in five starts, including the suspended game against the Giants, to run my record to 12–9.

During that run I won the 200th game of my career, pitching a three-hitter against the Cubs at home to defeat Dave Hillman 3–1 on August 1. By September 10 I was 14–13 and started a game against Don Drysdale in Connie Mack Stadium. We knocked Drysdale out in the third inning, and I pitched into the ninth inning with an 8–5 lead before getting into trouble. Sawyer then brought in a rookie right-hander named Don Erickson to relieve.

Erickson was from Springfield and had graduated from Lanphier High. After my rookie year in 1948 I had returned home to Springfield and stayed with my parents. I helped coach the Lanphier basketball team that winter, and Donnie was one of the better players on the team. He was supposed to be quite a pitcher. One day he came over to the house to work out. It was freezing cold outside with snow on the ground, so we went up into the attic and played catch in the available space, which was about 45 feet. I quickly noticed that he had a delivery very similar to mine, what they later called drop and drive.

Don ended up signing with the Phillies and getting called up in '58 after pitching well in Tulsa. Against the Dodgers, Donnie retired the side in the ninth to save the ballgame and my 15th win, so Springfield, Illinois, and Lanphier High School got a win and a save that day.

I finished the year 17–14, losing three games 1–0 and one 2–1 along the way. I started 34 games, completed 21 (second in the league), and threw 270 innings. I put together a 10–5 record after my 7–9 start into July. My earned run average for the year dropped to a much more respectable 3.23, and so I spent the winter much more content and looking forward to pitching an entire season under Eddie Sawyer.

The 1959 season started very well as on Opening Day I defeated Don Newcombe, now with the Cincinnati Reds, 2–1, and even doubled to drive in our first run. It was my 10th Opening Day start and brought my Opening Day record to 5–4. Eddie Sawyer continued to send me out there every fourth day, and I racked up 257 innings, but the ballclub never gelled. Bob Carpenter had brought John Quinn in over the winter to replace Roy Hamey as general manager, and we became a team in transition. John Quinn had put together the pennant-winning '48 Braves as well as the Braves teams that won a World Series and two pennants, and lost in a playoff from 1957 to 1959. He was known as a trader and by early June had swapped Stan Lopata, Granny Hamner, and Willie Jones to three different teams, leaving only Richie, Curt, and me from the 1950 Whiz Kids.

We finished in the basement again at 64–90, winning five fewer games than the year before. We ended 23 games behind the first-place Dodgers and 7 back of the seventh-place Cardinals. I had a 9–9 record heading into a July 30 start against the Giants in old Seals Stadium. Pretty quickly I was 9–10. It was Willie McCovey's big-league debut and yes, he did go four-for-four against me, including two triples. I know because I was there.

People often talk about McCovey's memorable debut. They never mention, however, that the next time I pitched against the Giants in Seals Stadium, September 11, I beat Mike McCormick 1–0 on three hits. McCovey was 0–3. No one ever mentions that, so I thought I would.

The start after the "McCovey game" I beat Bob Anderson and the Cubs 2–1 in Wrigley Field to even my record at 10–10. Then I hit a rough stretch, losing five of six including an August 29 11–1 shellacking to Bob Friend and the Pirates to sink my record to 11–15. But I came back strong with four complete-game wins in a row, including a 2–1 four-hitter over Vernon Law and those same Pirates and the 1–0 three-hit shutout over the Giants.

The 2–1 victory over the Pirates involved one of the luckiest moments I ever had on a baseball diamond. The game had been a scoreless tie heading into the eighth inning when the Pirates squeezed a run home to take a 1–0 lead. In the bottom half Carl Sawatski singled with one out, and Eddie Sawyer told me to go ahead and hit. I ripped a rope to right field for a base hit. Roberto Clemente charged in from right and made a big scoop for the ball and, to everyone's surprise, missed the ball completely. Solly Drake, pinch running for Sawatski, scored from first base to tie the score, and I made it all the way to third. Joe Koppe, our shortstop, was next, and he singled to drive me in with the go-ahead run.

I went out for the top of the ninth with a 2–1 lead. The first batter was Rocky Nelson, a pinch-hitter for Law, and he singled to center. Roman Mejias went in to run and he made it to third on Bob Skinner's single to center, with Skinner taking second on Ashburn's throw to third. I now had runners on second and third with no outs and Dick Groat at bat. I got ahead of Groat two strikes and then plunked him in the shoulder when I tried to come inside.

Clemente was the next batter. If you want a definition of a pitcher's jam, I had it. Bases loaded, nobody out, and Roberto Clemente at bat; that is a jam. I then went 2 and 0 on Clemente; that is really a jam.

Although I rarely did this when I was behind in the count, I decided to throw Roberto a curveball. Roberto took one of his huge swings and hit a soft line drive off the end of the bat right to me. I caught it and threw to third to double off Mejias. Dick Stuart was the next hitter, and I got him to pop one about a mile straight up. Joe Lonnett, my catcher, caught it, and I had a 2–1 victory.

I've never gone from the crapper to the palace so quickly. To have Roberto Clemente up with the bases loaded and no one out in a one-run game and get out with a win was close to a miracle.

Roberto Clemente, by the way, became one of my favorite people, but I can't say he impressed me the first time I saw him on a baseball field. Branch Rickey drafted him for the Pirates out of the Dodgers organization in 1955, and that is when he made his big-league debut. I thought Roberto ran awkwardly, sort of clippity-cloppity, flailed his arms all around, and had a very unorthodox batting stance. He just did not look very fluid. I remember Mayo Smith telling a group of us, "Boy, that kid is an outstanding prospect."

I thought to myself, "You've got to be kidding, Mayo." I thought the kid was in the wrong sport. He just didn't seem to have a rhythm for baseball.

Well, Roberto was unorthodox, but he proved that he could really play the game. As he played and improved, I began to think maybe he had the right rhythm and it was the rest of us that lacked it. He could hit shots to all fields, was a great right fielder, and possessed a cannon for an arm.

Early in his career Roberto seemed to have a chip on his shoulder and tended to make a controversy out of everything. I think he had the feeling that as a kid out of Puerto Rico he had suffered from some discrimination, and maybe he had. In 1960 the Pirates won the pennant and Roberto's teammate Dick Groat was named Most Valuable Player. Roberto also had a fine year and let it be known that he thought that he should have won the award. But as he became an established star those rough edges smoothed out, and I learned firsthand what a fine, giving person Roberto was.

In the mid-sixties I flew into Pittsburgh one day for a Players' Association meeting. I walked off the plane at the Pittsburgh airport and was heading to catch a cab to the meeting when I saw Roberto standing in the terminal. I had never met Roberto off the ballfield or talked with him, but he recognized me and said, "Robin, how are you?"

I said, "I'm fine, Roberto."

"Where you headed?" he asked.

I said, "I'm going down to the ballpark for a meeting."

He said, "Well, let me take you."

He had his Cadillac nearby, so I got in and we drove down to the ballpark. The drive into town was the first time I had a conversation with him. It was about a 40-minute drive to Forbes Field, and when we got there he started to just let me out at the curb by the entrance.

I said, "No, go ahead and park, Roberto. I'll walk in with you."

He said, "Oh no, no, no. I have to go back out to the airport and pick up my wife. I was waiting for her to come in off a flight."

I thought, my goodness, I'm not sure who I would have done that for. Here was a guy whom I'd never met except for playing ball against him, and he drove me all the way down to the ballpark from the airport and then went back to pick up his wife. I don't know of a nicer gesture that anyone has ever done for me. After that, anytime anyone might say something negative about Clemente, I would interrupt and say, "Wait a minute. You are talking to the wrong guy. I know the real Roberto Clemente."

Roberto was just a very giving, caring individual who was a great ballplayer to boot. His tragic death on New Year's Eve 1972 at the age of 38 while trying to get relief supplies to earthquake victims in Nicaragua showed the world what I already knew.

The Pirates' manager in those years was Danny Murtaugh. Some guys just look and act like managers. They have the bearing and presence that says they are in control. They also have good players. Bobby Cox and Joe Torre, to me, look like managers. Eddie Sawyer, Walter Alston, and Ralph Houk did as well. And so did Danny Murtaugh.

Danny and I went way back. He played second base for the Pirates the first game I pitched in the big leagues in 1948. As a player he didn't have a lot of natural ability, but he was a scrapper. He was a solid infielder and a spray hitter who usually made contact. He was also a very witty guy, as I first learned in 1949.

On May 22 that year, I was beating Elmer Riddle and the Pirates 6–1 in the ninth inning on a blustery Saturday afternoon in Pittsburgh. With two out Murtaugh came to bat. I fell behind him 2–0 and threw him a fastball right over the plate. The Pirates had shortened left field in Forbes Field a couple of years earlier to take advantage of the power of Hank Greenberg and then Ralph Kiner, and the wind that day was blowing out in what seemed like gale force. Danny connected and hit a soft fly ball that just floated over the fence, scraping it as it came down barely on the other side. I could not believe that ball had left the park.

The next day Murtaugh walked by me and said, "Howya doin', cuz?"

I said, "C'mon, Danny."

He said, "No, no. When I hit a home run off you, I'm going to call you cousin."

I guess he had something. Danny hit only eight home runs in 2,600 at-bats in his big-league career. Until he died in 1976 he called me "cuz" because of that wind-blown home run in 1949.

Danny's sense of humor surfaced during his managerial career with regard to Dick Stuart, the Pirates' first baseman in the late fifties and early sixties. Dick could really tattoo the ball and had hit 66 home runs with Lincoln, Nebraska, in the Western League. But he was prone to slumps, and during a prolonged one the hometown fans were getting on his case. Once when he popped up yet again, the boos really came cascading down from the stands. According to the story, Dick retreated to the dugout and walked over to Murtaugh, asking, "Skip, how come they are always booing me?"

Without missing a beat, Danny said, "They're not booing you. They're booing me for playing you."

Danny Murtaugh was a beautiful man and a fine baseball manager.

Of course, those Pirates teams that Murtaugh managed in the late fifties were strong clubs, and his 1960 team won the pennant and the World Series against the Yankees on Bill Mazeroski's dramatic home run. But for most of the early and mid-fifties the Pirates were decided also-rans.

Duffy Daugherty, the legendary Michigan State football coach, was an assistant football coach when I was at Michigan State, and he was a big baseball fan—in fact, he would sometimes hang out in the bullpen when I played in college. Duffy was originally from Pittsburgh, so when I made the big leagues he made a standing $1 bet with one of his buddies from home every time I pitched against the Pirates. I guess he did pretty well for a number of years, because I had good success against the Pirates. But then in the late fifties, when the Pirates became a contender, Duffy told me, "I've called off the bet. They're too good now."

* * *

That four-game win streak near the end of 1959 made me 15–15 going into a season-ending series with the Milwaukee Braves, who were locked in a tight pennant fight with the Dodgers. I got beat at home 8–5, giving up three runs in the top of the ninth, and then lost to Spahn in Milwaukee 3–2 to end the season on a down note. As a result, I finished 15–17 with 19 complete games in 35 starts. I threw two shutouts but also got hit around some as my earned run average climbed to 4.27. I was still the winningest pitcher on the club. Curt missed virtually the entire year with arm trouble, and Jim Owens and Gene Conley, whom we acquired from the Braves in the Stan Lopata trade, both won 12 games.

We had acquired 25-year-old second baseman George "Sparky" Anderson from the Dodgers organization before the '59 season. Eddie Sawyer played Sparky the entire year at second base. He hustled and played hard every day but hit only .218. At the end of the year, Eddie called Sparky in and told him, "I appreciate your effort, but I'm afraid you just are not a big-league ballplayer."

As a result, Sparky went back to the minor leagues with Toronto and soon got into coaching and managing in the minors. I next saw Sparky during spring training in 1967 when I was in the minor league camp with Reading. I asked, "How you doing, Sparky?"

"Aw," he said, "I'm not going to manage anymore. I can't stand the umpiring. They are just driving me crazy. They really get to me. I'm just going to be a coach and let it go at that."

Needless to say, I was surprised when he took the Cincinnati Reds job three years later in 1970 because I thought he was serious. Of course, Sparky became one of the most successful managers in baseball history, leading both the Big Red Machine of the seventies and the Detroit Tigers in the eighties to

World Championships. He is in the Hall of Fame, and it is not for his playing. I asked him about our conversation in later years, and he told me he had been serious at the time but that he learned to control himself better and not let the umpires get to him so much.

After our second straight last-place finish in 1959, there was not much room for optimism for 1960. In January, John Quinn traded Richie Ashburn, who had slumped to .266 in '59, to the Cubs for infielders Alvin Dark and Jim Woods and pitcher John Buzhardt. He made a number of other deals as well, trying to stop our slide, and acquired players like Johnny Callison, Tony Taylor, and Tony Gonzalez who would become Phillies mainstays in the future. But our slide continued, beginning on Opening Day when I lost to the Reds at Crosley Field 9–4. I didn't have it, and Eddie took me out in the fifth inning, something he rarely had to do.

That night we flew back to Philadelphia to begin our home season and awoke the next morning to learn that Eddie Sawyer had resigned as manager, one game into the season. When asked why, he tersely responded, "Because I'm 49 years old, and I want to live to be 50." Eddie had something there. We were not a good club and, furthermore, it was pretty clear that Eddie and John Quinn did not see eye to eye about running a baseball team.

John Quinn acted quickly and brought in 34-year-old Gene Mauch, who had been managing the Minneapolis Millers in the American Association. Mauch had spent nine years in the big leagues as a utility infielder, but this was his first major league managerial position. Not that it really mattered much. Managers cannot do much without talented players, and so we spent most of the season battling the Chicago Cubs for seventh place. The Cubs won the battle by one game, and we continued our string of winning five fewer games than the previous year, finishing 59–85, 36 games behind the champion Pirates.

Curt Simmons and I began the year rooming together on the road, and we were in San Francisco in early May when Gene Mauch called to the room and said he was coming up. When Gene arrived he was very emotional and said, "Curt, we've decided to release you."

Curt just stood there and said, "OK, if that is what you've decided." Although Lefty was upset, he just did not show much emotion. For Gene Mauch, that was a tough message to deliver.

But in his 13th season with the club, Curt was gone. He went home to Philadelphia but wasn't there a week before Solly Hemus, the manager of the St. Louis Cardinals, called. Solly had been with the Phillies and thought that Curt could still pitch. He was right. Lefty worked out for the Cardinals, they signed him, and for most of the next seven years with the Redbirds, he was an effective starting pitcher. In 1964, at the age of 35, Curt won 18 games and lost only 9 to help the Cards to the pennant. Lefty finally pitched in the World Series that year, 14 years after missing the Whiz Kids' Series in 1950.

Shortly after Curt was picked up by St. Louis, the Cards came to Philadelphia for a doubleheader. One of our coaches told Jim Owens, one of our starting pitchers, that Jim was going to pitch the easy game, meaning the game Curt Simmons was throwing for the Cardinals. It was the kind of offhand remark someone could make because Curt had not pitched well for the Phillies and had yet to pitch much for the Cardinals.

So Owens went out and lost 1–0 to Curt. After the game, Jimmy came into the clubhouse, threw his glove into his locker, and said, "Thanks a hell of a lot for the easy game."

After Curt's release, I was the last of the Whiz Kids still with the Phillies. I really struggled along with the team early in 1960, and on June 1 I was 1–7. One day I was warming up for a start in Connie Mack Stadium in front of the dugout, as we used to do. As I finished and started walking to the bench, I heard a familiar voice say, "Hey, kid."

I looked up and it was Cy Perkins. I had not seen Cy for a long time. I said, "Cy, how are you?"

"I haven't been feeling too good, but I had to come out and watch you warm up. You're throwing good. I was worried about you, but you are all right. Some people don't understand what a good delivery you have. Just keep pitching." Then he turned and left, and I don't think he stayed for the ballgame. It would be the last time I ever saw Cy.

It was amazing the effect that visit from Cy had on me, just knowing that one person believed in me. I pitched much better for the rest of the year, finishing 11–9 for an overall record of 12–16. I probably should have had Cy move in.

Although I was pretty sure the team and I had hit rock bottom in 1960, 1961 proved me wrong on both counts. We opened the season against the Dodgers in Los Angeles. The day before the first game, Gene Mauch and I attended a banquet, and he was asked who his Opening Day pitcher would be. He said laughingly, "Robin Roberts. He is my Opening Day pitcher and he may never win another game."

I know Gene really didn't mean anything by that remark, but as the season wore on and I didn't have a victory, I began to think, "By golly, he might have been right, I may not win another game." I was 0–7 when I finally beat the Giants on June 5 in Candlestick Park 3–2. I gave up a two-run homer to Chuck

Hiller in the bottom of the second, but Pancho Herrera, our first baseman, hit a three-run dinger in the top of the third off Mike McCormick to give us a lead that I managed to hold for the rest of the game. It wasn't easy. In the bottom of the ninth the Giants had a runner on third with two outs. The batter hit a high hopper over my head. Our shortstop, Ruben Amaro, came across and made a fine play to get to the ball and throw the runner out at first. To me, it was an all-time great play because it finally got me my first win.

Bob Lemon was our pitching coach that year. When a pitcher is going as bad as I was that year, nothing works. The night before the game against the Giants, Bob and I were sitting in the hotel bar together. I generally just drank a couple of beers, but this night Bob suggested that I order a vodka gimlet. It tasted like 7-Up. I think I had three. After I won the game, Bob came over and suggested that maybe the vodka gimlets were the answer. I didn't agree, but I didn't win another game.

That win was my 234th and last as a Phillie. I know it was tough for everyone with the Phillies to watch me go through such a difficult year, and of course it was rough on me, especially with the team having so much trouble winning. I even managed to get injured and go on the disabled list for the first time in my career. On July 2 I was locked in a 1–1 duel with Don Drysdale in Connie Mack Stadium after five and a half innings. In the bottom of the sixth I singled and then took off for second on a 3–2 pitch to Johnny Callison. He hit a sharp grounder to Junior Gilliam at second, and I slid hard into the base trying to take Maury Wills out and break up the double play. Maury jumped in the air making me miss, and I hooked my leg on the bag and stretched some ligaments.

I hobbled off the field, out of the game, and my leg really swelled up in the clubhouse. After I rested it for a week, Gene tried me in relief against the Cubs in Wrigley Field. I threw an inning, but my leg was not much better, so the club placed me on the 30-day disabled list. After all the pitching I had done for so many years, it was really difficult for me to not pitch for 30 days. I worked out before the games, running and stretching, and then had to go upstairs to the press box to watch the games, because if you were on the disabled list you could not be in the dugout once the game began.

It was a long 30 days. The night before I was to come off the list, John Quinn, the general manager, told me, "We'd like to leave you on the disabled list for the rest of the year."

I said, "C'mon, John. Thirty days without pitching is about all I can stand."

"Well," he said, "we'd like you to stay on the disabled list."

As I think back it might have been a good idea to just rest for the balance of the season, but at the time I thought to myself, "Wow, how low have I sunk?" For the first time I thought I did not really fit in with the Phillies.

Quinn did take me off the disabled list, but the team was in the middle of what would become a major-league-record 23-game losing streak. We finally broke the streak on August 20 when John Buzhardt beat the Braves 7–4 in the second game of a doubleheader. We were very firmly entrenched in the basement, and as the season wore down, I pitched less and less. There was a two-week period in September in which I didn't pitch at all.

The team had a long road trip to California near the end of the season. Because I had not been pitching and the team had brought up a number of young guys from the minors, I went up to Gene Mauch and said, "Gene, if you're not going to pitch me on the trip, I'd just as soon stay home." I thought it would save the Phillies money and I wouldn't have to go out and just sit around in California.

"Well," Gene said, "I'll talk to Quinn about it."

The next thing I knew I got a phone call from Bob Carpenter, telling me to come see him before the next day's game. When I went to see him, he said, "What's this about you refusing to go on the trip tomorrow?"

I said, "Oh, no, I didn't say that. I just asked Gene, 'If you're not going to use me, why don't you leave me home.' That is all I said, Bob."

He said, "Well, you get on that plane like everyone else."

I said, "Fine. I was just making a suggestion. I wasn't trying to cause any trouble. I only wanted to stay home because I haven't been pitching." So I went on the trip and didn't pitch much. At that juncture there was certainly friction between the organization and me, which I'm sure I contributed to.

When I pitched it was mostly in relief. My last game as a Phillie was a microcosm of the season for both me and the team. On September 28 I relieved in the fourth inning against the Dodgers in Connie Mack Stadium. We were already down 3–0, and I held Los Angeles scoreless until the seventh when they scored five unearned runs on three errors. We lost the game 10–0 as Don Drysdale shut us out on six hits.

For the year I finished 1–10 and the club ended 47–107, 46 games behind the first-place Cincinnati Reds and 17 games from the seventh-place Chicago Cubs.

It was pretty clear that I would not be in the Phillies' plans after that dismal season, and in December Bob Carpenter called to tell me that the Yankees had picked me up on waivers. It was difficult to have my career with the Phillies end like that after living in the community with my family for so many years and pitching for the club for so long. It was quite an adjustment to have my relationship with the Phillies end. For many years, I had worried about everything involving the club, not only on the field, but off the field, like whether we were drawing well. I felt that I was part of the Phillies family and that I would be part of the family because I always had been.

When I left I reflected on all those years and the role I'd had with the organization, like rooming with Bouchee or members of the Dalton Gang or speaking to men's groups and churches in the winter when the team asked me to. But I wanted to continue to pitch so much that I did not consider it a negative thing that my time with the Phillies was over. My relationship with the Phillies had become uncomfortable, and I understood I was going somewhere else to continue my career. That is what I wanted because I still thought I could pitch effectively, even after that awful '61 season.

CHAPTER 11

With the Yankees Oh So Briefly

I had always appreciated how nice it was to live with my family in the town in which I played. I knew it was going to be more difficult playing in a different town. Mary and the boys had always joined me for spring training. But after spring training Mary always had our four boys by herself until school was out for the year. She should have gotten an award. Now when school was out Mary would pack the boys and herself and drive to whatever city I was pitching for and set up a home for us in a rental property until school started, when she would reverse the process and drive the boys back to Philadelphia. Baseball wives, then, as now, simply do not get enough credit for keeping the family going while the man of the house is off playing ball.

Curt Simmons, who was now with the Cardinals, and I worked out together in the winter before the 1962 season just as we always had, throwing in a gym to each other. In late February I reported to the Yankees' spring training camp in Ft. Lauderdale to prepare for the 1962 season. Mary and the kids came with me, and Mary set up home for us. She had arranged for the kids to be in school there for the six weeks of spring training.

The '62 Yankees were the defending World Champions and were coming off the memorable year when Roger Maris and Mickey Mantle had challenged Babe Ruth's single-season home-run record of 60 with Roger breaking it on the last day of the season. Whitey Ford had won the Cy Young Award with a 25–4 record, Ralph Terry was 16–3, and Luis Arroyo had 29 saves and a 15–5 record out of the bullpen. The infielders Moose Skowron, Bobby Richardson, Tony Kubek, and Clete Boyer were in their prime. Yogi Berra and Elston Howard behind the plate were not too shabby either.

At one point in spring training the Yankees traveled to Tampa for three games against teams training in that area. While we were there, I received a call in my hotel room from Larry Shenk, the Phillies' public relations director, asking me to meet Bob Carpenter, John Quinn, him, and some media for lunch at the Holiday Inn in Tampa located at the entrance to the causeway to Clearwater where the Phillies still trained. He told me that they were going to retire my Phillies uniform number. I thought, "Well, isn't that something."

So I went and had lunch, and they gave me my uniform top and told me that they were retiring my number. In later years the Phillies invited me to Veteran's Stadium on the occasions when they retired Steve Carlton, Richie Ashburn, and Mike Schmidt's numbers, and there would always be sixty thousand people in the stands. I would remember back to when the Phillies retired my number at a luncheon at the Holiday Inn in Tampa in 1962. It was a nice lunch.

Ironically, Johnny Sain was the pitching coach for the Yankees. Of course, Johnny was the one who said he didn't know how I'd gotten them out when I threw hard. But my pitching for the Yankees that spring was not particularly impressive. I was competing with some good young pitchers like Jim Bouton, Roland Sheldon, Marshall Bridges, and Al Downing as well as veterans like Bud Daley and Jim Coates. The Yankees did give me a chance to pitch in spring training, and I felt like I was rounding into shape as the spring wore on.

Mickey Mantle was starting his 12th season with the Yankees, and it was his team. He was the leader on the club and a fun-loving character. One time during spring training I was on the team bus waiting to leave for one of our road trips. Mickey was always the last one to jump on the bus, and as he got on he noticed Elston Howard, who was black, sitting in the first seat. Mickey walked by and then came back and said, "Ellie, get to the back of the bus where you belong." Elston replied that Mickey should do an impossible act, and Mantle laughed and headed for the back of the bus himself.

The Yankees were Mantle's team and everyone knew it, but they were still a team first. Practices were completely team oriented, the way they were early in my career with the Phillies. For example, in batting practice each hitter got two bunts and five swings and that was it. One day Jim Coates, who really threw hard, was pitching batting practice. Mickey took his five swings and never hit the ball out of the batting cage. After his last swing, he threw his bat to the ground and, as he ran to first, growled, in very strong language, that he wished Coates would throw that hard in regular-season games. But the point was that Mantle took only five swings like everyone else.

Coming into the American League for the first time, I really didn't believe that Mantle could be the equal of National Leaguers like Willie Mays, Hank Aaron, or Stan Musial. It was easy to see that he had real talent, but he limped as he ran and I wondered just how good he could be. In the fifties there was a tremendous rivalry between the two leagues, and Mickey, although he had nailed me for that gargantuan blast in the '55 All-Star Game, experienced rather indifferent success in those games. I later figured out that he was such a team player that the annual trip to the All-Star Game was sort of a lark for him.

We opened the 1962 season against the Baltimore Orioles in Yankee Stadium. We were losing 2–1 in the top of the eighth, and I was sitting in the dugout next to Jack Reed, a reserve outfielder. I mentioned to Jack that we had better get it going, that we needed to score some runs or we were about to lose. Jack's reply was classic. He said, "Don't worry, Mickey hits this inning."

In the bottom of the eighth, Roger Maris walked and Mickey hit one into the bullpen to give us a 3–2 lead. I looked at Jack, and he said, "Mickey does that all the time." Luis Arroyo came in and got the Orioles out in the ninth, and we had a 3–2 win. I began to understand; although playing in New York was in some ways a big advantage for a great baseball player, Mickey's ability to handle the pressure and consistently rise to the occasion was something very special. There was a reason the Yankees won all those pennants and World Championships during Mickey's career.

Later that same opening week we traveled to Baltimore to play the Orioles there. On Friday night Whitey Ford pitched and won a tough ballgame. After the team bus got back to the hotel, Jack Reed, who was my roommate, and I started to go to the coffee shop to get something to eat. Whitey asked, "Where you headed, Robin?" When I answered that Jack and I were going to grab something to eat, he suggested we go with Mickey and him.

The four of us grabbed a cab to an Italian restaurant and arrived close to midnight. The Yankees had won, Whitey had won, and I am sure Mickey had done something to contribute. The day's work was complete, and Whitey would not pitch for four more days. It is difficult to sleep after you've pitched anyway, and Whitey and Mickey were wound up. We all ate, drank, talked, and mostly laughed the night away. By quarter to six in the morning we were still talking and laughing. I was not in the habit of staying up like that because I generally liked to get my sleep. But I enjoyed that evening immensely, as much as any I can remember in baseball. We finally got back to the hotel about 6:45 in the morning, and I thought that these guys sure knew how to relax. With all the pressure and all the limelight, they knew how to get away from it all and have a good time.

Mickey had a wonderful sense of humor, made to order for the game of baseball. One of the best stories about Mantle involved Pedro Ramos, who pitched for the Washington Senators for many years. One day Ramos struck Mickey out to end a ballgame. The next day Pedro asked Mickey to sign the ball he had struck out on. Mickey obliged and Pedro was quite pleased.

About a week later Mickey hit a long home run off Ramos. As he rounded third, completing his home-run trot, Mickey hollered to Ramos, "I'll sign that one for you, too, if you can find it." Great story. I hope it was true.

The Mick was a gamer. Later when I was with the Orioles, I pitched against him a number of times. In one game, I had a 2–1 lead late in the game. I walked Mickey and he immediately stole second to get into scoring position. Mickey had great speed but stole only 153 bases in his career. I would bet that every one of them was in a tie or one-run game when the extra base meant something.

After the series in Baltimore we returned to New York for a homestand. I was out in right field shagging fly balls during batting practice one day when Jim Hegan, one of the Yankees' coaches, came out and said, "Robin, Houk wants to see you." Ralph Houk was the Yankees' manager.

I had earlier mentioned to Mary that Ralph had not said much to me. I think it was because he did not have much good to say. So after Hegan spoke to me I assumed that Houk was going to release me, and I was right. When I arrived at Ralph's office, he said, "This is the worst thing I've ever had to do in baseball. We've decided to release you."

I said, "Fine," and got up to leave. I really did not want to sit and discuss it. As I was walking out, Ralph said, "I'd like to shake your hand. I enjoyed having you on the team and I'm sorry it didn't work out."

I said, "I'll shake your hand, Ralph, but I'll tell you something. There's nobody here who's a better pitcher than me other than Whitey. He might be. But I feel bad that I didn't get an opportunity to pitch." And with that I left, went into the clubhouse, packed my belongings, and went home to Philadelphia.

The next morning, a Saturday, I was at home having breakfast with Mary and I said, "You know, I've got to call Houk. I wasn't very nice yesterday." So I called him and got right through to him at the ballpark. I said, "Ralph, I'm sorry about yesterday. I really did feel terrible, but I've been thinking about it and I understand. I am sorry that I popped off a little."

Ralph said, "Don't worry about it, Robin. I understand that you were very disappointed."

It was a sad situation. I'd been a pretty good pitcher for quite a few years, and the Yankees made the decision to release me a week into the season without giving me the chance to pitch. And it looked like neither the worst team in baseball nor the best team thought I could still pitch.

CHAPTER 12

New Beginnings

After the Yankees released me early in the 1962 season, I went home, very unsure of my future. I was 35 years old and had a wife and four boys.

Soon after I got home, the phone rang. It was Cy Perkins. I had not spoken to him for almost two years, since he came out to watch me warm up in 1960 when I was struggling for the Phillies.

"What are they trying to do to you, kid?" he asked.

"I'm not sure," I said.

"Don't let them run you out of the game. You'll be pitching shutouts when you're 40," he said.

"Thanks, Cy," I said.

"I'm telling you, kid, don't you dare quit. There's no way you can't keep pitching."

It is hard to describe how much that call from Cy meant after two teams had given up on me. I still thought I could pitch and still wanted to pitch, and Cy's call really picked me up.

I soon received a call from a representative of the Tokyo Giants, wanting me to come to Japan to pitch. I thanked him but said no thanks. I did not want to disrupt my family to go to Japan, and besides, I thought I could still pitch in the major leagues. As a result, I called Freddie Hutchinson, the manager of the Cincinnati Reds, after I had been home a few days. The Reds were in town playing the Phillies, and I told Freddie that I would like to work out for him.

Freddie said, "Fine Robin, I'd like to see you. How are you feeling?"

I said, "I'm fine. I didn't fit in with the Yankees, but I can still pitch."

"Well," he said, "come on out and throw for me at 4:00."

I got there a little early and got Maje McDonnell to catch me. I got good and loose, and at 4:00 Hutchinson came out of the dugout. He said, "Are you loose?"

I said, "Yeah, I'm good and loose." Then I threw five or six pitches and Freddie said, "That's enough. You're throwing good, aren't you?"

I said, "I feel good, Freddie. My arm's fine."

"I'd like to have you," he said. "I'll give you 10 straight starts." Hutch then told me to contact Bill DeWitt, the Reds' general manager, about my contract and then join the team in Pittsburgh, where it was heading next.

I was very excited about the prospect of starting for the '62 Reds. They were the defending National League champions and were a very solid club with players like Frank Robinson, Vada Pinson, Leo Cardenas, Bob Purkey, Joey Jay, and Jim O'Toole. So I called Bill DeWitt and he said, "Freddie wants you to join us. What do you want for a salary?"

"Well, I was making $33,500," I said.

"Aw, I can't pay you that kind of money. I've only got one player making $30,000."

I said, "I need that kind of money to break even."

He said, "Well, I'll give you $15,000."

I said, "I can't sign for $15,000."

"Well, that's it. That's what I can give you," he said.

So that was that. I would have loved to pitch for Cincinnati, but I just could not take that kind of pay cut to do it.

I then called Lee MacPhail, who was the general manager of the Baltimore Orioles. Of course, Baltimore is very close to Philadelphia, and playing for them would allow me to commute from my home. Lee invited me down, and I warmed up with Darrell Johnson, one of their catchers. Lee then called me and offered me a contract at my old salary, so I signed as an American Leaguer for the first time.

The 1962 Orioles were a team with talent with guys like Brooks Robinson, Gus Triandos, Jim Gentile, Russ Snyder, Jackie Brandt, and 21-year-old Boog Powell. They had a young staff with good arms including Chuck Estrada, Milt Pappas, Steve Barber, and Jack Fisher. Future Hall of Famer Hoyt Wilhelm was as good as they come out of the bullpen. Billy Hitchcock, a former American League infielder, was the manager. But even with all that talent, the Orioles were not able to win in 1962, and we struggled, finishing in seventh place in the expanded 10-team American League, eight games under .500.

My first American League appearance came on the road on May 21 against the Cleveland Indians. Billy Hitchcock brought me in from the bullpen in the fourth inning in relief of Hal Brown and Wes Stock, with the Orioles down 7–2. I threw two scoreless and hitless innings before being lifted for pinch-hitter Earl Robinson. We eventually lost 10–7.

That effort earned me a start six days later on May 27 against the Boston Red Sox in Fenway Park, my first visit to that venerable ballpark after 13 years in the big leagues. I pitched pretty well, pitching seven and two-thirds innings before leaving with the game tied 2–2, and I found myself in the regular starting rotation.

My first start against the Yankees was in Yankee Stadium on June 11. Boog Powell had hit two home runs the night before to beat the Yankees. In his first time up that day, Bud Daley, the Yankees' pitcher, drilled Boog right in the head. They had to carry him off the field, and as I sat on the bench I thought about how in the National League when that happened, the opposing pitcher would then throw right at the head of the first batter he faced. Roger Maris was the first batter when I went out to pitch the next inning so I threw the ball high and tight, right at Roger's head. Down he went, then he picked himself and his bat up and started for the mound.

I wasn't eager to bust my hand, but I knew I would take a swing at Roger as soon as he got to me. Fortunately, Hobie Landrith, my catcher, jumped on Roger's back and they wrestled a little, but nothing else happened. I ended up pitching into the eighth inning and won my first game in the American League 5–3. It was special to beat the Yankees, not only because of my brief association with them but also because they were the Yankees and were the defending World Champions.

The next day during batting practice Roger came walking by and asked, "Why me?"

I said, "Roger, you're the first guy that showed up. If it had been Mickey, he'd have gone down. You can't throw at our guys and not expect us to knock you down."

I didn't generally knock hitters down just to loosen them up at the plate. The only time I ever threw at a batter because he was hitting me was against Ted Kluszewski in the mid-fifties. Big Klu was a powerful man with huge, muscular arms. He had nailed me for two home runs in Crosley Field his first two times up. The third time I drilled him in his right arm. The ball dropped at his feet, and he picked it up and flipped it to me as he jogged to first. Somehow I don't think I scared him.

Brooks Robinson was not yet 25 years old when I joined the Orioles but already was a fielding legend at third base. Brooksie was not one of those gifted guys who could run like the wind or throw hard. He could just play baseball. He had wonderful baseball instincts and great quickness and just did everything right. Brooks Robinson was a pleasure to watch play baseball every day.

Brooksie taught me a lesson in late June in a game against the Chicago White Sox in Memorial Stadium in Baltimore. In the very first inning with two outs and a 2–0 count, Joe Cunningham laid a surprise bunt down the third-base line, trying for a base hit. I went over to pick the ball up, when I heard, "Look out!" Brooks Robinson gloved the ball and threw Cunningham out at first, all in one motion. As I walked to the dugout, Brooksie patted me on the butt and said, "Stay out of my way, old man. I'm good on that play." So I did from then on. I also went on to win the game 3–1, scattering five hits to beat Juan Pizarro.

Billy Hitchcock kept me in the starting rotation for the rest of the year and I won my share and lost some tough one-run games. I lost two straight one-run games to Jim Bunning and the Tigers in early July and later, on August 1, hooked up in an 11-inning duel against Jim Kaat and the Minnesota Twins. The score was tied 1–1 in the top of the eleventh when Jim Kaat himself hit a triple to drive in the lead run. Vic Power drove Kaat home, and I was a 3–1 loser. Every time Jim has seen me in the many years since, he brings up that game-winning triple.

The sportswriter Dave Anderson once asked me who I thought deserved to be in the Hall of Fame who is not, and my answer was Jim Kaat. Not only did he win 283 games, including 20 or more three times, he was among the best fielding pitchers of all time. He won 14 Gold Gloves, second only to Brooks Robinson's 16. In that 11-inning game in 1962, we had the bases loaded with two out in the eighth inning when Brooks Robinson hit a shot right up the middle. Kaat caught the ball with lightning reflexes and threw Brooks out at first to end the inning. That ball was smashed, and if anyone else had been pitching, two runs would have scored and I would have been the winning pitcher. That is a sad story.

In late August the Yankees came into Baltimore for a five-game series, a doubleheader Friday and Saturday and a single game on Sunday. We were not going anywhere, but the Yanks were in a pennant race with the Minnesota Twins, so the games were important to them. We swept both doubleheaders, and on Sunday I started against Whitey Ford. Tony Kubek hit a home run off me in the top of the second to put the Yankees up 1–0, but Brooks Robinson smacked one of his own in the bottom of the inning to tie the score. Whitey was tough on left-handed hitters and had been particularly rough on Jim Gentile, our free-swinging first baseman. Jim, however, touched Ford for a homer in the fourth to put us ahead 2–1, and that is the way it ended—2–1 as I scattered five hits. The Orioles had swept the five-game series against the World Champs.

In September we played the Kansas City Athletics and, lo and behold, Granny Hamner made a relief appearance for the A's and got us out for a couple of innings. Granny had always fooled around with a knuckleball. In fact, I had hurt my shoulder once trying to hit it in batting practice when we were with the Phillies. Granny had been managing in the minor leagues and began putting himself into games and throwing his knuckleball. I guess it helped that he probably wouldn't take himself out. He had gone 13–2 there and the Athletics, who were in ninth place and going nowhere, called him up.

After the game, Granny came up and asked, "Hoss, what do you think?"

I said, "Ham, you look like a shortstop to me." He laughed even though I wasn't very supportive of his pitching career. The Athletics weren't either; they released him shortly thereafter.

As for me, I pitched well for the Orioles in 1962, finishing 10–9, and I started to learn what an earned run average was. That was because I finished second in the league with a 2.78 ERA, behind Hank Aguirre of the Tigers and just ahead of Whitey Ford of the Yankees.

Over the winter I attended a baseball banquet in Columbus, Ohio, to receive an award. Afterward I was getting on the elevator to go up to my room when I ran into Ralph Houk and Tommy Henrich, who were getting off the elevator. Ralph said, "Where are you going, Robin?"

I said, "I'm just going up to go to bed."

Ralph said, "C'mon and go with us," so I did. We had a good visit and conversation. Ralph really felt bad that I hadn't gotten a chance to pitch for the Yankees, maybe especially since I had later shown that I could still pitch. I knew, however, that I was caught up in a numbers game because the Yankees had so many good young arms. I had not pitched that well in the spring, and the Yankees had a decision to make, which was almost inevitable given the circumstances. They made it and I was disappointed, but I understood their decision. But it was good to get to talk to Ralph and let him know that I had no hard feelings.

I came back to an improved Orioles ballclub in 1963. We had added Luis Aparicio to play shortstop, Boog Powell was starting to come into his own, and Steve Barber won 20 games. I started 35 ballgames, threw 251 innings, and ended with a 14–13 record. We moved up to fourth place, 10 games above .500, a significant improvement over 1962.

Milt Pappas was just 23 years old as the '63 season began and was already in his sixth season as a starting pitcher for the Orioles. He was a fine pitcher but was happy to come out of the game if he had a one-run lead after five or six innings. If he had a five-run lead, he would stay in and finish the game. He told me one day, "I'm not paid to win, I'm paid not to lose." In a close ballgame, Milt's elbow would start hurting, but that never seemed to be the case if he had a big lead. It really detracted from the kind of pitcher he could have been. He didn't do so badly anyway. In a 17-year career he won 209 games against 164 losses. But he doesn't get the respect that he should, and it is mostly his own fault.

Milt was one of the first pitchers that Paul Richards babied when Paul was the Orioles' manager. With all those young arms, Paul was one of the first to start counting pitches. I'm not sure how many pitches they got, but Milt, Steve Barber, and Chuck Estrada generally were limited as rookies to how many pitches they could throw in a game.

Our new shortstop, Luis Aparicio, was a wonderful talent who was a veteran of seven years with the Chicago White Sox. He had a powerful arm and a great delivery, and he threw hard in warm-ups every day. I used to ask him, "Hey, Louie, who is counting your pitches?"

Louie was also an exceptional base stealer. I used to think that a base runner ought to steal on a bad count for the hitter, like 0–2 or 1–2 when the pitcher is trying to make a good pitch to get the hitter out. In that situation, it may be a pitch that is hard for the catcher to handle, giving an advantage to the base runner. But base stealers are afraid of pitchouts on those counts, so they want to steal when the pitcher is behind in the count and can't pitch out.

I would say to Louie, "Don't steal on 2–0 or 3–1, let the guy hit."

Louie would say, "No, no, I know they're not going to pitch out."

I cranked up some good games in '63, winning four starts in a row in May, including four-hit 6–1 and two-hit 2–0 wins over the Washington Senators. In late June I shut out the Los Angeles Angels 10–0 and then pitched into the fourteenth inning before losing to the Kansas City Athletics 3–1. On July 15 I hooked up against Gary Peters of the Chicago White Sox in Comiskey Park. Gary had overpowering stuff and ended up striking out 13 Orioles batters with no walks on the way to a 4–0 victory. The hard-hitting Robin Roberts broke up Gary's perfect game with a bloop hit over Nellie Fox's head at second. Every time I see Gary he reminds me that I cost him $1,000 because the White Sox used to give a $1,000 bonus for a no-hitter.

Two weeks later I saw Mickey Lolich for the first time. I started against him and his Detroit Tigers and could immediately tell that he had a good hook and a good fastball. Dick McAuliffe doubled home Billy Bruton to give the Tigers a 1–0 lead in the top of the first, and that was the only run either team scored until the bottom of the ninth. With one out Al Smith pinch hit for me and singled. With two out Dick Brown hit for Russ Snyder and blasted a two-run homer and I was a winner, 2–1. I pitched a two-hitter and Mickey allowed

186

only three hits, two in that ninth inning. Lolich was a rookie, but I could tell he was going to be a fine pitcher.

I was not so fortunate against the Tigers late in the season in Tiger Stadium. I was up against Jim Bunning, and Johnny Orsino popped a two-run home run in the third to put me ahead 2–0. I had a one-hit shutout with two outs in the bottom of the eighth when Gates Brown pinch hit for George Smith. He worked the count to 3–2 and fouled off about five pitches. He finally walked on a pitch that could have gone either way. Up came another pinch-hitter, a young kid I had never seen before. He was a rookie named Willie Horton. Young Willie hit a low fastball into the upper deck for his first major league home run to tie the score 2–2.

The game continued until the bottom of the tenth inning when, with one out, the Tigers' Gus Triandos knocked a fly ball into the bleachers and I lost 3–2 even though I had given up only three hits. At least I had another start before the end of the year so I didn't have to sit through the winter thinking about Willie Horton. I ended the year with a 6–3 victory over the Senators in a game in which my old Whiz Kid teammate Steve Ridzik, making a successful comeback with Washington, pitched a scoreless inning in relief.

Dave McNally was a rookie that year and, like a lot of first-year pitchers, struggled some against big-league hitters. Near the end of the year he came up to me and said, "Robin, why don't you ever talk to me about pitching?"

I said, "Well, Harry Brecheen is the pitching coach, Dave."

"Well, you never say anything."

"It's not my job," I said.

"Well, what do you think?" he asked.

I said, "I'll tell you one thing. You don't throw your fastball enough when you are ahead of the batter. These guys can hit a curveball when they are looking for it, and you've got a good one. A curve is fine to start a batter off with or when you're behind the hitter, but when you're ahead you need to throw some fastballs."

"I'm not fast enough like you."

I said, "Fine, but I'm telling you, you don't throw your fastball enough when you're ahead of the hitter."

Five years later, I was retired from baseball and in the investment business when McNally won 20 games for the first time. I called to congratulate him and said, "It's Robin, Dave. Congratulations on a fine year."

He said, "You know, I am fast enough."

I guess if you play for 18 years like I did, you ought to be able to have some insight into the game.

* * *

Going into 1964, I really thought the Orioles had a good enough club to win the pennant. Hank Bauer, the crusty ex-Yankees outfielder and ex-marine, was the new manager, and we had a great young pitching staff and a strong every-day lineup. Boog Powell was entering his third year as a regular and making giant strides each year. He was hampered by still having to play out of position, in the outfield. Boog was a natural first baseman, but the Orioles had Jim Gentile stationed there in 1962 and 1963. Then before the '64 season the club traded Jim to the Kansas City Athletics for Norm Siebern, who also was primarily a first baseman. As a result, Boog was still stuck in the outfield.

Whenever I would see a young talent like Boog, I would always wonder what Cy would have said about him. Part of my special relationship with Cy was talking about and appreciating talented new ballplayers, and I just carried that on after Cy was no longer there. Boog had hit 15 and then 25 home runs in his first two years. One day during spring training in '64, Boog, Norm Siebern, and I were sitting around after working out and I said, "Boog, would you like to hit 40 home runs?"

Boog said, "Yeah, I'd like that."

I said, "Get right up on the plate. You'll take a few shots in the ribs, but get right up there and look for the fastball. They can't throw you the curve there because they can't see the catcher. Just look for the fastball."

Well, Boog did get right up on the plate that year and finished with 39 home runs. The last day of the season he came over to me and said, "Old man, you lied to me. You said I'd hit 40 homers. I only hit 39."

Boog did later tell me that he wasn't going to do that anymore and was going to move back from the plate. He really considered himself a left-center-field hitter and was more comfortable back a little bit. Some guys, like Frank Robinson, stayed up on the plate their whole career, but it wasn't for Boog even though he really hit some shots when he was up on the dish.

I really enjoyed Boog. He was fun. He loved to play ball and then go out and have a good time. Jerry Adair, our second baseman, and Boog were great country music fans. Late in the '64 season I shut out the Yankees in New York. After the game Boog came up and said, "Robin, we'll take you with us."

I said, "All right, Boog, I'll go along." So the three of us went to a country music club somewhere in New York and had a great time, drinking beer, talking, and listening to country music. We got in about 6:00 A.M.

When the Orioles played a night game followed by a day game in Washington, we stayed overnight at the Shoreham Hotel rather than driving back to

Baltimore. Once the club roomed Boog with me after one of those night games in Washington. Pretty soon Boog started putting a sheet up between our beds. I asked him what he was doing and he said, "I can't sleep at night. I'll read and smoke my cigarettes and you can sleep in your half of the room." So I went on to sleep and when I woke up the next morning, he was still lying in bed reading. Pretty soon we got up and went to breakfast and Boog still hadn't slept a wink. That afternoon, Boog hit three home runs against the Senators.

Several years later Boog again hit three homers in a game in Fenway Park in Boston. I had retired from baseball, but I called Boog and said, "Hey, I know who you slept with the first time you hit three home runs. Who'd you sleep with this time?"

He laughed and said, "Robbie, you won't believe it. I slept with my wife."

After the 1964 season, Boog finally got to play first base, and he held down that spot for the Orioles for the next 10 years, before spending his final years with Cleveland and then the Dodgers. He was a big guy but a marvelous first baseman who never received the credit he was due for his fielding. Boog always jokes about the famous play behind third that Brooks Robinson made in the 1970 World Series against the Cincinnati Reds. That play is often shown on highlight films, but no one ever notices that Boog made a great pickup on a low throw from Brooks to nail the runner. Boog jokes, "I really made the play of the year and no one ever mentions it."

I started the 1964 season with three strong outings but had only one win to show for it, a 1–0 shutout over Dave Morehead and the Boston Red Sox on April 23 in Memorial Stadium. My fourth start was to be on May 3 against the Cleveland Indians in Baltimore. A couple of weeks earlier I had received an invitation to a dinner on May 2 at the Waldorf-Astoria Hotel in New York honoring all the people who had appeared on the cover of *Time* magazine. I had been on the cover in 1956 and, of course, it had been a great thrill. Bob Hope was to be the speaker, and they were going to show a video of each guest and introduce each of them.

When I got the invitation I didn't think there was any way I could go since the dinner was in the middle of the baseball season, so I threw it in the trash. While the kids were still in school I commuted to Baltimore from my home in Philadelphia during homestands, so a couple of days later I was at home when Mary said, "You know what? We didn't get an invitation to the big dinner at the Waldorf where they are honoring everyone who has been on the cover of *Time*."

I said, "You wouldn't want to go to that, would you?"

Mary said, "Oh, I would absolutely love to. Can you imagine all the famous people who will be there?"

So I made a quick calculation and figured out that I could attend the dinner because we had an afternoon game the day of the dinner and I wasn't pitching until the following day. I went into our back room to use the phone and call the people at *Time* and said, "I made a big mistake. Would it still be possible for my wife and me to attend the dinner at the Waldorf?"

The people at *Time* said that would be fine, although they wouldn't be able to have a video of me because it was so late. I went back to Mary and told her that I'd thrown away the invitation but that I had just called and it was all set for us to attend anyway.

When we arrived at the cocktail party we looked around and didn't know anyone except the photographer, whom I knew from the ballpark. He came over and said, "Robin, is there anyone you would like to have your picture taken with?"

I asked Mary, and she said she would love to have her picture taken with Adlai Stevenson, her favorite politician. I introduced myself to Adlai, although I don't know if he remembered attending the special night my hometown of Springfield gave me in St. Louis when he was governor of Illinois. In any event, we had our picture taken together. Later on when we received a copy of the photo in the mail, we were surprised to see that Senator Everett Dirkson's head was in the photo as well. Dirkson was from Illinois also, and I guess he wasn't going to let Stevenson have a photo opportunity without him.

The banquet itself dragged on and on as they introduced everyone and Bob Hope still had not spoken. I finally went up to Bob and introduced myself, saying, "I'm sorry, Bob, but I can't stay to listen to you talk. I've got to pitch tomorrow in Baltimore." So Mary and I left and drove back to Philadelphia.

The next day I drove down to Baltimore and pitched against a young rookie named Tommy John. I lost 3–0 as John pitched his first career shutout. Tommy would go on to pitch 26 years in the big leagues and win 288 games. His name would become forever associated with the ligament-replacement surgery that successfully extended his career. Today each year any number of pitchers undergo "Tommy John surgery" to repair ligament damage in their elbows.

We had a lot of young arms in Baltimore in '64, including Milt Pappas, Steve Barber, Dave McNally, and 19-year-old Wally Bunker who won 19 games and lost only 5 for us in his rookie year. We also picked up veteran lefty Harvey Haddix in a trade with Pittsburgh. Harvey and I had been team-mates with the Phillies for two years, and although he was only about 5'10", I was always amazed at how hard he could throw. He is of course famous for

the 12-inning perfect game he threw for the Pirates against the Milwaukee Braves in 1959 before losing the game in the thirteenth on Joe Adcock's home run. He was tough out of the bullpen for the Orioles that year, making 49 appearances and compiling a stingy 2.31 earned run average.

Harvey was a good athlete, as I learned one afternoon in 1957 when we were teammates with the Phillies. We were out in the bullpen during the game, and for some crazy reason several of us decided to see who was the best at the standing broad jump. So between innings, we drew a line in the dirt and started leaping like frogs. None of us could beat Harvey, even though he was the smallest guy out there. He really had some spring in his legs.

The next day, by the way, Bob Carpenter called me into his office and read me the riot act. Even though we were only conducting our "contest" between innings, it seems that the TV cameras caught us in the act. I got chewed out even though I was lousy at the standing broad jump.

Harvey and I roomed together on the road in '64. We were in Los Angeles to play the Angels when I got a call from Leonard Tose inviting me to his stepson's bar mitzvah at the Beverly Hills Hotel. Leonard would later become the owner of the Philadelphia Eagles. He lived in L.A. at the time, but I had known his older brother Louis and him when they had earlier lived in Philadelphia. I told Leonard that I couldn't come because we had a night game and wouldn't get back to the hotel until 11:30 or quarter to twelve. Leonard said, "That's all right. We'll still be here. I'll have you picked up at the hotel."

I generally went out for some eggs after a night game. When we got on the bus that night to go to our hotel, Harvey Haddix asked, "Roomie, where are we going tonight?"

I said, "Leave it up to me, Harvey."

When we got off the bus at the hotel, a limousine driver came up and said, "Mr. Roberts, Mr. Tose sent me to pick you up."

I said, "Fine," and motioned Harvey to come with me. He drove us to the Beverly Hills Hotel, and we had a great time visiting with Leonard and his guests and eating steak with all the trimmings. A little after 1:00 I said good-bye to Leonard, and the limousine took us back to our hotel. When the driver let us off, Harvey looked at me and said, "That's the damnedest thing I ever saw. You sure took care of dinner." Well, we didn't have eggs that night.

Harvey and I were connected in another way that summer. His wife, Marsha, was pregnant with their third child that summer, and she went into labor on one of our trips to the coast. It would often happen that way with ballplayers and their wives, and in this case my wife went to the hospital with Marsha when she had the baby.

* * *

Led by Brooks Robinson; our new shortstop Luis Aparicio; Boog Powell; starting pitchers Milt Pappas and Wally Bunker; and a great bullpen led by Dick Hall, Stu Miller, and Harvey Haddix, we played very well all year and were in the thick of a three-team pennant race with the Yankees and the White Sox. Brooksie had one of the finest years I ever witnessed, winning the MVP, hitting .317, driving in 118 runs to lead the league, and catching every ball hit in the vicinity of third base. He helped propel us into the lead in August, but the Yankees, managed by Yogi Berra, came to Baltimore and swept a three-game series to take the lead for good.

We were still in the pennant race, however, and headed to the coast to play the Los Angeles Angels. I had a bad outing and lost the first game of the series to Fred Newman, 7–1. The weather in L.A. was cool and dry at night, just beautiful for playing baseball. But after the L.A. series we flew to Washington for a series with the Senators. I pitched the first game against Buster Narum, and it was hot, humid, and muggy. I pitched the first two innings, and then in my first at-bat in the top of the third I knocked one right over first base for a base hit. I rounded first, and as I headed into second, the whole stadium started swaying. I was down on all fours and the umpire asked, "What's wrong, Robin?"

I said, "Boy, I'm really dizzy." Eddie Weidner, the trainer, came out and eventually helped me into the dugout. They took me back to the training room and hooked me up to a glucose IV. They called an ambulance to take me to the hospital. I got into the ambulance still hooked up to the glucose IV, and the ambulance driver ripped through the streets of Washington like it was life or death. I sat up in the back and said, "Hey, buddy, take it easy. I'm all right." He was scaring me half to death. We made it to the hospital where they kept me overnight for observation and then released me.

Hank Bauer started me again six days later, on September 15 against the Twins in Baltimore. He relieved me with one out in the seventh in a 1–1 game we eventually lost 2–1.

Then I didn't pitch at all for 12 days. Of course, I didn't say anything to anybody, and no one told me why I wasn't pitching.

Finally near the end of the season we went to Cleveland for a series with the Indians. Out of the blue Harry Brecheen, our pitching coach, came up and said, "Robin, you'll be starting tomorrow night."

That was fine with me, and I ended up shutting out the Indians 3–0 on three hits for my fourth shutout of the year. After the game we headed to the

airport to fly back to Baltimore. As I got off the bus, Hank Bauer looked at me and said in his gruff way, "Hell, I didn't know you could still pitch."

That was about as much as Hank ever said to me. A few years after I retired from baseball, Hank asked me at an Old Timers' Game in New York, "Robin, why couldn't I talk to you?"

"Henry," I said, "I don't know. I had that problem other places, too."

That was very true. Other than to say hello I never had a real conversation with any of my managers, whether it be Steve O'Neill, Terry Moore, Mayo Smith, Gene Mauch, Ralph Houk, Billy Hitchcock, Bauer, or later Luman Harris, Grady Hatton, or Leo Durocher. As I will relate, the one time I did talk to Leo I got suspended. Actually Mayo Smith did come to me a few times and ask me about certain players or who I thought should be playing, but I wasn't comfortable giving him my opinion. I would say, "I don't know, Mayo. That's not my job. You're the manager."

I think that because I never said much to anybody some people regarded me as aloof. I was not trying to be aloof, but I was just going about my business in a way that had worked for me. I didn't think I needed to explain anything. I wanted the ball and wanted to win and just never bothered anyone. That lack of communication probably didn't help me late in my career.

Hank started me again in the last game of the season in a very strange game against the Detroit Tigers in Baltimore. The fog rolled in so thick early in the game that the outfielders could not see the ball. A couple of balls were hit to center field that Jackie Brandt never saw until they hit the ground. The Tigers outfielders couldn't see the ball either, and we scored six runs in the second inning against Joe Sparma. The umpires kept the game going only because it was the last game of the season and everyone was headed home for the winter afterward. I pitched five innings and left the game ahead, 9–4. Harvey Haddix came in to relieve me. As soon as he did, wouldn't you know, the fog lifted. Harvey could still throw hard, so it was fortunate for the Tigers that it did. He held them scoreless for four innings, and I ended up as the winning pitcher in the great fog game.

I had a good year all told, winning 13 and losing 7 in 31 starts with a 2.91 earned run average. I threw 204 innings and tossed four shutouts. Wally Bunker won 19 with only 5 losses, and Milt Pappas was 16–7, helping us to a 97–65 third-place finish, just two games behind the pennant-winning Yankees and a game out of second behind the White Sox.

The 1964 season is, of course, the year the Phillies blew a 6½-game lead with only 10 games to go. In the process they lost 10 straight games, and it reminded me so much of what the Whiz Kids had gone through in 1950. The

'64 team was unable to turn it around like we did in Brooklyn on the last day of the 1950 season and is forever remembered as the team that blew the pennant. Gene Mauch was criticized for pitching his two aces, Jim Bunning and Chris Short, on short rest during their bad stretch. That also reminded me of 1950 and how often Eddie Sawyer pitched me the last week of the season. I'm sure that if I had lost that last game in Ebbets Field everyone would have second-guessed Sawyer for trotting me out there so much on short rest. It just struck me again how close we came to blowing the 1950 pennant. But for Richie Ashburn's throw and Dick Sisler's home run, the Whiz Kids could have had the same sad ending as the 1964 Phillies.

There were a number of ironies surrounding the National League pennant race in '64. Curt Simmons helped pitch the St. Louis Cardinals to the pennant, winning 18 games and beating the Phillies late in the year in the midst of their losing streak. He would finally pitch in a World Series, 14 years after he missed the 1950 Series because of military duty. Also, Dick Sisler managed the Cincinnati Reds the last one-third of the season after taking over for the ill Freddie Hutchinson. The Reds ended up tied with the Phillies for second place, one game behind the Cardinals.

I felt that I had contributed significantly to the Orioles' success in 1964 but, even so, I could tell that I was not really in Hank Bauer's plans when I reported to spring training for 1965. With all the young arms in camp like Milt Pappas, Steve Barber, Dave McNally, Wally Bunker, John Miller, Darold Knowles, and a kid named Jim Palmer, Hank just did not use me much that spring.

We had a young outfielder in camp named Paul Blair. Anyone could tell right away that Paul had a lot of talent and could play, but he seemed to always be clowning around on the field. One day during batting practice I was in left field shagging flies and I noticed that Paul was over in center fooling around with a catcher's mitt. I walked over to him and said, "Young man, what are you doing? Go get your fielder's mitt. What are you doing clowning around out here with a catcher's mitt?"

Paul kind of turned around and walked away. The next day at the ballpark Paul came up to me and said, "You're trying to help me, aren't you?"

I said, "Well, I'm glad you figured it out."

I never saw Paul with a catcher's mitt again, but he went on to have a fine major league career and was one of the best center fielders of his time.

Once the season started I wasn't in the regular rotation, but early on I stepped in to start for Milt Pappas in a game against the Red Sox in Boston. It turned out to be a wild game. I gave up five runs in the first couple of innings, but Bauer let me hit anyway, and I got a base hit over third with the bases loaded to drive in a couple of runs and tie the score. Hank eventually took me out and brought in a 19-year-old rookie named Jim Palmer in relief. The kid threw two scoreless innings in what was his first big-league appearance. Before he was through 19 years later, he would win 268 games and earn a place in the Hall of Fame in Cooperstown.

The Orioles had me room with Palmer that year. He was a bonus baby that they had to keep on the major league roster, and he didn't pitch much. Jim was a nice young man and I was literally twice his age. One night we were in our room in L.A. about 11:30 trying to go to sleep and Jim asked me, "Old man, why don't you tell me about pitching?"

I said, "Throw the hell out of the ball and go to sleep."

Jim likes to tell that story today. He later told me that was some of the best advice he ever received.

After that game in Boston I was pretty down, however. I had not been pitching much, and after that performance it didn't look like I would be pitching any more. I did not want to just take up a spot on the roster. If I wasn't going to be able to contribute, I didn't want to be there. The next morning we flew back to Baltimore to start a home series against the Red Sox. Milt Pappas' arm was still bothering him, so I started for him again in Baltimore. I pitched a complete game and won 4–2 over a young pitcher named Jim Lonborg. Not only that, I got a base hit with the bases loaded to drive in the tying and winning runs.

Five days later I started against Pete Richert and the Washington Senators and beat them 6–3, throwing another complete game. I was now a starting pitcher again, and four days later I shut out the Yankees 5–0 in Yankee Stadium. Mickey Mantle was the second batter in the bottom of the ninth inning. When Mick walked to the plate, I noticed that he said something to my catcher, John Orsino. He then popped up sky high to Brooksie at third, and I got the next hitter out to end the game. John came out to congratulate me and said, "Did you notice Mantle talking to me when he came to hit?"

I said, "Yeah, what was that about?"

John said, "Mickey told me, 'Tell Robin he's pitched a helluva ballgame.'"

That was the type of thing that I most enjoyed about competing. I wasn't someone who jumped around or was demonstrative, but I enjoyed the competition and appreciated others who competed in the same way. I guess I was a sportsman, and it made me feel good about my chosen profession when someone like Mickey Mantle recognized me in that way. So Mickey taking the time to tell Orsino that I'd pitched a good game was really satisfying to me.

We next traveled to Minnesota, and I pitched on three days' rest against the Twins who were on their way to the American League pennant. I beat Jim Kaat 5–1 for my fourth consecutive complete-game win, allowing only a home run to Harmon Killebrew.

We returned home to Baltimore to play the Detroit Tigers. Before my start on May 10, I threw in front of the dugout to Sherm Lollar, the bullpen coach who warmed me up before every start. Sherm had caught for 18 years in the big leagues, was a few years older than I, and was someone I respected, related to, and enjoyed being around.

Sometimes my arm would act up and I'd have a little catch or stiffness in my shoulder and would have trouble getting loose. Occasionally, I would have to pitch two or three innings before I could work that catch out and really feel good. I was having difficulty getting loose before my start against the Tigers that day, and after about 10 minutes Sherm came up and said, "Let me tell Hank [Bauer] to warm somebody else up. You're not throwing like you have been."

I said, "Aw, I'll be all right, Sherm. I'll work it out."

Sherm said, "You dumb SOB. This is really stupid."

So I went out to pitch the ballgame, and I guess in the first inning at least it was stupid because Al Kaline hit a three-run homer. But then I finally got loose and started popping the ball and only gave up two more runs the rest of the game. Still I lost 5–4 to Mickey Lolich.

I've often thought maybe I should have listened to Sherm. But I just couldn't say about five minutes before the game that I couldn't pitch. That was just not me. If they gave me the ball, I went out and pitched until somebody came and got me. There was only one time that I actually asked to come out of a game, and that also occurred with the Orioles. I started a game in Minnesota against the Twins on a bright sunny day with the temperature in the 70s. I was pitching a good game, but in the seventh inning a norther blew in and the temperature dropped about 40 degrees in just a few minutes. I went out to warm up for the bottom of the seventh and was so cold that I could not throw at all. I actually called Harry Brecheen, the pitching coach, out and said, "Harry, this is the first time I've ever had to do this in my life, but I can't throw." So they brought a relief pitcher in to finish the game.

With that one exception, if anybody came to the mound and asked me if I was all right, I always said yes. If they told me to be honest, I still told them I was fine, because I always thought I was, except for that one time in Minnesota.

The game in 1965 against the Tigers started a bad stretch where I often had trouble getting loose and lost six in a row, although one was a 1–0 game to Cleveland's Jack Kralick in which I allowed six hits. I had another good outing on June 17 against the Yankees' Jim Bouton, pitching into the ninth inning before leaving with the game tied 1–1. We eventually won 2–1 in 16 innings. But after a mediocre start against the Red Sox on June 22 I was in the bullpen and not pitching much at all.

Back when I signed with the team, I had told general manager Lee MacPhail that if there was ever a time that they didn't want me to be a regular starting pitcher, they should just tell me and I'd go on home and be with my family. Maybe it was a little selfish, but I had always been a regular starting pitcher, and if I wasn't going to pitch I did not want to just take up a place on the bench. I did not enjoy going to the ballpark to watch my team's games if I wasn't going to contribute. In any event, Lee agreed to release me if that ever happened.

So just before the All-Star Game, I said to Harry Brecheen, our pitching coach, "Would you ask Hank if he's going to use me any more after the All-Star break?" I didn't tell Harry, but if Hank was not going to use me, I planned to call Lee MacPhail and get my release and go on home. I knew Lee would honor our agreement.

After the All-Star break, Harry said, "Naw, you're in the same spot." This is probably where I should have just gone and talked to the manager directly, but I didn't. It just wasn't my way to make waves. As a result, I never had a conversation with Hank about pitching at all.

I then called Lee MacPhail and reminded him of our understanding. Lee said, "Well, let's talk about it. Come in and see me tomorrow on the way to the ballpark."

When I went by his office the next day, he had my release prepared. Lee told me, "I did promise you this. I thought it over and this is probably for the best."

I did say, "Lee, you might try one thing. Maybe you could call John Quinn [the general manager of the Phillies] because Lew Burdette is sitting around with the Phillies like I am here. As long as I'm at home, I could sit around in the Phillies' bullpen if Lew could come over here."

I think Lee actually called Quinn, but apparently John didn't like my idea, because I was released by the Orioles. I went home to Philadelphia and wasn't there three days when I got a call from Paul Richards, the general manager of the Houston Astros.

Paul said, "How are you feeling?"

I said, "Paul, I was pitching all right and then I had a bad streak when I wasn't pitching well. I still feel fine. The Orioles just decided to go with younger people."

He said, "How would you like to come pitch for me?"

I said, "I would enjoy that. I think I can still pitch."

"What would it take?"

I said, "Well, I was making $33,500. I'll come if you pay me on that basis the rest of the year and give me a $10,000 bonus if you want me back next year."

Paul said, "That's fair enough. Join us in Milwaukee."

So I did join the Astros in Milwaukee in early August but did not pitch against the Braves. We returned to Houston, and on August 9 I started my first game for the Astros against, of all teams, the Philadelphia Phillies. The crowd was more than thirty thousand in the Astrodome and, ironically, Lew Burdette started for the Phillies. It was also the first game ever played on AstroTurf.

The Astrodome had opened at the beginning of the year, replacing the temporary Colts Stadium. In fact, I was with the Orioles when they played the first day game in the Astrodome in the preseason. The field was grass and the roof was clear, to allow the grass to grow. During the game Boog Powell, playing left field, lost a fly ball in the glare of the roof. That was first time the Astros organization knew they had a problem. They then painted the roof light blue to try to reduce the glare. It did, but the grass would not grow under the blue roof. Apparently the grass got sicker and sicker as the year wore on. The team decided it had to do something and installed artificial turf, called Astro-Turf, in the infield while the Astros were on the road trip during which I joined the team. I pitched the first game after that road trip, and the infield was Astro-Turf while the outfield was still the sick grass.

When the game started my new teammates jumped all over Burdette for four runs in the first inning and I had my good rhythm all day. I breezed to an 8–0 victory, scattering four hits in a complete-game shutout. I even hit a double and scored a run. It was a big game for me, my first game for the Astros and pitching against the Phillies.

After the game, Paul Richards asked me what I thought about the Astro-Turf. One ball had been hit back at me that sort of skipped, so I suggested that he might consider cutting a dirt strip from the plate back to the mound like ballparks had in the old days. That would have created a couple of edges between the turf and the dirt, so that may have just caused another problem.

A week later I started against the Pirates and old rival Bob Friend in the Astrodome and threw another four-hit shutout, winning 3–0. Five days later I started against the Cubs in Wrigley Field and, with great support, won again, 9–2 over Dick Ellsworth. In fact, I extended my scoreless streak to 24 innings before the Cubs touched me for two runs in the seventh inning. Five days later

I was in Connie Mack Stadium starting my first game in Philadelphia as an opposing pitcher. I was matched against then Phillies ace Jim Bunning, but neither one of us was particularly sharp. I left in the seventh with the score 4 to 4, and my new teammates, led by a home run from Eddie Kasko, scored two more in the eighth to win 6–4, although I got a no-decision.

John Bateman was one of the catchers with the Astros that year. He was a youngster but in his third season with Houston. Before the first time he caught me, he asked me what signs I wanted and what I threw. I said, "Well, one is a fastball, and if I just go into my motion it means I'm throwing a low fastball. If I shake it off, I want to throw either a high fastball or a curve. Then put down one again or two and we'll go from there."

John said, "OK. What else?"

I said, "That's else. That's my act."

I know that I was easy to catch because I threw only two pitches and had good control, pitching to the corners. After the game, I was sitting by my locker when Bateman came over and said, "Robin, will you do me a favor? Call all the young pitchers over here and let's show them how you did it."

I said, "Johnny, I'm not the pitching coach."

John said, "No, really. Do it for my benefit. These guys have all got four pitches. They don't need four pitches."

John was correct. Those young guys with live arms, like Larry Dierker, didn't need four pitches, but it wasn't my place to tell them.

Our road trip concluded against the Mets in Shea Stadium, and I started on August 31, the only time I ever pitched there. Frank Thomas hit a three-run homer in the first against Mets starter Larry Miller, but the Mets scored two in the bottom half and the lead was quickly down to 3–2. Thomas homered again in the third to extend the lead to 4–2, and I settled down and held the Mets scoreless until the bottom of the ninth when they added a third run. Luman Harris brought Jim Owens, my old Phillies teammate, in for the final two outs, and I had my fourth win in five starts for the Astros, who had been victorious in all five of my outings.

In the sixth inning of that game, I broke off a sharp curve to Charlie Smith, another former Phillie. I generally didn't have that sharp a curveball, and I guess that one was too good, because I felt something pop in my elbow. I kept pitching, but I could tell something was wrong with my arm. I could still throw my fastball all right, but my curve left something to be desired.

My next start was back in Houston against the Los Angeles Dodgers and Sandy Koufax. Sandy was in the process of leading the Dodgers to the pennant and World Championship and would finish the year with a 26–8 won-loss record and a minuscule 2.04 earned run average. The game drew a crowd of almost fifty thousand, the largest until then in the Astrodome. Maybe a few of them were there to see Koufax.

Dick Farrell was supposed to start for us, but as we got off the plane the night before coming in from New York, Lum Harris asked me if I could pitch the opener against the Dodgers. I said, "Sure, but I thought Dick was supposed to pitch." I didn't even know who was pitching for the Dodgers at that time. Lum indicated that Dick's arm was bothering him, so I said I'd be happy to start.

That evening I went to dinner with Eddie Kasko, a veteran infielder with the Astros. Eddie was about five years younger than I was, but he had been around the baseball block and we tended to hang out together. We were enjoying a couple of beers before the food came, talking about various things. By then I knew that Sandy Koufax was starting for the Dodgers. All of a sudden, Eddie said, "You can't wait for tomorrow night, can you?"

I said, "Yeah, Eddie, I like to pitch in those kinds of games. I don't know whether I'll win or not, but I generally pitch well in big games." Maybe I'd had more than two beers, but I also said, "I'll probably get a couple of hits off Sandy."

It turned out I was psychic. Koufax retired the first eight Astros hitters, so I came up with two out in the third inning. I'm not sure what Sandy threw me, but I hit a line shot to left field for our first base hit of the game. The Dodgers had scored a run off me in the top of the third, and it remained 1–0 until the bottom of the seventh inning. With one out, Ron Brand, our catcher, singled and was sacrificed to second by Lee Maye. Then Bobby Lillis, our shortstop, singled to right-center field to drive in Ron and tie the score, taking second on the throw to the plate. That brought me up with two out. I was batting right-handed, and Sandy started pumping fastballs at me, so there was no way I was going to hit anything to left field this time. But I hit one right over the first-base bag into right field to drive in Lillis with the go-ahead run, although Ron Fairly in right threw me out at second as I tried to stretch the single into a double.

Well, I had my two hits off Koufax and the lead, 2–1. I retired the Dodgers in order in the eighth inning and went out to pitch the ninth, still holding on to that slim advantage. Maury Wills was first, and I got two strikes on him. Then he poked a little dunker over third for a single. Wes Parker was next, and he bunted down the first-base line near home plate. Ronnie Brand thought it was going to go foul and was letting it go, but I could tell that it wasn't, so in desperation I picked it up and flipped it to first. I hit Parker on the shoulder, so when the dust settled the Dodgers had runners on second and third and no outs. I got the next batter, Willie Davis, to pop up to the infield, so then I had one out. Then Ron Fairly popped up as well, so I had two outs and still had the lead.

At this point, Lum Harris decided we needed to have a meeting on the mound to discuss how to pitch to the next Dodgers hitter, Lou Johnson. I didn't really care to have discussions on the mound when I was pitching because they interrupted my concentration and never really added anything useful. So we had this big meeting, and I was kind of standing on the back of the mound thinking about how I was going to pitch to Lou Johnson. Then Lum told me, "Don't let Maury steal home."

I had a fairly quick windup and delivery, and no one had ever stolen home on me in 17 years, so I thought that was a really odd statement. In the meantime, Walter Alston had sent up Junior Gilliam to pinch hit for Lou Johnson. Junior hit a rope on my first pitch over Rusty Staub's head in right field for a double to drive in both runs. Jim Lefebvre followed with a single to score Junior, and we lost the game 4–2, after being one out from a victory.

Of course, that ballgame made me remember the first time I ever saw Koufax. The Phillies were playing the Dodgers in Ebbets Field in 1955, and I noticed that the young left-hander who was pitching batting practice was so wild he was having trouble hitting the batting cage. Carl Furillo, the veteran Dodgers outfielder, happened to be over by our dugout, and I asked, "Carl, who is that kid?"

Carl, speaking in the vernacular of the day, said, "Aw, some Jew kid. He'll never be a pitcher as long as he has a hole in his ass."

Several years later after Sandy became a big winner I saw Furillo and said, "Carl, I noticed that the Dodgers haven't hired you as a scout yet. I guess that's because of your assessment of Koufax as a pitcher."

Carl laughed and said, "I couldn't believe how that kid developed."

After the game against Koufax, my arm never felt right for the rest of the year. I had four more starts and pitched pretty well in all of them, losing to the Dodgers and Don Drysdale in L.A. 5–2 behind some shaky defense and defeating the Cardinals and Ray Sadecki 4–2 in the Astrodome on the last day of the season. I finished with a 5–2 record and an ERA well under 2.00 for the ninth-place Astros.

I wasn't that big a fan of AstroTurf, but I loved pitching in the Astrodome. The fences were pretty far back and the place was air-conditioned, so it was a pleasure to pitch there. I thought I could pitch in the Dome until I was 50.

Even though the Astros finished in ninth place, I couldn't believe my eyes at the young talent on the club. They had guys like Larry Dierker who was just 18 years old, 21-year-old Rusty Staub, outfielder Jimmy Wynn, and second baseman Joe Morgan, who was in his first full big-league season. I really enjoyed watching those young ballplayers. I had noticed that Joe Morgan was short-arming the ball from second base with the result that some of his throws ended up in the dirt and didn't have much on them. Second basemen often end up short-arming their throws because on the double-play pivot at second they are in a big hurry to get their throw off and get out of the way of the oncoming base runner.

One day I was standing next to Joe while he was fielding ground balls during batting practice and I said, "Joe, you're too good a hitter to be taken out for defense. You need to follow through when you throw to first. You're short-arming the ball."

Years later when Joe was inducted into the Hall of Fame, he told that story. He said, "You know, Robbie was right. I wasn't following through. But I never had any trouble after Robbie pointed it out to me."

Anyone could see that Joe was a great talent. Even though I was out of baseball, I couldn't believe it when the Astros traded Joe to the Cincinnati Reds after the 1971 season. It was probably the best trade the Reds ever made.

The Astros also had a young 19-year-old slugger named Nate Colbert whom they had drafted from the Cardinals organization. In batting practice, Nate would hit balls to the far reaches of the Astrodome, but the club never played him. He just sat on the bench during games. One day I was sitting on the bench next to him after he had rifled shots all over in batting practice and I said, "Nate, why don't they play you?"

He said, "I don't know, man. I wish I knew."

Nate later was selected by the San Diego Padres in their expansion draft and went on to have a good career there. In fact, in 1972 he hit five home runs and drove in 13 runs in a doubleheader against the Atlanta Braves.

* * *

After the season, Paul Richards came to see me and said, "We'd like to have you back next year."

"Fine," I said.

"That means I owe you a $10,000 bonus."

I said, "Yessir, that's right."

He said, "Well, we'll give it to you if you get your arm operated on."

I was 39 years old and in those days, before arthroscopic surgery, arm operations were pretty major procedures without the success they have now. I wasn't at all excited about having my arm operated on, so I said, "I'm not sure I want to do that. Let me go home and think it over."

So I went home to Philadelphia and quarterbacked the neighborhood touch football games like always. My elbow started swelling up, and that convinced me that I had some chips in there that had to come out. So I went to Houston to have the surgery. I had three bone chips, and after the operation, Dr. King, the surgeon, came in and told me, "I got two chips out without any problem but I couldn't get the other one." Unfortunately, as it turned out, I think that was the chip that was causing the problem.

Paul Richards came to see me in the hospital after the surgery and brought me a $10,000 check, so I was set to pitch for the Astros in 1966. My arm never did come all the way back, however. My elbow remained stiff, although I did not have any pain.

We opened the '66 season on April 12 against the Dodgers in Dodger Stadium. Dick Farrell was slated to start for us against Claude Osteen, who was pitching the Dodgers opener because that was the spring that Sandy Koufax and Don Drysdale staged their joint holdout. I wasn't sure what my role with the team was going to be but just assumed that when Grady Hatton, who was the new Astros manager, told me to pitch, I would pitch. In any event, I was sitting in front of my locker before the game when Grady came up to me and asked, "Can you pitch?"

I said, "I thought Dick was pitching."

"Naw, he's got a sore arm."

So I said, "Yeah, I can pitch, Grady."

That was the way my 13th Opening Day start came about, by default. I pitched pretty well, giving up two runs, one of which was earned, in seven innings before being taken out for a pinch-hitter behind 2–1. Osteen pitched a little better, and we ended up losing 3–2.

After the game I went out for a late dinner with Bob Silvers, my friend from the army who had moved from Chicago to L.A. We visited into the wee hours and I got back to the hotel about 3:00 A.M. The next afternoon I was by my locker when Grady Hatton asked to see me in his office. He said, "I've got to fine you."

I said, "What do you mean, Grady?"

"Well, you missed curfew." I didn't even know when curfew was because normally I was in early and did not stay out late.

I said, "Grady, I pitched Opening Day when I didn't know I was going to pitch. I lost a tough ballgame and went out afterward with an old friend and talked until 3:00 A.M. I wasn't going to sleep anyway, and you aren't going to use me today. And you're going to fine me?"

Grady said, "That is kind of silly, isn't it?" That was the end of it; I didn't get fined.

My next start on April 18 was also against the Dodgers. The opposing pitcher was a rookie just two weeks past his 21st birthday making his big-league debut. His name was Don Sutton. Unfortunately for me, I helped get Don's big-league career off to a good start. I was knocked out in the fifth of a 6–3 loss. Sutton pitched eight innings to get his first major league win. Over the next 22 years he would win 323 more games. He would be elected to the Hall of Fame in 1998.

I pitched well in my next start, on April 23 against the San Francisco Giants, but Gaylord Perry pitched better and I lost my third start in a row, 2–1. I followed with two more good outings, defeating Nelson Briles and the Cardinals 4–2 and on May 4 shutting out the Cubs in the Astrodome 4–0 on a seven-hitter. After a rough outing against the Mets, I beat the Cubs again 4–2, this time in Wrigley Field. It would be my last win as an Astro. I got knocked around in my next couple of starts, although I pitched a quality game against Don Drysdale and the Dodgers, leaving after seven innings with the score tied 2–2. But my elbow just never felt right, and as a result, I didn't have the good wrist action that put movement on my fastball. My rough outings were beginning to outnumber my good ones.

CHAPTER 13

Can We Go Home Now?

The Astros released me on the Fourth of July, 1966. My arm was not bothering me after the surgery, but it didn't have much flexibility and I had not pitched well the previous couple of weeks. Grady Hatton was the manager that year. He called me in and said, "Robin, we are going to release you."

I'd been released before. I said, "Grady, you can't release me."

He looked at me with a puzzled expression and I said, "It's July Fourth. You can't release a guy on the Fourth of July."

Grady said, "What?"

Then I said, "Just kidding. Just kidding. I understand."

So when I went home to our little rental house in Richmond, a suburb on the west side of Houston, and told Mary I'd been released, she said, "Robin, can we go home now?" Mary was more than ready to get back to Philadelphia where we had spent so many years and had so many friends.

The Atlanta Braves happened to be in town when the Astros released me. Ken Silvestri, one of my old Whiz Kid teammates and a former catcher, was one of their coaches. Hawk was special. For eight years Ken, whom we affectionately called Hawk because of his small nose, warmed me up before every game. And he treated every game like it was Game 7 of the World Series. He had an infectious enthusiasm all the time. Hawk would hold his glove low and on the outside corner, and if you hit it warming up, he would get excited and yell, "That a boy, Robbie! They'll never touch you with that stuff!" He would also pitch batting practice to the pitchers anytime and did the work of about eight guys. Although Hawk hardly played, he had been very important to the success of the Whiz Kids.

So I called Ken up and said, "Hawk, will you do me a favor? Will you come to the ballpark early tomorrow and let me throw to you?"

Hawk said, "Sure, I'll do that."

I said, "Hawk, if I can't throw anymore, tell me to go home."

Hawk said, "Sure Robbie, I'll be honest with you."

So the next day I warmed up with Hawk and got good and loose. Afterward I said to Hawk, "OK, now tell me to go home."

Ken said, "Are you kidding? You throw better than seven of the guys we've got on our staff."

I said, "Hawk, you're not kidding me?"

He said, "No, I'm not. Don't you give up."

The next day we were packing the car and the phone rang. It was John Holland, the general manager of the Chicago Cubs. Freddie Fitzsimmons, the Cubs' pitching coach, had gotten sick and John wanted me to come replace him. I told John, "I'll come if I can still pitch. Put me on the active roster and I'll be your pitching coach."

John said, "All right, you can pitch."

But if Kenny Silvestri had told me to go home, I would have packed it in. I think. Or maybe I would have wanted a second opinion.

So after John Holland called I went to my wife and said, "Mary, we've got to go to Chicago. The Cubs want me to come pitch and be their pitching coach." Poor Mary just rolled her eyes, so we finished packing the station wagon.

Mary and I and our four boys headed to Chicago instead of Philadelphia. We stopped the first night at a Holiday Inn in East St. Louis, Illinois. Our station wagon was packed to the gills and we were so tired that we didn't unpack it. When my son Robbie went out to the car the next morning he discovered that someone had broken into it and taken all of our belongings. The only thing they left was my bag with my glove and baseball spikes. I guess the thief wasn't a ball fan. Or maybe he was.

So we went to Chicago with just the clothes on our backs, checked into the Edgewater Beach Hotel, and I reported to the Cubs.

The 1966 Chicago Cubs were managed by 61-year-old Leo Durocher and were headed for the cellar. We had some real talent on the pitching staff with Ken Holtzman and Bill Hands, both of whom would become 20-game winners later in their careers. Dick Ellsworth had won 20 but was struggling. Cal Koonce and Bob Hendley were solid; in addition, my old buddy Curt Simmons was on the staff, working out of the bullpen and as a spot starter.

Overall, we had the nucleus of a fine ballclub with Billy Williams in the outfield and an infield of Ernie Banks, Glenn Beckert, Don Kessinger, Ron Santo, and Randy Hundley. They would rise to third place in 1967 and 1968 and lead the way for most of 1969 before a late-season collapse paved the way for the Miracle Mets to win the division.

I joined the club during the All-Star break. The White Sox and Cubs used to play an exhibition game the day after the All-Star break, and so that was my first day on the job. I was out in the bullpen in Comiskey Park watching our game with the White Sox when a big, lanky kid with the Cubs asked if he could throw for me. I said sure because I'd never seen him pitch before. He threw about 10 or 15 pitches and I told him, "You've got to be kidding."

He said, "What do you mean, Coach?"

I said, "I didn't know you threw like this." He had super wrist action and his ball really moved.

"Aw, but I'm not fast enough," the kid said.

I said, "Don't worry, you're plenty fast enough. I used to have that kind of stuff."

The kid was Ferguson Jenkins. Leo was using him mainly in relief that year, but Fergie was just not yet confident about his stuff. He was getting hit around sometimes trying to throw too many breaking pitches. I kept encouraging him.

That Cubs team had three future Hall of Famers on it: Fergie, Billy Williams, and Ernie Banks, not to mention Ron Santo, who may get in one day. It also had a fine young catcher named Randy Hundley.

After the break we traveled to Pittsburgh to play the Pirates in Forbes Field. Leo started me on Sunday, and they had a tough lineup, with Roberto Clemente, Willie Stargell, Donn Clendenon, and Matty Alou, who was on his way to a batting championship. With two outs in the bottom of the ninth I led the Pirates 5 to 4. Pittsburgh manager Harry Walker sent Jerry Lynch up to pinch hit. Lynch was the best pinch-hitter in the league, so Leo came to the mound and Randy Hundley came out, too, from his catcher's position.

"Don't let this SOB beat you," Leo said. That's all he said, and he turned around to walk back to the dugout.

So I said, "Hey, Leo. What do you want me to throw him?"

"Aw, curve that SOB."

So I threw Lynch a curve, and he hit a rope to right field for a base hit. But then I got Manny Mota out to end the game.

As I'm walking off the field, Ron Santo came up to me all excited. He said, "Robin, that's the first time since I've been with the Cubs that we've had a guy pitch a complete-game victory in Forbes Field." I found that hard to believe because Santo had been with the Cubs for seven years, but it must have been true or he would not have made such a big deal about it.

Afterward we flew back to Chicago. I was sitting in the rear of the plane by myself when Hundley walked back and asked if he could sit with me for a spell. I said, "Sure, but I want to tell you something first. You're as good a catcher as I've ever pitched to. You can really catch."

After he thanked me he said, "I really liked what you did when you asked Mr. Durocher what pitch he wanted you to throw to Lynch. You know, he is always getting on me for calling the wrong pitches."

"Randy," I said, "if they call them, it can't be the wrong pitch. That's why I asked Leo, so he couldn't second-guess me. But no matter. Leo thinks you are a fine catcher or else he wouldn't start you every day."

The next day back in Chicago I went up to Leo and said, "You know, Leo, Randy Hundley is a fine catcher, but you've got him scared stiff of you."

Leo said, "That kid, why he doesn't even swear. The strongest thing he says is 'Judas Priest.'"

I said, "But you must know how good he is because you catch him every day."

"Oh, he's a dandy," Leo said.

"Well, he's really uncomfortable with you. From now on, why don't you just tell me when you want to tell him something and I'll tell him for you?"

"All right," Leo said. He never said another word to Hundley the rest of the year, and Randy relaxed and played with much more confidence.

After a while, I noticed that Randy tried to pull everything, which was really silly in Wrigley Field where the power alleys were only about 365 feet. We were playing the Giants in a doubleheader on a beautiful summer day, and I was out in the bullpen early, before even batting practice. Randy came out and said, "Hey, how you doin', Coach?"

"Fine, Randy," I said. "Hey, you know when you pull all those balls foul down the left-field line? That means you can't hit the outside pitch. Why don't you pretend the shortstop is the left-field foul line? That will keep your shoulder in."

Randy hit three home runs that day in the doubleheader. He ended up having a fine big-league career, but it could have been even better. For four years he caught virtually every game for the Cubs. But injuries really caught up to him, and he was never really healthy for the rest of his 14-year career. In his prime, he was outstanding defensively, could throw with the best, and had real pop in his bat. And he said "Judas Priest."

I also soon noticed that Fergie Jenkins, who had all the talent in the world, wasn't working out very hard when the pitchers ran and stretched. We had a veteran outfielder on the team named George Altman who was very well respected, so I asked him to do me a favor. "George," I said, "tell Fergie to shake his ass. He's not doing much running or anything. I don't want to tell him that he's got to do what everybody else does, but he's got to come up with his own routine and work a little bit."

About a week later George came up and said, "I told him, Coach."

Near the end of the year we went into Atlanta to play the Braves. We started Fergie in that series, his first start in a long time. He beat the Braves 5 to 1, striking out nine and walking only one. He came over to my locker after the game and said, "Hey Coach, I am fast enough."

"And the right guy knows it now," I said.

The next year, Fergie won 20 games, the first of six straight 20-game-win years. Fergie obviously had a lot to do with the Cubs' success in the late sixties and early seventies. He ended up with 284 major league wins and a spot in the Hall of Fame. Because I ended up with 286 wins, I told him years later, "Fergie, it sure was nice of you to win only 284."

My second start for the Cubs came four days after my win over the Pirates, on July 19 against the Cincinnati Reds in Wrigley Field. I went into the ninth leading Jim Maloney 2–1, but Gordy Coleman doubled in the tying run to send the game into extra innings. I pitched through the eleventh when Leo pinch hit Joey Amalfitano for me, and the game eventually went 18 innings before Don Pavletich homered to win for the Reds 3–2.

I had earned a spot in the rotation and went up against Bob Gibson and the St. Louis Cardinals on July 23. I pitched well again and was down 2–0 after eight innings, when Lee Thomas pinch hit for me. But Gibson completed his shutout and we lost 4–0. That was my last good start in the big leagues.

I had some rocky outings after the game against Gibson and earned my way to the bullpen. As the season wound down I was doing more coaching and less pitching. The Cubs were headed for a 10th-place finish and Leo understandably was getting the young staff some experience.

On August 29 we played the Braves in Atlanta. Fergie and Tony Cloninger of the Braves hooked up in a pitching duel that went into extra innings tied 2–2. Leo brought me into the game in the bottom of the thirteenth inning, and I held the Braves without a run. In the top of the fourteenth George Altman came through with a two-run pinch-hit single to drive in Adolfo Phillips and Ron Campbell and put us into the lead 4–2. I got the Braves out again in the bottom of the fourteenth to record the win. It was the 286th and last victory of my big-league career.

It also made me the only pitcher in major league history to have beaten the Boston Braves, the Milwaukee Braves, and the Atlanta Braves. I don't know if there is a prize for that, but I'm the only one, and I guess it is a record that won't be broken.

Leo Durocher was certainly a good manager, but I was not comfortable with his style. I had of course competed against Leo much of my career and pitched for him in the 1955 All-Star Game. Leo liked to be in control of everything and was the consummate second-guesser. He was a competitor and would do anything to win.

While I was Leo's pitching coach, we really clashed one hot, muggy night in Philadelphia. The Cubs were in last place, but Kenny Holtzman was pitching a fine game for us, leading 2–1 in the seventh inning. With two outs he came to bat and hit a ground ball up the middle. Kenny ran hard to first, but Phillies shortstop Bobby Wine made a good play and threw him out. Kenny then leaned over to get his breath and put his hands on his knees for a moment.

All of a sudden, and I don't know why, Leo started ranting and raving at Holtzman from the dugout. "Look at you, look at you. You been smoking too many cigarettes?"

Well, it was a hot, humid night and Kenny had been pitching all evening in a tight ballgame. So after Holtzman came back to the dugout and Leo kept talking I walked over and said, "Say, Leo, stay off his ass. He's pitching a helluva ballgame."

Leo turned toward me and said, "You getting on me?"

I said, "I think it's ridiculous getting on him like that. That's crazy."

"You can't talk to me like that. Get outa here. You're suspended."

So I went into the clubhouse, and the Phillies' visitors' clubhouse man, Teddy Kessler, who had been there forever, asked, "What's wrong?"

"Ted, you won't believe this. Leo's just suspended me." So I got dressed and headed out to the airport. The Cubs had a charter back to Chicago, and so I got on and sat in the back of the plane and waited for the rest of the team.

It turned out that the Phils tied the ballgame in the eighth inning. My buddy Curt Simmons came in to relieve, and Ernie Banks hit a home run in the top of the tenth. Curt got them out in the bottom half to win the game.

Curt had heard about me, so he came back to sit with me when he got on the plane. "Whaddya done now?" were his first words.

I said, "Aw, don't worry about it, Lefty. It'll be all right." So that's the last we talked about it on the flight back. Leo never came back to see me and never said a word.

My family and I were still staying at the Edgewater Beach Hotel in Chicago. We had an off-day the next day, which was Thursday. I was concerned about how I was going to explain to my boys about how their old man, the pitching coach, had gotten suspended by the manager. That morning I had my son Robbie run to get a paper so I could read about my suspension. There was nothing in it about my row with Leo. That night I bought one of the evening papers—still not a word. Same thing Friday morning. We had a game that afternoon, so I went out to Wrigley Field and asked Yosh Kawano, the clubhouse man, where Leo was. Yosh told me he was in the training room, getting his hair cut.

We had a catcher, Don Bryant, who was also a barber. So there is Leo in the training room with a sheet around him, getting his hair cut. I said, "Hey, what do you want me to do?"

"Meet me in my office."

I went to wait for him, and he finally came in and closed the door. He looked at me and said, "Robin, you can't get on me; I'm the manager."

I said, "Leo, you're a hundred percent right; I was a hundred percent wrong. You're the manager and I shouldn't get on you."

"Aw, forget it. Don't worry about it. Go get your uniform on."

I started to go out the door but stopped and said, "I want to thank you, Leo. I've got four boys and this game has been good to me." Needless to say I was greatly relieved. I wasn't looking forward to my sons' reading about their old man getting suspended.

There were only two or three weeks left in the season, and that was the last conversation we had about it. Just like Leo said, I could forget it. Once it was over, it was done. So Leo was more than fair with me. Of course, with the club in last place, it did not make a lot of sense for Leo to suspend his pitching coach, especially for defending one of his pitchers.

When the season ended I was in the hospital from a bleeding ulcer attack caused by a certain teammate's pizzas, which were delivered to the clubhouse after games. Cubs general manager John Holland called me there and asked me if I would come back just as the pitching coach. I said, "Mr. Wrigley doesn't have enough money to pay me to work for Leo."

"Is he that bad, Robin?" John asked.

"He's a helluva manager," I said, "but I'm just not comfortable around him." I respected Leo, but we just had different personalities. Furthermore, I did not want to just coach. I could stand the travel and being away from my family if I was pitching but not to coach.

And I thought I could still pitch. It is what I did for a living. I pitched. I didn't have any other interests. Everybody thought I was going for 300 wins. I thought I was going for 350. I wasn't going to stop at 300.

I suppose I was remembering that streak with Baltimore in 1965 when I threw four straight complete-game victories or the stretch with the Astros that year when I won four straight complete games. For the year I had eight complete games in 25 starts and a 2.78 earned run average. Those were good numbers for anyone, especially a 39-year-old.

In 1966, after my arm operation, I struggled and my arm felt stiff all year. But Ken Silvestri told me I was still throwing well, and when I got home after the season and started playing touch football with the kids, my arm felt really good, better than it had all season. Then I knew I really didn't want to quit.

The Phillies had a farm club in Reading, Pennsylvania, in the Double A Eastern League. Reading was only a little more than an hour commute from my house in Philadelphia. So I called Phillies owner Bob Carpenter and told him I would like to pitch at Reading the next year until June 15. If nobody picked me up by that date, I would go home and retire.

Bob agreed, so I went to spring training in 1967 with the Reading Phillies. They were managed by Frank Lucchesi who later managed in the big leagues for the Phillies and the Texas Rangers. Dallas Green was the pitching coach, and of course he was the Phillies manager in 1980 when they finally won the World Series.

When the season started my first game was against Williamsport. It was cold as hell and I lost 1–0. We later traveled to Pawtucket to play the Red Sox farm team there. I went out to the mound in the first inning and there was a big hole in front of the pitching rubber. It looked like it had been there a while. I pitched in front of the rubber, so I told the umpire, "I can't pitch with that hole there. Get the ground crew to fill it in."

The ground crew came out with one of their spreaders and put a little dirt in the hole, but it wasn't going to do any good unless it was packed down. So I got their tamper and sprinkling can and got down on my hands and knees to pack the dirt into the hole. Then I got up and pitched and won the ballgame 5 to 3. I suspect that the young kid pitchers were just pitching with that hole because they thought that was the way it was supposed to be. But I knew I couldn't pitch with a big hole in front of the rubber.

My final game was June 15 against Williamsport in Reading. I pitched eight innings, and we won the ballgame 5–3. For the year I had won five, lost three, and pitched two shutouts. I had 65 strikeouts and only five walks and a 2.25 earned run average. Afterward I showered quickly and went in to Frank Lucchesi and said, "Thanks, Frank, for the opportunity."

Frank started to tell me to stay, but I said, "No, I said I'd go home June 15 and I am."

I got in the car to drive home to Philadelphia. After the way I had pitched, I could not believe that no one wanted me to pitch for them. During the drive I started to think about Cy Perkins, who had died in 1963. I remembered that when the Yankees released me in 1962 he had told me that I would pitch a shutout when I was 40. I thought, "Cy, you old son of a gun, you didn't tell me it would be in York."

He had also told me early in my career that I was the next 300-game winner. It occurred to me driving home that Cy was right about that one, too. I had won exactly 300 games: 9 at Wilmington, 286 in the majors, and 5 at Reading. But somehow, I don't think that is what Cy had in mind.

CHAPTER 14

The Players' Association

There is probably nothing more boring to a true baseball fan than to read about baseball's labor problems, which have plagued the sport since the 19ᵗʰ century. Baseball fans love the game because of what happens on the field and in spite of what goes on off the field. But I played such a large role in the development of the Players' Association that I will tell the story of its origins.

My first exposure to labor problems in baseball occurred just before the Opening Game of the 1950 World Series. My teammates and I were very excited to be in the World Series. Just before we were to leave the clubhouse in Shibe Park to take infield, Granny Hamner, our shortstop and representative to the Players' Association, came in and said, "Nobody take the field until we settle something with the commissioner and the presidents."

We were not sure what was going on, but we stayed put. It turned out that Gillette had, for the first time in baseball history, paid Major League Baseball $1 million for the right to sponsor the World Series. Ham and Tommy Henrich, the Yankees' representative, had been meeting with Commissioner Happy Chandler and league presidents Ford Frick and Will Harridge about where that money should go.

The players' pension was new and on shaky ground financially. Happy Chandler agreed that the $1 million should go directly to the pension fund, and Ham came back into the clubhouse and told us, "It's all right. We've settled it."

That was my only brush with player/management relations until 1952 when Granny stepped down as the Phillies' player representative and my teammates asked me to succeed him. My manager, Eddie Sawyer, suggested that it would not be a good idea for me to accept. Because I was such a prominent member of the Phillies, Eddie wanted me worrying just about pitching. But because my teammates had voted for me, I thought I should represent them.

The first meeting I attended as the Phillies' player representative was at the Broadmoor Hotel in Colorado Springs. The discussion among the veteran players in attendance like Walker Cooper, Terry Moore, and Ralph Kiner focused on solidifying the pension fund. As a result of that meeting, my main interest as a player representative was increased funding of that plan.

The first real controversy that I was involved with came after the new television contract for the World Series and All-Star Game was negotiated in 1953. The rights fees went up to $3 million, and naturally the players expected that most of that money was going into their pension plan. The owners, on the other hand, wanted to stay at the $1 million level.

Ralph Kiner of the Pirates and Allie Reynolds of the Yankees were the player representatives for each league. They had arranged for the team player reps to meet in Atlanta with Ford Frick, who had become commissioner when the owners failed to renew Happy Chandler's contract at the end of 1950. Allie Reynolds had asked J. Norman Lewis, a New York lawyer, to help us in the negotiations. However, Ford Frick told us that he would not meet with us with a lawyer in the room.

As a result, the player representatives had a discussion about whether we should accept Frick's condition. I argued that we should because I assumed Frick would be representing the best interests of baseball and not just the owners. I said, "Let's keep our lawyer outside of the room, and if we need his advice on something, we'll just halt the meeting and go talk to him."

The other player reps thought that was a bad idea and voted against meeting with the commissioner. The vote was almost unanimous, except for me and one or two others. So we did not meet with the commissioner; instead we all flew home without resolving the issue.

In retrospect, that should have been my first hint that the commissioner was not neutral. But at the time, I thought the commissioner had a unique role to look out for the best interests of baseball, and I did not want to do anything that would take away from that. I refused to view the commissioner as just a mouthpiece for the owners, but I now believe that it was a big mistake for Ford Frick to refuse to meet with us with our lawyer in the room.

In fact, although I was not aware of it at the time, one of the reasons that the owners chose to not renew Happy Chandler's contract at the end of 1950 was because they thought he was too sensitive to the players' concerns. Awarding the television money to the players' pension fund may have been the last straw.

After the events in Atlanta, Allie Reynolds and Ralph Kiner used J. Norman Lewis to work with John Galbreath and Hank Greenberg, who represented the owners, to work out a compromise agreement. They agreed that 60 percent, or $1.8 million, of the new television revenues would go to the players' pension fund. This represented an increase from the previous $1 million, but the owners now received 40 percent of the World Series and All-Star Game television revenue.

By now it was clear that whenever a new television contract was negotiated there would be controversy about how much of it went into the pension fund. At least a new television contract would not be negotiated for a number of years.

After the 1954 season, Ralph Kiner was traded to the Cleveland Indians in the American League, and the player representatives elected me to succeed him as the National League rep. Although the television negotiation was down the road, the player representatives still had meetings with the owners to request such things as improvements in clubhouses and dugouts.

The owners were responsive to these kinds of requests. For example, I learned that the visitors' clubhouse in Connie Mack Stadium was really inadequate. I had never been in it, but the player reps from other teams complained about it. They were particularly unhappy that visiting players had to walk through the crowd to get to the playing field.

I told Phillies owner Bob Carpenter about the complaints, and he invited me to take a look with him. The clubhouse was very small and was a mess, and the players did not have any way to get to the field without walking through our fans. Bob told me, "All right. I'll work on it."

A few months later he called me and said, "Come on out and look what we've done." I rarely went to the ballpark in the off-season, but I went this time and met him there. He had widened the clubhouse by 10 or 12 feet and had a tunnel dug from the clubhouse to the dugout so that the visiting players could avoid walking through the fans.

Afterward we went for lunch and Bob told me, "You know, that really worked out for both of us. We've created more box seats that we can sell because of the way we reconfigured the space outside the visitors' clubhouse." I thought how nice it was that the clubhouse remodeling had benefited both parties.

The more time I served as National League players' representative, the more I ran into issues that I had no real training to handle. For example, we attempted to negotiate a six-year free-agency rule. In our proposal, a player could sign with whomever he wanted after six years in the big leagues. Upon signing another contract, he would be bound for another six years. We also proposed that the players have representatives on the committee that chose commissioners. The commissioner and the owners did not seriously consider these requests and tabled them both.

217

I knew that the television money would continue to escalate and that we also had licensing issues to deal with. So I began to believe that the Players' Association needed a full-time, permanent director to handle the pension and licensing negotiations. At that time, only active players could serve, causing a lack of continuity.

After the 1959 season I went to a Players' Association meeting in St. Louis, intending to resign as the National League representative. I wasn't pitching very well, and I thought my role with the players was detracting from my performance on the mound. I believed certain things should be accomplished but was frustrated that I did not know how to get them done. So I told the group that I was resigning but urged them to hire a full-time executive director to work with and represent us. I figured it would cost each player about $125 a year to do so.

The group indicated that they would look into it, but nothing happened. At that juncture, I really got out of the Players' Association business. I was no longer even the team representative. I did follow what the association was doing but no longer had an active role. Of course, I was a member as a player. The Players' Association did appoint Judge Robert C. Cannon of Milwaukee as their legal counsel during this period.

Then, in the fall of 1964, I suddenly realized that a new World Series television contract was about to be negotiated and that it would involve more money. I felt strongly, especially because I had been involved in the haggling over the distribution of the television money in 1953, that the Players' Association needed someone to negotiate with the owners. In addition, the players' pension fund had never received anything from the nationally broadcasted *Game of the Week*, and I wondered if the owners were bidding down the World Series and bidding up the *Game of the Week* contract because they did not have to share that with us.

The Players' Association was having its regular meeting in Houston that winter, so I called Bob Friend, who was the National League player rep, and asked if I could speak at the meeting. He said sure, so I flew to Houston. I was able to convince the reps that we really did need to hire a full-time executive director.

Of course, I had no conception or idea about free agency, attacking the reserve clause, or setting the stage for work stoppages and strikes. None of that ever entered my mind. I could just see that the organization needed a full-time director to negotiate with the owners for our pension fund and to negotiate licensing rights.

As a result, I was appointed to a search committee along with Jim Bunning and Harvey Kuenn to come up with candidates. It soon became apparent that

Judge Cannon, the association's legal adviser, had a lot of support among the players to become executive director. Judge Cannon was a great baseball fan who reputedly really wanted to be commissioner.

The owners and the players had been very comfortable with Cannon in his role as legal adviser. I simply did not believe, however, that he was the right man to become executive director of the association. I also talked to Chub Feeney, president of the Giants. I thought Chub would have been an excellent choice, but he wasn't much interested in the job. I also contacted Senator Charles Percy of Illinois, but he had no interest.

As the search proceeded, the leading candidates were Judge Cannon; Bob Feller, the pitching great who had retired from baseball in 1956; John Gabel, the actuary for our pension fund; and J. William Hayes, a Washington lawyer. None of these men really excited me, however, to fill the position I envisioned.

As it happened, I thought of George William Taylor, a professor at the Wharton School of Business in Philadelphia. I had never met Professor Taylor but had read about him in the newspaper from time to time. He was frequently called to mediate in labor disputes, so I thought he might be a good source for candidates. I was just sitting at home one day when I decided to call him to see if he could recommend someone.

I picked up the phone and called. He said he followed baseball and knew who I was. I told him what I wanted, and he said that he was going to a convention and would talk to some people and call me the next week when he returned. He did call and said he had a couple of people in mind and would call me again in a couple of days after he had visited with them.

When Dr. Taylor next called he said that Lane Kirkland, who became head of the AFL-CIO where he served for years, was not interested. Marvin Miller, however, was interested in the job. Dr. Taylor had known Miller since serving with him on the War Labor Board in the 1940s. At this juncture Miller had been a ranking official with the United Steelworkers of America Union for more than a decade. Marvin called me shortly thereafter, and we discussed the job.

Then in December 1965, the search committee—Jim Bunning, Harvey Kuenn, and I—met with Miller in Cleveland. I am not sure whether Bunning and Kuenn thought meeting with Miller was a good idea or not, but they went along without complaint.

I was impressed with Marvin and thought he was just who the Players' Association needed to deal with the owners. During our meeting in Cleveland I told Marvin that I would back him 100 percent as long as I had his assurance that he would never lead the association out on strike.

Miller told us that he had no intention of ever leading a strike on baseball. I also told Marvin that I could envision a time in which the pension fund would receive $15 million a year. At that time, it received around $5 million a year. After that meeting, we put Miller on the list of candidates to be voted upon by the player representatives.

The committee next sent out the list of candidates with their qualifications to the commissioner, who was then retired air force general William D. "Spike" Eckert. We asked him to check the list and to strike anyone he thought was not an appropriate candidate. Having heard nothing from the commissioner, we then sent the list of candidates to the player representatives.

One day in the middle of all this Mary announced to me, "You know, you're cutting your own throat." She thought that I was so involved in getting an executive director for the Players' Association that it would come back to haunt me, and maybe it has. At the time, I thought that I was working through the commissioner's office and assumed that he was in charge of the game and could call a halt to anything not in the best interests of baseball.

In any event, we set up a meeting in New York to formally vote to establish the office of executive director and then to vote to nominate a candidate. The players would then vote to ratify our nomination after the nominated candidate made a tour of spring training sites to meet the players. The list we distributed included Judge Cannon, Bob Feller, John Gabel, J. William Hayes, and Marvin Miller.

In January 1966 we did meet in New York and agreed to create the office to be based in New York City for a minimum of five years with a $50,000 annual salary. Next on the agenda was to vote to recommend to the players who should become the association's first executive director. There were 20 votes cast because at that time there were 20 teams in the major leagues. Judge Cannon received 13 votes, Marvin Miller received 6, and there was 1 vote for one of the other candidates.

I was very uncomfortable with Judge Cannon but thought that the process had been fair and if he was the choice, I would just have to live with it. So I recommended that we have another vote to make it unanimous, and we did.

Bob Friend seemed pleased after the meeting because he favored Judge Cannon. I had supported Marvin Miller and so Bob said to me, "Well, we won."

I said, "That's fine, Bob. But the day you realize that he won't take the job the way we set it up, you let me know and we'll have another election."

It is odd that I would say that, but I was positive that Judge Cannon was not going to move to New York. I wished I had asked the Judge beforehand, but I had assumed others, who supported him, had talked to him.

The meeting in New York took place on a Saturday, and afterward I went home to Philadelphia. Bob Friend and Judge Cannon had dinner on Saturday night, and Sunday morning I got a call from Bob. He said, "How did you know that?"

I said, "What do you mean, Bob?"

He said, "Well, the judge not only won't move to New York but he wants us to match his judicial pension. I told him, 'Look, you sat there when we talked about all of this and you didn't say anything.' Then he told me he couldn't take the job under these circumstances. Robin, you were right. I can't believe that this happened."

I said, "Don't worry about it. Let's just set up another meeting."

As a result, we scheduled another meeting of the player representatives for March in Florida. In the meantime, I was calling Marvin Miller to urge him to continue to be a candidate. He was reluctant until I asked Bob Friend to call him. Bob now supported Marvin, and when Marvin understood that, he agreed to allow us to resubmit his name.

The player reps met again on March 6, 1966, in Miami. I had called General Eckert to invite him to sit in on our Florida meeting. General Eckert instead sent Lee MacPhail. Because Eckert had no experience in baseball prior to being selected as commissioner, the owners had appointed Lee to serve as his executive assistant for one year. It did not take long to proceed to a vote, and this time the reps overwhelmingly voted for Miller.

After we nominated Marvin, he agreed to visit all the spring training sites and meet with the ballplayers to explain his plans for the association. Then the players were to vote to ratify him as the first executive director.

I was very excited about Marvin becoming the executive director, and I really wanted him to win ratification. At that time baseball players had no facial hair, not even mustaches. They were a pretty conservative group. Marvin had a little pencil-thin mustache, so I said to him before he started visiting spring training camps, "Marvin, I wish you would shave your mustache off. I don't want anything to work against you."

I guess Marvin thought my request was ridiculous, and perhaps it was. In any event he didn't do it.

Marvin started at the training camps in Arizona, and he apparently ran into some opposition from some of the players. Larry Jackson and Ron Santo of the Cubs and some other players were very leery of Miller's union background. They saw baseball as a game, not a business that needed a union. The California Angels trained in Palm Springs, California, and were quite hostile to Marvin. Veteran players like Buck Rodgers, Lew Burdette, Jimmy Piersall,

Joe Adcock, and Jack Sanford were critical of unions and of me. Adcock, who was finishing a long playing career and would later become a manager, accused me of setting up a lifetime job for myself. Joe, of course, had never talked to me about the Players' Association, and for him to say that was not only untrue but unfair as well.

Eddie Mathews of the Braves was another prominent player who spoke out against me. In a way, I could understand their opposition. They had not been involved with the player representative system and really did not understand what we were trying to accomplish.

Marvin was a little discouraged when he came to Florida after meeting with the clubs in Arizona. The voting out there had been disastrous. But the tide turned when he came to the Florida camps. I was in Cocoa Beach with the Houston Astros, my last spring training as a major league ballplayer. We traveled to West Palm Beach for a spring training game with the Braves. As I was running sprints in the outfield before the game, I looked up and saw Eddie Mathews jogging toward me. I was unsure what was on his mind because he had been critical of my role in hiring an executive director. I was also unaware that Marvin was appearing before the Braves players that day. Eddie had left Marvin's meeting, saw me, and came out to talk. He said, "Robin, I apologize for what I said. I think this guy is someone we need."

I said, "Don't apologize, just vote for him."

The teams in Florida did vote heavily in favor of Miller, and he received a much more positive reception than he had in the west. The final tally was announced on April 13 and was 489 to 136 in favor of Marvin.

With the favorable vote, Miller was finally ready to take office. But he had no office space, office equipment, or secretary. The association's records consisted of the minutes of some of our meetings but little else. Undeterred, Miller ended up in New York City in Frank Scott's office before getting permanent office space of his own. Frank was a players' agent and was hired by the association to develop our licensing contracts and help administer our meetings.

After Marvin was elected, I called him to discuss whom he might name as general counsel for the Players' Association and suggested Richard Nixon. I thought that it just made sense to have a New York law firm as the association's counsel and thought Richard Nixon would be an ideal choice. I knew that Nixon was a real baseball fan and his firm, Nixon Mudge Rose & Mitchell, was highly respected. I did not consider who had what political affiliation but just believed that Nixon would add credibility to the Players' Association in its dealings with the baseball owners.

Apparently Marvin thought that it was a horrible idea for me to ask him, a liberal Democrat and career union man, to work with a conservative Republican like Richard Nixon. In any event, Jim Bunning and I went to New York and had lunch with Nixon to see if he would be interested in the job. Nixon was very enthusiastic but indicated that he might have other plans. History shows that he in fact did.

After our lunch, I called Marvin and reported Nixon's interest to him. With my encouragement, Marvin even went to see Nixon himself. Finally Marvin said to me, "I think it would make more sense for me to have my own man as general counsel."

I said, "Marvin, if that is what you want, that is fine." I meant it when I said the decision was his, and so in January 1967 Marvin brought in Dick Moss, a colleague from his steelworker days, as general counsel.

I was happy that Marvin was in place. He was smart and energetic, and the Players' Association now had a full-time executive director to represent and negotiate for it. I enjoyed the competition and the teamwork of baseball, and I wanted the players to be able to play and not worry about the off-the-field issues. And that is what we had accomplished with the hiring of Marvin Miller. Of course, I did not anticipate just how his hiring would change base-ball forever.

I was out of baseball after Marvin came on board, working in the invest-ment business in Philadelphia. In fact, for a couple of years I had very little contact with anyone in baseball. Then, one Friday afternoon, I received a call from Jim Bunning, who was then the National League player representative.

Jim said, "Robin, they are after your boy."

I had noticed that whenever there was any controversy about Marvin, he was my boy. When things were going smoothly, I never heard that. I said, "What do you mean, Jimmy?"

He said, "We are having a big meeting in New York tomorrow with all the player representatives and quite a few players. Some of the players are dis-gruntled, and some of the owners are trying to get us to get rid of Marvin."

I said, "Well, what do you want me to do?"

Jim said, "Why don't you come up and sit in on the meeting?"

I did attend the meeting the next day at the Biltmore Hotel in Manhattan. Among the players were some who had obviously been talking to their owners and wanted to get rid of Marvin. I was sitting in the back of the meeting room next to Milt Pappas, who had been my teammate in Baltimore. After a while I asked Milt if he would introduce me to the group so that I could speak.

He did, and I got up and said, "Fellows, I am sitting here listening to this discussion and want to remind you why we hired Marvin Miller in the first place. There were two major reasons. One was the pension. He is to make sure we get our share of the television contracts for our pension. The other was to develop our licensing rights. I imagine that is difficult, but he is making progress and I think our licensing fees will grow and grow.

"I understand that some of you have club owners who think that Marvin is a little tough on them, but I don't think that is the case. Overall, I believe Marvin will be a real asset to the Players' Association. I think that any conversation about getting someone to replace him is really silly because he is the right man for the job.

"I just wanted you all to know that. I thank you for letting me talk to you."

I left the room and caught a cab to the train station to go home to Philadelphia. I was getting ready to catch my train when I saw Davey Johnson coming toward me. Davey was the Baltimore player representative and later the manager of the Mets, Reds, Orioles, and Dodgers. He said, "Well, you sure ended that meeting."

I said, "What do you mean, Davey?"

He said, "As soon as you left, they forgot about getting rid of Marvin Miller and stopped the meeting."

Of course, Marvin eventually took on much more than the pension and licensing for the Players' Association. At the time of the Players' Association's first strike in 1972, only the benefits package, health insurance, and the pension fund were at issue. I had, of course, been following the negotiations in the newspapers and was concerned about the possibility of a strike. I remembered that when the search committee first interviewed Marvin in Cleveland in 1965 he had assured us, in response to a question from me, that he had no intention of ever leading the players out on strike.

When the strike occurred I immediately called Marvin. His first words to me were, "I've been expecting your call."

I said, "I can't believe this happened. I was so confident that you would never let it get to this point."

He replied, "Well, the players forced me to do it," which I thought sounded ridiculous.

After that first strike, it seems to me that Marvin became a much more confrontational, combative union head. He was very comfortable in that contentious climate where the two sides were negotiating hard and fighting over every issue. That kind of adversarial environment had been his life, and he was excellent operating in it.

I do wish that Marvin had been a little more temperate and had displayed more reverence for the game of baseball and the place it has in this country. I was a little disappointed and surprised that Marvin did not have that feeling about baseball; he was just doing a job representing ballplayers regardless of his impact on the game. When we hired him, I never imagined the role of executive director of the Players' Association would develop in the way it did.

Of course, the owners had a lot to do with the way that the labor wars developed in baseball. Looking back, it is absolutely clear that, after the owners fired Happy Chandler in 1950, the commissioners, beginning with Ford Frick, have simply represented the owners and not the best interests of baseball. And from the beginning when they resisted any change to baseball's status quo and later when they tried to undermine the hiring of Marvin Miller, they created an adversarial system that, unfortunately, still predominates.

Few owners ever sat down with Marvin Miller and had a conversation with him. When Ruly Carpenter became president of the Phillies in 1972, I went by to congratulate him. Ruly was Bob Carpenter's son and had been around baseball all his life. I told Ruly, "One of the first things you ought to do is call Marvin Miller in New York and tell him you'd like to come up and have lunch with him."

Ruly thought that was the worst idea he had ever heard. "I wouldn't sit down with that guy for anything," he said. Later Ruly's father, Bob, was in the hospital a couple of times, and each time I called to wish him well. Both times all Bob could say to me after all those years I pitched for him was, "You and that SOB Marvin Miller. I'd like to wring your necks." And I was just calling to wish him well. Ruly and his dad's attitude was typical; the owners just had no use for Marvin and regarded him as their sworn enemy. I do believe that some owners attempted to be civil to Marvin, but they were in a real minority.

In 1966, I was with the Houston Astros while the Players' Association was considering hiring Marvin. One day I was in our locker room in the Astrodome about 15 or 20 minutes before the start of a game. Bob Lillis, our shortstop and the Astros' player representative, came in and said, "Robin, you better get down to the dugout. President Giles is talking about your boy."

With something going wrong, Marvin was my boy again. So over I went and Warren Giles, who was the longtime president of the National League, had his back to me as I came up the stairs to the dugout. He was talking to several players about how Marvin was a Communist and how a union would ruin baseball, but he did not see me. Then he noticed the players looking past him at me, and he turned and saw me.

Mr. Giles and I always had a good relationship from all those years I pitched in the National League. He looked at me and said, "Oh Robin, how are you?"

"Mr. Giles," I said, "I'm fine. I'd like to ask you one question. Have you ever met Marvin Miller, Mr. Giles?"

"No, I haven't, Robin," he said.

"That's what I thought," I said, and I turned and went back to the clubhouse.

The idea that Marvin Miller was my boy has dogged me ever since. Once I was about to tee off at a golf tournament put on by the Baseball Hall of Fame in Cooperstown. Bowie Kuhn was commissioner and was announcing the players, and when it came to my turn he said, "Robin Roberts. Here is the guy responsible for Marvin Miller getting into baseball."

I certainly do not deny it. But I do find it curious that at the time we were conducting our search and I was sharing our list of candidates with the commissioner's office and with the owners, no one called me to talk about Marvin Miller. They were certainly talking to other players about what they thought of Marvin Miller, as Warren Giles did that day in the dugout in Houston, but I did not hear from anyone, although we had an open process and solicited input from everyone.

I believe I had established a good reputation in baseball as one who respected the game and one who would certainly never do anything to hurt it. I can only believe that they assumed getting a full-time executive director and hiring Marvin Miller was all right, because no one called me to tell me any differently.

Once at a Hall of Fame induction weekend, Chub Feeney, who was then National League president, came up to me and said, "Robin, they've given you a lot of malarkey about Marvin Miller, haven't they?"

"Well, I've learned to live with that, Chub," I said.

"You know, no one ever remembers that you were representing the players. I think you may have done a good job."

Well, I know that financially it certainly did turn out well for the players. I remember that at our original meeting with Marvin in Cleveland I said that I could envision when the pension fund would receive $15 million a year. When that happened Marvin called me to remind me of our early conversation. The pension now receives at least $85 million a year.

I do regret that the game of baseball and the fans have taken some real hits over the past 30 years or so while the owners and the Players' Association have duked it out.

I do not think that the owners really gave Marvin a chance after he was hired and that he reacted to their treatment of him with his bulldog mentality. Later, I think that Marvin lost sight of everything but doing battle with the owners.

I got an insight into Marvin's view of his position once when I went to see him with a suggestion after he had been in his position for about 10 years. I was long retired from baseball but was concerned with the off-field behavior of some of the young guys breaking into the big leagues. In the old days the veterans tended to mentor the rookies and let them know what was expected of a big-league ballplayer. That had sort of broken down, and because relations between the owners and players had become so fractious it did not appear that the clubs could say much to players about their behavior.

I explained this to Marvin and suggested that he consider hiring a public relations firm from New York that would advise young ballplayers who reached the major leagues about how to act and conduct themselves. I thought it was something that someone really had to do, but Marvin's response was that he wasn't into public relations, so that was the end of that.

On another occasion after I retired, Ralph Kiner and I went to a meeting with Marvin and the Players' Association about increasing the retired players' pension. There was a lot more money going into the pension fund, and we thought it would be appropriate to increase the pensions of the retired players. During our conversation, Marvin made the statement that he did not feel any responsibility to anyone who had played before he became executive director and who had not been through the strikes.

Frankly, Marvin's statement made me sad. He often acted like he was just a hired union gun who had a very narrow view of his job and was not at all concerned about the welfare of the game of baseball. His actions, in addition to those of a group of self-interested owners, have created an atmosphere of irreconcilable conflict that has substantially harmed the place of the national pastime in our society. Both sides represent monopoly interests. The Players' Association represents all major league baseball players. The owners represent Major League Baseball. There are no rival players' associations or professional baseball organizations.

Each side has acted in the self-interested way of monopolists with the result that the fans who support the game are left out in the cold. The commissioner has not for a very long time been an independent arbiter and protector of the game. In fact, today's commissioner is an owner. Thus, when disputes arise, there is no independent entity to resolve the issues and represent the fans.

I firmly believe that baseball needs a strong independent commissioner to look out for the best interests of the game and to protect the public interest. The owners and the players have made it clear that they are always going to try to advance their own self-interests. When we created the executive director's position for the Players' Association, I just assumed the commissioner was in place to ensure that decisions were made in the best interests of the game and not to advance the position of one group or the other.

I envisioned that the commissioner would work with the executive director and the owners, not against the executive director and for the owners. That certainly was the original model for the commissioner under Judge Landis.

To their credit, the owners and Players' Association later did increase the retired players' pensions even though they had no obligation to do so. I worked on a committee with then representatives Jim Bunning, Early Wynn, Gerry Moses, and Donald Fehr, who succeeded Marvin as the executive director, to gain a commitment from the Players' Association. The association then secured the agreement of the owners to provide the increase.

After Peter Ueberroth was named commissioner, he asked me if I thought Marvin Miller would be fair with him. I said, "Yes, I think he will." But I think I was wrong. By that time, I don't think Marvin Miller would have been fair with anyone in authority in baseball. He had his own agenda and his own way of accomplishing it, usually involving resorting to the courts or leading the players in a work stoppage.

Each time the courts got involved in baseball disputes or the players struck, I knew baseball was losing, no matter what the ultimate result. I just do not believe that baseball, with its special, unique role in American life as the national pastime, should be treated like any other business.

Of course, no one has asked for my opinion or my help for a long time, although I have offered my opinion unsolicited from time to time. I was shocked when the players struck in 1994 and the owners canceled the World Series. I just could not believe that those two groups were arrogant enough to take the playoffs and World Series away from the fans. My phone bill in September 1994 was more than $500. I called all the owners; I called Donald Fehr, the executive director of the Players' Association. I called the commissioner. I called the league presidents. I called everyone involved in the failed negotiations to try to get them to accept binding arbitration. And then, when they refused, I called to tell them how arrogant and stupid they all were.

I still cannot believe how the owners and the Players' Association hurt the game of baseball in 1994. But fortunately the game is so much a part of the fabric of American life that it is very resilient, in spite of the efforts of those two groups. I still watch every game I can because not only is it a wonderful game to play but it is a wonderful game to watch.

Of course, baseball will continue on its current path because of the way it is structured. As long as the commissioner is selected by and represents only the owners, no one is looking out for the best interests of the game. The owners and players will continue to slug it out through collective bargaining every time the labor agreement is up for renegotiation, each side seeking only its own selfish interests and ignoring the fans.

CHAPTER 15

Life After Baseball

I came home from Reading on June 15, 1967, and I knew it was over. It sounds crazy now, but I had no contingency plans for what I was going to do after baseball. I enjoyed playing so much and didn't have any real aches and pains. I honestly thought I was going to pitch until I was 45. I thought I could still pitch when I left Reading, but you've got to have a team that wants you, and that was what I was lacking.

The Cubs had offered me a job as pitching coach for the 1967 season before I decided to go to Reading, but I was not really interested in all that travel and time away from my family if I couldn't pitch, so that didn't seem to be a real option.

Bob Bast, a good friend who is a lawyer, suggested that I take mediation training. At the time, that did not interest me, but in retrospect I sometimes wonder if that would have been a good role for me.

I did have to figure out how I could make $40,000 a year to support my family in the manner we had become accustomed to. I sat around for about three months, not knowing what to do. Curt Simmons and I were part of a group that had purchased the Limekiln Golf Course in suburban Philadelphia. Curt split the year between the Cubs and the California Angels, and after the end of the baseball season he and I spent the fall working on the golf course. It was an old course that needed a lot of work, and I could rake and pick up trash. Curt was pretty handy with a chain saw, so I left him to that.

I knew I had to go get a job doing something, but I really couldn't figure out what on earth I could do. Finally, I got a call from a friend named Jim Castle who had a small investment business going with his partner John Cannon. They offered me a job for a salary of $25,000 to work in their firm.

That was a large part of the money I needed. About the same time, I was approached by a radio station in Philadelphia, WPEN, to do a morning sports show. In the off-season for a couple of years in the fifties I had done the *Robin Roberts Sports Club* on WCAU-TV in Philadelphia. I had also done some radio work with a disc jockey named Jack Pyle, who was a baseball fan. In any event, the WPEN folks agreed to pay me $15,000 to do three sports reports a morning. So I would get up about 5:30, drive downtown, arriving by about 6:30, and then do the sports at 7:00 A.M., 8:00 A.M., and 9:00 A.M. I was still a big sports fan and generally already knew what had happened the day before, so it was pretty easy for me. Then I would head to the investment firm in Flourtown in suburban Philadelphia and work until 5:00. Later on Cannon and Company was acquired by Janney, Montgomery, Scott, a brokerage firm downtown, so then I worked in downtown Philadelphia.

Those got to be pretty long days, and I eventually told Mary that once I got up to $40,000 from the investment business I was going to get out of the radio business. After about three years I was able to stop doing the morning sports reports. I enjoyed the investment business, although I didn't know anything about it when I started with Cannon and Company. But I learned pretty quickly; we sold computerized sinking-fund information on bonds. John Cannon and I divided the top 100 banks in the country and made calls on their portfolio managers, trying to interest them in our product. Periodically we would travel all over the country, talking to those large-portfolio managers.

I did fine in the investment business and worked in the industry for about 10 years, but it never absorbed me the way baseball always has. Baseball was so much a part of my life for so long, which is one reason that I can remember games that I pitched 40 or 50 years ago. There is not much about my baseball career that I don't remember. I can remember games I played in grade school, the score, who made the winning run, everything about the game. After spending my life in sports and baseball in particular, it was difficult to transition into the business world. I showed up for work every day, however, and worked hard at it. I was just never totally comfortable in that environment even though the people I worked with were great.

One afternoon while I was at Cannon and Company I got a call from my old teammate Granny Hamner who was unemployed at the moment. Ham called everybody "Hoss." He said, "Hoss, can you get me a job?" Ham had no experience in the investment business, but I got his phone number and said I would call him back. I then called Bob Carpenter, the Phillies' owner, and said, "Bob, don't you have a job for Granny Hamner?" I explained that Ham had called me and was looking for work.

Bob said, "Have him call me."

I called Ham back, gave him Bob Carpenter's number, and said I thought Bob might have something for him. Ham said, "I'll only work on my terms."

I said, "Ham, you have no friggin' terms." So he called Bob Carpenter and worked for the Phillies for the rest of his life. Granny Hamner was a baseball guy.

After I retired from coaching college baseball in 1986, Granny was named to be the Phillies' minor league coordinator because Larry Rojas, who held that position, had heart-replacement surgery. Ham called me and said, "Hoss, I need some help." He wanted me to be the Phillies' pitching coordinator for the minor leagues. I worked out an arrangement with Bill Giles, the Phillies' president, and signed a two-year contract to help Ham.

Larry Rojas recovered quite rapidly and soon resumed his role as minor league coordinator. I then spent two years as a man without a role. As it was, I didn't think the Phillies had many minor league pitchers who were big-league prospects. Michael Jackson was one who had potential and went on to have a nice major league career. There were two or three others who made it to the major leagues briefly. In any event, after my contract was up, I was not rehired.

Earlier, in 1972, Ruly Carpenter, only 32 years old and the son of Bob Carpenter, became president of the Phillies, succeeding his father. Ruly had always been around the Phillies clubhouse, and I had always had a good relationship with him as he grew up. I called Ruly, congratulated him, and told him I would love to talk to him about becoming the general manager with him at the helm of the organization. Ruly said he would consider what I might do with the organization and call me back. A few days later he did and said that his father and he would like me to come down and have lunch with them the following week. Then, the day before the scheduled lunch, Ruly called again and said, "My father decided that maybe we shouldn't have lunch after all." So that was that.

I later learned that Wister Randolph, who was a vice president of the Phillies, had talked to Bob Carpenter right after I retired from baseball and asked, "Don't we have a position for Robin now that he has retired from baseball?"

Bob reportedly replied, "Who's going to take care of me when I get old?" When I heard that remark I thought it was a little uncalled for. It is strange, but I never talked to Bob Carpenter about working with the Phillies. Of course, I didn't realize until later when I called Bob in the hospital to wish him well and he growled at me about Marvin Miller how upset Bob was and continued to be over my involvement with the Players' Association.

Shortly thereafter I did interview with Ruly Carpenter for the Phillies' manager job, as did Andy Seminick, Richie Ashburn, Jim Bunning, and Danny Ozark, a longtime coach with the Dodgers. The club hired Ozark, and he had a successful run for almost seven seasons, winning three National League East titles. It was clear to me that my interview was just a courtesy Ruly extended me.

Another time I talked to the Philadelphia 76ers about their general manager job. I interviewed and then they sent me to a psychiatrist who asked me a bunch of questions. I apparently didn't pass the psychiatric test because I never did hear back from the Sixers.

A little later I was approached by Ed Piszek, who had started the Mrs. Paul's Frozen Foods Company, which had done so well in Philadelphia. He asked if I would be interested in helping him run a minor league hockey team in Philadelphia. At the time, the Philadelphia Flyers were the hottest ticket in town and Eddie believed that a minor league team downtown would be attractive to the many hockey fans in the area. So my oldest son, Robbie, and I worked for the team, called the Philadelphia Firebirds, for about a year. The team did not draw well, however, and so I decided to return to the investment business.

Shel Gordon, an executive with Lehman Brothers whom I had met while working in the investment business, offered me a job with their money management group. I traveled to their Wall Street offices in New York three days a week and also traveled quite a bit to try to secure pension funds for Lehman to manage. I worked with very good people once again and worked hard, but it is not something I can say I really enjoyed.

One evening I expressed a little dissatisfaction to Mary. She pointed out that I was doing well financially. I agreed, but I was 50 years old and told her that I just could not see myself working in the investment business the rest of my life.

Ironically, soon after in the fall of 1976 I received a phone call from Dick Bowers, the athletic director at the University of South Florida in Tampa. He said that Bobby Richardson, the former Yankees second baseman, told him to call me. Bobby was coaching the University of South Carolina baseball team and had turned down an offer to move to South Florida but suggested that I might be interested. I had my degree from Michigan State, and I was eligible to coach Division I college baseball.

I told Mary that the South Florida job would be for a lot less money than I was making in the investment business but that I would sure like to go down and take a look at it. Mary rolled her eyes again. She was not sold on the idea but agreed for me to go check it out. So I went down to interview and see if it made sense to make that career change and coach college baseball.

Dick Bowers offered me the job, so I returned home and told Mary that I would like to take it but that I was not going without her and Jimmy. Our youngest boy, Jim, was the only child still at home full-time. We had lived in Philadelphia for a long time and raised our children there. Most of our friends were in the area, and so it was a big move at that time of our lives, but after Mary and I went down and looked at the Tampa area, she was on board.

I was excited about coaching at the university. I had coached my sons Robbie and Danny for two years on an American Legion team at Plymouth-Whitemarsh Township near our home in Philadelphia and enjoyed the experience. About that time Jim Buckley, the baseball coach at Germantown Academy where the boys went to school, decided that he wanted to coach the girls basketball team instead. Germantown's athletic director, Jack Turner, asked if I would like to coach the baseball team as a volunteer. So I coached Germantown Academy for four years and had some good teams. I was able to coach my sons Danny and Ricky at Germantown. Danny was a scrappy second baseman and Ricky was a jack-of-all-trades who loved to hit.

During those years, Germantown had a first-rate pitching prospect named Timmy Lewis. At one point I called Bobby Richardson at the University of South Carolina to tell him about the young man. Bobby told me that he never signed a kid that he didn't see personally, so I invited Bobby to come up and watch Timmy pitch. Unfortunately, both games Bobby was supposed to see were rained out.

I prevailed upon Bobby to offer Lewis a scholarship anyway, telling him that he could really pitch. Bobby did and Lewis went on to become the winningest pitcher in the history of the University of South Carolina. I'm sure Bobby remembered all that when he recommended me for the South Florida job.

Jack Butterfield had been the South Florida baseball coach, but George Steinbrenner had offered him a job with the Yankees organization in September. So South Florida needed a baseball coach in a hurry, and I was able to step in. I had a part-time assistant, Jeff Davis, who had been with the program and would prove to be invaluable to me.

Shortly after it was announced that I had taken the South Florida job, I got a call from Ron Polk, the coach at Mississippi State. As we were talking he said, "You really have to have an operating budget of at least $125,000 to have a chance to run a good program. I just hope you have that in mind. You just can't attract the right kids without that kind of budget." I had to laugh to myself because my budget when I started at South Florida was $5,000 a year.

I coached at South Florida for eight years, worked hard at it, and had a lot of fun. I particularly enjoyed the on-field parts, practice and the games. I don't think I was much of a recruiter; I used to tell the boys and their parents that I was a collector, not a teacher. If they couldn't play when they came down to South Florida, I'm not sure how much better they were when they left. When I had good players, I could coach and we could compete with anyone.

235

In 1982 we had a fine team and finished with a 49–13 record. We won the Sun Belt Conference tournament and went to the NCAA regionals in Miami where we defeated the University of Florida before losing to the University of Miami and Stetson. The first baseman on that team was my son Jim, who made the All–Sun Belt Conference team and had an outstanding year. Jim was one of a number of fine ballplayers on that team. Jon Cook was outstanding behind the plate. Timmy Carr at second was great, and Randy Wilson pitched and played third. He had talent and was really a fighter. We had a strong outfield and solid shortstop. Somehow I was a good collector that year.

It is not that I didn't recruit at all. For example, I recruited Paul O'Neill out of high school in 1981. He was a highly regarded pitcher, outfielder, and basketball player, and I had heard all about him and visited him at his home in Columbus, Ohio. He signed with South Florida, but we had to wait for the major league draft to see if he was going to turn professional or go to college. He called me after the draft and told me he had been drafted in the fourth round by the Cincinnati Reds. I said, "Paul, it's a great life. If you get $50,000, I can see no reason why you shouldn't sign. You've got good ability and you'll probably make a good living."

After he negotiated with the Reds he called me and said that the Reds would pay him only $40,000. I told him, "Well, I think you are shortchanging yourself, but good luck." Of course, Paul went on to play in the major leagues for 15 years for the Reds and the Yankees, appearing in six World Series and five All-Star Games. I believe he signed one four-year contract for about $20 million and played for about $6 million his last year with the Yankees. It is not about the money, but Paul certainly had a fine career and reaped its rewards.

I had four guys who played for me at South Florida who made the big leagues. Chris Welsh was a left-handed pitcher who played for the Padres, Expos, Rangers, and Reds in a five-year major league career. Chris was a fine athlete who probably could have been an everyday ballplayer, although he only pitched for me one year. He now announces Cincinnati Reds games.

Tony Fossas pitched three years for me and then pitched in the big leagues as a left-handed relief pitcher for many years. Tony was drafted after his junior year and was offered $8,000 to sign a professional contract. He called me for my advice. I said, "Tony, let's think about how much $8,000 is. You pay your taxes and buy yourself a car but have no money left for gas. Why don't you come back to school and be one of the first Cuban boys to have a college degree."

Tony came back, pitched his senior year, signed a professional contract, and pitched in the minor leagues for 11 years before getting his chance in the major leagues. He made the most of it, pitching a dozen years in the big leagues as a left-handed relief specialist before retiring after the age of 40. And he has a college degree.

Tim Hulett was an all-round athlete at Lanphier High School in Springfield, Illinois, where I had gone to school. He played only one year for us but was a fine ballplayer who hit 17 home runs in 1986 for the Chicago White Sox and played five full seasons with the White Sox and Baltimore Orioles.

The best athlete I ever coached was Scottie Hemond, who became the number one draft choice for the Oakland Athletics in 1986. He had a solid big-league career but never had the success that he might have. Guys like him who have big-league ability really do stand out on a college team.

My other association with college baseball was through my son Danny, who was the head coach at West Point for 17 years. He is West Point's winningest baseball coach. My Mary has seen more baseball games than any woman in the history of western civilization. Danny's Army teams always made a spring trip to Florida, but Mary finally quit going to his games. Danny asked his mother why, and Mary said, "Your pitchers throw to first base too much." Amen.

When I was coaching, I kept things on the team simple and had only two rules. First, if my players didn't go to class, they could not practice or play. I had the professors let me know if they were cutting class so I could enforce the rule. The second rule was if they were late for practice, they had to run 30 pole-to-poles in the outfield.

Once the guys knew the rules, there were very few problems. On one occasion a professor called to tell me that one of my players had been cutting class. When the player showed up for practice, I said, "Hey, Brad. We don't need you today."

He said, "Why, Coach?"

I said, "Hey, I told you about missing class." It was the last class the young man missed. Later on the same kid was late to practice one day. He came in and said, "Hi, Coach," and went out and ran his 30 pole-to-poles. I never had to say a word. And it was the only time anyone was ever late for a practice.

One year we were playing one of the most outstanding baseball programs in the country. During batting practice the other team's coach came over and asked if he could speak with me a moment. He said, "I have some kids that register for classes and then never go. What can I do?"

I answered, "Well, you don't play them." Apparently he had never thought of that.

College sports are so popular and the athletes are so much in the limelight that it seems that their education often takes a backseat to their participation in athletics. But I do not understand why student-athletes are not required to attend class if they want to represent their universities in athletic events. When I attended Michigan State, I never missed a class, unless it was because of team travel. Neither did my teammates, with rare exceptions. Unlike today, none of us assumed that we were headed for a professional sports career, and we valued the education we were receiving. I have loved playing sports my entire life, but I have always been proud of the education I received at Michigan State.

We had some fun while I coached at South Florida. We tried to win and were competitive, but a little humor didn't hurt and may have helped the guys relax. Once we were playing St. Leo's University in a practice game and our pitcher, Larry Grubbs, gave up a monster home run in the ninth inning to lose the game 2–1. Larry had pitched a fine game but this ball was hit so far that it went through some goal posts on an adjacent field. Afterward when I got the players together I couldn't resist saying, "Hey, Larry, I gave up a lot of home runs but I never threw one that went that far."

Another time, I put a pinch-runner in who promptly was suckered by the hidden ball trick. This was when the Soviet Union–Afghanistan War was going on, and when the young man came back to the dugout, I said, "I don't know why they are fighting in Afghanistan and there are 900 million Chinese who don't give a damn. But I'll tell you one thing. When I put you in to pinch run you had better know where the damn ball is."

During my years at South Florida our Sun Belt Conference rivalry with the University of South Alabama added some spice to the competition. South Alabama was coached by former big leaguer Eddie Stanky, who was still "the Brat." Eddie had a full scholarship program and produced some fine teams. We were only able to beat them for the conference championship one time, but just about every other year we went down to the wire with them. Every game between us seemed to be a nail-biter, and Stanky would do whatever he could to win. One time we were beating them in Mobile, and as he went out to the mound to talk to his pitcher he told the umpire, "Just because he's in the Hall of Fame, you don't have to give him every pitch."

When they were at home, he would dress about 40 kids, even though you could have only 22 on the playing roster. One year we had a pretty serious ruckus with them in Mobile, and there were some real punches being thrown. We quickly found that we were seriously outnumbered because of all the guys Stanky had suited up who came racing in from their bullpen. That was typical of Stanky; he always wanted the advantage.

The next year Stanky had retired. Before the first game when we went to play at South Alabama, their new coach asked if I minded if he suited out his extra players. I was holding a fungo bat at the time and said, "Yeah, that'll be all right, but if we have a fracas like we did last year, I'm coming after you with this fungo bat."

Stanky's players really liked him, especially the hitters. Lance Johnson, who played for Stanky and then made the major leagues, told me that he loved the guy. A close friend of Stanky's once told me that off the field Eddie was a real nice guy. I said, "Well, I've never met him off the field." Of course that was not true, but it was a good line.

We played the University of Florida, Florida State, and the University of Miami every year and had an unbelievably poor record against those programs except for 1982 when I had that outstanding team. We beat all three of them that year. When I had good players I really improved as a coach. Funny how that works.

I enjoyed coaching at South Florida, but after eight years I was ready to stop collecting ballplayers and start playing more golf, so I stepped down after 1986. I'm still reaping some benefits from my college coaching years, however. Every month or two Mary makes some clam dip and Jon Cook, who caught for me at South Florida, and Jeff Davis and Kevin Maronic, two of my assistant coaches there, show up at our house to argue about sports. I really get a kick out of our "discussions" and like to think that the three of them enjoy my company. But they probably come because of Mary's clam dip.

* * *

I am amazed at how often I've run into baseball fans from Brooklyn in the years since I left pro ball. As I have described, I pitched many crucial games against Brooklyn during my career with the Phillies. The Brooklyn fans were a special breed, rabid and completely loyal to their Bums.

The Dodgers had the Dodgers Sym-phony, a little band that tried to harass the opposing team during the games. When a rival player would ground out, the band would play a little tune as he jogged back to the dugout. Then when he sat down, the drummer would accentuate it with a big loud bong. Del Ennis would come back from grounding out and almost sit down, then go get a drink of water, then stand for a while to see if the drummer would get tired of waiting for him to sit. Finally, Del would sit down and the drummer never missed, no matter how long it took. There would be a loud bong, and Del would get the biggest kick out of it.

That rivalry with the Dodgers has seemed to follow me all my life. Just a few years ago, I went to a restaurant in Manhattan to have dinner. Our waitress, who happened to be black, started smiling when we sat down. When she brought our order she asked, "You're Robin Roberts, aren't you?" When I said I was, she said, "Oh, I used to hate you." I asked her if she was from Brooklyn, and she said, "Of course. You used to try to get my Jackie out."

Danny Kaye was from Brooklyn and a huge baseball fan. He used to travel occasionally with Leo Durocher when Leo was working as a broadcaster for the *Game of the Week*. I pitched a shutout in Milwaukee on one *Game of the Week* and afterward Danny Kaye came by my locker to say hello. I was sitting having a beer with Maje McDonnell, and so we got Danny a beer and just sat and visited.

Years later Mary and I were driving into Reno with some friends from the investment business. We passed a billboard that announced that Danny Kaye was playing at one of the local establishments. My friend's wife saw it and told us that Danny Kaye was her favorite entertainer of all time. When we got to our hotel room I mentioned to Mary that it would be fun to surprise her. I called the casino where Danny was performing, and they put me right through to his room and he answered the phone. I told Danny that Mary and I were in town with one of his most devoted fans. He immediately offered to get us a table for the show that night right in front of the stage and told us to come backstage after the show.

We went and enjoyed the show. Then we went backstage to his dressing room and found him sitting in nothing but his shorts. He told us to come in and so we talked and laughed with him for about 20 minutes before going back to our hotel.

Eli Wallach is also from Brooklyn. I learned this spending a pleasant evening with him and his wife, the actress Anne Jackson, one night in New York. I was there to make an appearance on Warner Wolf's local sports show to promote an upcoming Equitable Old Timers' Game. I was sitting in the green room prior to the show. Eli Wallach came in and recognized me, even though we had never met. He said, "Robin, I'm from Brooklyn and I sure used to root against you."

After the show he asked, "Why don't you join Anne and me for dinner?" I was just headed back to my hotel so I said, "That would be great." We had a nice dinner and talked a lot of baseball, and at the end of the meal Eli said, "We are going to watch a private showing of a new movie called *Terms of Endearment*. Why don't you come with us?" So I accompanied them to a small theater that had about 120 seats and watched the screening. Afterward I thanked them, said good-bye, and headed back to my hotel. I never have seen Eli again, but I certainly spent a pleasant evening with him and his wife, especially considering that he was from Brooklyn.

Sometime later I learned that the Pulitzer Prize–winning historian Doris Kearns Goodwin wrote in her best-selling memoir *Wait Till Next Year* about how as a little girl she had wished that I would fall down some steps so that I couldn't face her beloved Bums. She grew up a devoted Dodgers fan in Rockville Centre on the south shore of Long Island.

One day a few years ago I was visiting with Eddie Cardieri who had been one of my assistants at South Florida and had then succeeded me as the head coach. I was telling him that sometimes it seemed to me that everyone I meet is from Brooklyn when Eddie started laughing and said, "Hey Coach, I'm from Brooklyn, too." I rest my case. Everybody is from Brooklyn.

Although Spencer Tracy is from Milwaukee and not Brooklyn, I had an interesting encounter with him as well during my playing days. It was while I was with the Phillies and we were playing the Dodgers in Los Angeles. Our announcer, By Saam, knew Stanley Kramer, the Hollywood director. By asked me to go with him and watch part of the filming of *Judgment at Nuremburg*, which starred Spencer Tracy. When we arrived at the studio, Tracy's brother visited with us because he was a real baseball fan. The scene they were filming involved Spencer walking down a long staircase and saying a couple of lines. When he got to the bottom of the staircase, he said, "Cut that, Stanley, let's do it again." Then he walked back up the stairs to do the scene again. As Tracy was climbing the stairs, Kramer turned to us and said, "You know, he'll do an entire movie and not have two of these cuts. He's amazing how he can do a scene on the first try."

Tracy was satisfied with the second take and then came over to visit with us. His brother introduced us, and Spencer said to me, "How many times have you thrown a pitch when you would like to say, 'Cut, let's do that over'?" That seemed like an awful good idea to me.

Another guy not from Brooklyn whom I enjoyed meeting was country music legend Charley Pride. Charley was quite a pitcher and outfielder with the Memphis Red Sox in the old Negro Leagues. He once pitched against Henry Aaron and Willie Mays. I told him that I wished that he had kept playing and that they had gone into singing. Charley also told me that he singled off Warren Spahn in an exhibition game. Spahnie promptly picked him off. The next time up he doubled. Spahnie promptly picked him off second. Charley needed Maury Wills to help him on his base running. Charley is the best singing baseball player I've ever known, and I enjoy his company.

One morning, I was eating breakfast alone at the Chase Hotel in St. Louis when a young man came up and introduced himself. He said, "Robin, I'm Jonathan Winters and I love baseball." I asked him to join me and we had an enjoyable breakfast. That evening I saw him perform at the Chase for the first time. A little later he was in Philadelphia and attended one of our doubleheaders. Between games he came in and put on a comedy skit in the clubhouse. He is certainly a funny man. I'm not sure whether we won the second game or not, but we were relaxed.

The last time I saw Jonathan I was leaving the clubhouse in Philadelphia. A man called, "Hey, Robin." It was Jonathan, and he wanted me to meet his son. Winters is one of many entertainers who are real baseball fans.

* * *

After I retired from baseball I enjoyed going to Old Timers' Games from time to time. Once when I was still in my forties I played in an Old Timers' Game in Shea Stadium. My brother John was along, and they put us up at the Roosevelt Hotel in New York and then provided a bus to the ballpark. Casey Stengel was on the bus, and once the bus started he got up and just started telling stories. The bus ride took the better part of an hour, and Casey never stopped talking. He had the whole bus in stitches the entire time.

Casey managed my team. I noticed during pregame warm-ups that our first baseman, Frank McCormick, who had been a great player for the Cincinnati Reds in the late thirties, really could not see the ball. The game began, and Frank soon missed a ball thrown right to him at first. I went over to Casey and said, "Casey, I watched Frank during infield. He can't see the ball."

Casey immediately started out of the dugout saying, "Time, time, time. We can't have a first baseman who can't see." Poor Frank was benched in the middle of an Old Timers' Game.

Later in the game I was on first base and Monte Irvin hit one right over the third-base bag. I could still run a little, so I took off for second base and just kept running, scoring all the way from first. As I went into the dugout, Casey hobbled up off the bench and met me at the steps. He put his hand out to shake my hand and said, "Roberts, you could have played for me." Ole Casey was into the ballgame, even in an Old Timers' Game.

Richie Ashburn played for the infamous '62 Mets and had an endless supply of Casey stories. One involved Frank Thomas batting for the Mets in the late innings of a close ballgame. All of a sudden Casey hollered from the dugout, "C'mon Frank, hit one over the canoe." Everybody on the bench was wondering what on earth Stengel was talking about. It turns out that there was a hot dog billboard on the front of the upper deck in the Polo Grounds that had a hot dog in a bun with some mustard on it. Apparently Casey's eyesight wasn't all that great so he wanted Frank to hit one over the canoe in left. But no one was really sure if Casey was serious or just playing a gag.

Of course there was the time that Marv Throneberry hit a shot into the gap with two men on and slid into third with an apparent triple. The opposition threw the ball in to first, and the umpire called Marv out for missing the bag. Casey went out to argue, and the second-base umpire came over and said, "Casey, he missed second base, too."

Throneberry was still on third, so Casey said, "Well, I'll say this. He didn't miss third because he's standing on it."

The '62 Mets lost 120 games, still a record for futility. They played the last game of the year against the Cubs in Chicago. In the ninth inning the Mets had no outs and runners on first and second. Their hitter hit a bloop beyond the infield, but Kenny Hubbs, the Cubs' second baseman, raced back and made a tremendous catch. Both the Mets' base runners were running, so Hubbs threw the ball to the shortstop at second base, who threw to first base for a triple play. That was how the Mets' season ended.

Whitey told me that after they filed into the clubhouse, Casey said, "Gentlemen, I gotta tell you one thing. This was a team effort. Nobody could lose this many games by themselves."

* * *

One of the relationships in my life that I most treasure is my friendship with James Michener. It came about in a most peculiar way. In the late sixties and early seventies a number of books that were negative about sports were published. In 1972 my friend Ed Piszek, who was a very successful Philadelphia businessman, called and suggested that we write a book focusing on the positive roles that athletics play in our society. I asked, "Do you write, Ed?" When he responded, "No," I said, "Well, neither do I, but let's try to get somebody who does."

I called Sandy Grady, who had covered the Phillies for the *Philadelphia Bulletin* but had become a political writer. He was covering the McGovern campaign in the presidential election and said that he would not be able to do anything until after the campaign. In the meantime Ed ran into James Michener at a cocktail party and expressed his frustration at so many people criticizing sports and told him about the book he would like to see written. In the course of the conversation Michener asked Ed if he had someone to write the book. When Ed said no, Michener indicated that he would be interested in undertaking it.

That conversation was the genesis of Michener's best-selling *Sports in America*, which was published in 1976. I first met Michener soon after he began work on the book and helped arrange interviews for him with guys like Chuck Bednarik and Bill White, who was a fine baseball player and later on the president of the National League. When the book was published Michener dedicated it to Ed Piszek; Joe Robbie, the owner of the Miami Dolphins who had been particularly helpful to him; and me. Of course, the book is now required reading for some university courses on sports in society. It is not just an apology for sports but successfully attempts to explain the role of athletics in our country.

Before I met Michener, Mary and I had read in the *Sunday Bulletin* that I had been one of his favorite ballplayers. He grew up with adopted parents in Doylestown, near Philadelphia, and had always followed the Phillies, even as a grown man. We became friends in the process of his writing *Sports in America*, and I always enjoyed his company and the fascinating stories he told about his experiences all over the world. In fact, his memoirs, *The World Is My Home*, is a wonderful book about his life's adventures.

One day we were discussing sportswriters and how today with all the competition in the media they seem more hostile to and less supportive of the athletes they write about. To make the point, I told Jim a story about Bob Considine, who was a well-known sportswriter for many years. In 1949 I was sitting in a hotel lobby in New York when a very well-dressed man came over and said, "Robin, I'm Bob Considine. I just want to tell you that I think you are going to be a terrific big-league pitcher."

I said, "Thank you very much." I don't think sportswriters do that sort of thing now, but I may be wrong. Considine had a television show in which he interviewed ballplayers, and he had me on several years later, but that was the only real contact I had with him. When I told Michener this story, he said that Bob Considine was one of his best friends.

Sometime later Ed Piszek called and asked if I could have lunch on a specific day. I said sure, and when the day came, Ed picked me up in his limousine and then we picked up Michener at his Doylestown home. Only then did I learn that we were going to New York to have lunch to help celebrate Bob Considine's 65th birthday. We drove to the 21 Club, and I spent three and a half hours listening to great stories.

Another time Michener, Piszek, I, and a group of friends spent a week fishing in Alaska. The only one who caught any fish was James Michener, and he wasn't even trying.

When in 1974 I was passed over in the election to the Baseball Hall of Fame, my friend Michener was greatly offended. He launched a letter-writing campaign of which I was unaware to the members of the Baseball Writers of America, the group of senior sportswriters who vote in the Hall of Fame elections each year. Apparently some of the writers took offense at Michener's efforts, or so he later reported to me. He felt very badly that he had somehow caused my election to be delayed another year, because I didn't make it in 1975 either. I doubt that was the case, but all is well that ends well because in 1976 I did get the call that I had been elected to the Hall of Fame.

As the years passed Mary and I became quite close to Jim and his wife, Mari. Once or twice a year we would see Jim and Mari socially. Jim was close to Stan Musial as well. Stan rented a place in St. Petersburg for spring training and threw an 85th birthday party for Jim there that Mary and I attended. On another occasion we were down in Miami to watch the West Point baseball team, where our son Danny coached, play Barry University on their spring trip. The Micheners were living near Miami while Jim worked on his book *The Caribbean*, and so we dropped by for a visit. It turned out that he was to throw out the first pitch for the first baseball game ever played at Joe Robbie Stadium, an exhibition game between the Montreal Expos and the Baltimore Orioles. This was before the Florida Marlins franchise began and before they reconfigured the stadium for baseball.

Jim had to use a walker most of the time, but he walked to the mound without it and threw the first pitch, which pleased him considerably. Afterward we all visited in Joe Robbie's box and talked baseball while the game went on. Jim once told me that the man who invented the walker must have been a genius.

When in the mid-nineties Paul Rogers and I decided to write a book about the Whiz Kids, I thought it would be quite nice if Jim would write the foreword for the book. I had not seen him for a number of years. By then he was living in Austin and in very ill health, having to have dialysis three times a week. I dropped him a note and heard nothing back for quite some time. I followed with another note and again received no response. At that point, Paul and I decided that Michener must simply be too ill to write, so we approached Pat Williams to write the foreword for the book. Pat is a unique individual who is a senior executive with the Orlando Magic and one of the leading inspirational speakers and authors of our time. He was

Ruly Carpenter's best friend as a kid and practically grew up in the Whiz Kids' clubhouse.

Pat penned a wonderful foreword and then one day, out of the blue, in the mail came a beautiful tribute to me from James Michener. We now had two forewords but it worked out superbly because Jim's piece was really directed toward me and my career, while Pat's emphasized the Whiz Kids. So we published both.

After the Whiz Kids book was published in December 1996, Paul and I traveled to Austin after a book signing party in Dallas to visit Jim and personally thank him. He was frail but was very pleased to see us. We had a nice visit for about an hour. It was the last time I saw that special man.

When Michener died there were two memorial services for him, one in Austin and one in New York City at the Metropolitan Club. I arranged to go to the service in New York with my son Robbie and my daughter-in-law Debbie, who has read all Michener's books. It was a memorable service with Walter Cronkite, among others, performing a eulogy. During the service, I sat next to Alan Simpson, the senator from Wyoming. I had met Senator Simpson in Washington, so afterward we visited. He asked, "Robin, why are you here?"

I explained to him and then asked him the same question. I knew that Michener had been an unabashed liberal and that Simpson had the reputation for being quite conservative politically. He told me that Michener had stayed with his family while they were making the television mini-series from his book *Centennial* and they had become very good friends.

Of course, they did not agree politically, but Simpson told me about a time when he was sponsoring legislation that Michener favored. Simpson was making his final speech in favor of the legislation in the Senate chamber and noticed that James Michener was among the people in the gallery. After the favorable vote, Michener came down and shook Simpson's hand and said, "You SOB, you finally got something right."

* * *

My election to the Baseball Hall of Fame in 1976 was a special occasion and took place 11 years after I retired as an active player. The rules require that a player is not eligible until he has been retired for five years, and so I was elected on my sixth year of eligibility. I never thought about the Hall of Fame while I played; it just didn't enter my mind. But after I retired I thought I might have a chance because I had won a lot of games and had a good career. In 1975 there was a lot of talk that I would be elected. Jack Lang, the veteran sportswriter who counted the votes, called me the night before the results were announced to tell me that I had not made it. Jack told me that was the first time he had ever done that.

The following year I received better news and was inducted with Bob Lemon, Freddie Lindstrom, Oscar Charleston, and Cal Hubbard. For the first time it rained on induction day and the ceremony was held inside the Otesaga Hotel. I followed Bob Lemon, who gave a beautiful, heartfelt acceptance speech, so I kept mine short, because Bob had expressed what I wanted to say so well. I introduced my family and thanked the people who had helped me so much, like Mary, my parents, C. B. Lindsay, Ray Fisher, Cy Perkins, Eddie Sawyer, and my teammates.

I've been back with my family on every induction weekend since. I like to see the old members and welcome the new ones. It is wonderful to be a part of such special occasions.

A number of years ago I was asked to join the board of directors of the Hall of Fame. About the only time we have made the news was when Pete Rose was placed on baseball's disqualified list. The board had to decide if someone on that list could be eligible for election to the Hall of Fame. Strange as it sounds, the board had never adopted a rule on that issue. Joe Jackson and his teammates who were accused of throwing the 1919 World Series had been put on the disqualified list by Commissioner Landis and had never been elected to the Hall of Fame, but until the Rose case came along, there was no formal rule against their election.

It seemed quite logical that someone on baseball's disqualified list should not be eligible for election to the Hall of Fame, and that was the decision we quickly reached. After the meeting, I called Rose's lawyer to tell him about the meeting. I explained that if Pete applied for reinstatement after a year, as the commissioner permitted him to do, and if he was taken off the disqualified list by the commissioner, he would then be eligible for election to the Hall of Fame. Of course, the Hall of Fame has nothing to do with who is or is not on the disqualified list, and that is the way it should be.

* * *

I enjoy playing golf and play in celebrity golf tournaments all around the country. Perhaps my most unique experience was while I was still in baseball, and it was totally unexpected. I was sitting at home in Philadelphia one Saturday evening watching it snow when I got a call from Frank Chirkinian down in Florida. Frank had produced the *Robin Roberts Sports Club* that I hosted for a couple of winters during my playing career and had moved on to CBS Sports where he was producing the *CBS Sports Spectacular* television show. Frank called everyone Bunky. When the phone rang and I heard, "Hey, Bunky, what are you doing?" I told him I was just watching television. Frank then asked if Mary and I would fly down to Florida the next day to play in a televised golf match for the *Sports Spectacular* show that was to be taped beginning on Monday. He indicated he would cover our expenses and I would get a new set of golf clubs out of the deal.

Frank had put together a pro-celebrity alternate-shot tournament that was supposed to pit Dow Finsterwald and Perry Como against Sam Snead and Ray Milland. Perry Como had taken ill and was not going to be able to play, so I was to be Perry's substitute. Mary and I flew down, and we began taping on Monday. The pros would drive, and then we would hit the second shot and continue alternating shots. It took, however, about 20 minutes between shots because of the logistical problems of getting the cameras in the correct positions. As a result, we could play only nine holes a day.

Finsterwald and I were down three holes after the first day. We went out to dinner that night and Frank said to me, "Hey, Bunky, you've got to shake yourself or else I'm not going to have enough footage for the show." He was concerned that under match play rules we would be eliminated well before we played all 18 holes. But we did better the next day and went into the final hole tied. We then won that hole and the match. It was the only time during those two days that we were ahead. Mary had a good time because we had dinner twice with one of her favorite actors, Ray Milland, who was a gentleman.

I have been fortunate to meet many interesting personalities and have interesting experiences because of my baseball career. One day while I was with the Orioles I was shagging balls in the outfield during batting practice, as I often did. The Orioles had brought some unsigned prospects in to work out and one young man ran toward first after taking his five swings in the batting cage, as was customary. But he kept running hard toward me in right field and when he reached me said, "Mr. Roberts, I'm Reggie Jackson." Reggie had been a high school football star in Cheltenham, near where we lived in suburban Philadelphia, so I said, "Reggie, I thought you were a football player." He said, "I am. I'm playing at Arizona State. But I'm going to play football one more year and then sign a pro baseball contract." The rest, as they say, is history.

The Phillies were, of course, very slow to sign black ballplayers, and for years I played against and watched players like Willie Mays, Henry Aaron, Monte Irvin, Ernie Banks, and so on. In 1960 the Phillies brought their best minor league prospects in to play intersquad games the last couple of weeks of the major league season. They would play in the afternoons before our night games. I enjoyed getting to the park early and watching some of these games. One afternoon at the end of an inning the shortstop for the team in the field came over to where I was sitting and said, "Are you Robin Roberts?"

I said, "Yes."

He said, "I'm Dick Allen. I would like to shake your hand." Actually, at that point he probably said that he was Richie Allen, but he later grew to hate the name "Richie" and demanded to be called Dick instead.

Dick Allen was the first black player for the Phillies who had the talent of the black stars we had played against for so many years. When I was with Baltimore, I pitched in a preseason game in Philadelphia. With two out in the first inning, up stepped Dick Allen. My 0–2 pitch hit the Coca-Cola sign on the top of the left-field stands. My shortstop, Luis Aparicio, came to the mound to tell me that was the hardest-hit ball he had ever seen. I will omit what I said to Luis in reply. The next time up Dick Allen struck out. He was then hitting only .500. That was his rookie season and his first home run in Connie Mack Stadium.

When I retired from baseball I was able to watch Dick Allen play quite often. He had many controversial moments that are well known to baseball fans. One day I was listening to the radio as the Phillies were about to play a doubleheader against the New York Mets in New York. Richie Ashburn announced that Dick Allen was not at the ballpark and no one knew why. But after the first game was over I decided to see if Dick had driven home from New York. I knew where he lived and went to his home. I knocked on the front door and his wife asked who it was. When I said, "Robin Roberts," she let me in. She said Dick was out getting sandwiches for her and the children and would be right back.

When he came in we went downstairs to talk alone. It is difficult for a white player to appreciate the problems, either real or imaginary, that a black player goes through. It was hard for me to understand why someone with Dick's ability couldn't just show up and play the game every day like other guys. He and I talked about his situation, and I wanted him to know that one Phillies fan was rooting for him to just show up and play the game. After that visit, nothing changed for Dick. He still had great talent and exhibited it on occasion. In hindsight I wish that Dick had seen Stan Musial play baseball day after day. Stan enjoyed the game so much that perhaps it would have rubbed off. But Dick is still a friend. He had a good career, but I wish it had been 18 years in Philadelphia.

* * *

After my retirement, I retained fond memories of teammates who were also friends, like Richie Ashburn (who didn't mind being called Richie). I first met Richie shortly after I reported to my first spring training in Clearwater, Florida, in 1948. I was a couple of weeks late because I was finishing up classes at Michigan State. I checked in at the Phoenix Hotel, got my room key, and found my room. As I entered, a young blond kid stood up and said, "Hi, I'm Richie Ashburn." I took one look at him, introduced myself, and said, "I'll see you in Cooperstown in a few years, Richie."

The last part, of course, is not true, but that meeting did begin a 50-year friendship with the man we called Whitey. For the next 12 years we would be teammates on the Philadelphia Phillies. I have described how the first two years, 1948 and 1949, we lived together at a rooming house Richie's parents operated for some of the single Phillies ballplayers. We played cards, argued, shot pool, argued some more, and ate Mrs. Ashburn's delicious cooking.

I quickly learned that Richie's behavior was not always conventional. One day I was driving us to the ballpark from the rooming house when I sailed through what I thought was a yellow light. A policeman pulled me over, advising me that I had run a red light. I was telling the officer that I thought the light was yellow when Richie piped up from the passenger seat, "No officer, you're right, the light was red." Thanks a lot, Rich.

On the ballfield Whitey could hit for average, run like the wind, and cover center field like a blanket. He led the league in putouts just about every year we played together. There is no doubt that I contributed to that because I threw so many fly balls. The only problem was that Richie was not tall enough to get the ones that ended up in the stands.

Richie was a tremendous competitor who hustled all the time, every day. He never thought a pitcher should retire him, and early in his career he would yell at pitchers after he made an out. He would holler things like, "How can you get me out with stuff like that" or "You ain't got nothing." It was really comical.

Few people remember how durable a ballplayer Richie was. He showed up to play every day and from 1950 through 1954 played in 730 consecutive games, the fifth longest streak in National League history. And I can attest that he played all out in every one of them, no matter what the score or where we were in the standings. His streak ended when he got the short end of a violent outfield collision with Del Ennis while chasing a Mickey Mantle drive in an exhibition game in Wilmington a couple of days before the 1955 season opener. Between 1949 and 1958 Richie missed only 22 games.

Richie was a great contact hitter, choking up on the bat and spraying the ball to all fields. He did not have much power, and his father used to get on him to "swing like a man." That, of course, was before Richie won two batting titles and finished second on two other occasions. I am glad Mr. Ashburn was not Richie's hitting coach.

Whitey usually only hit about two home runs a year, and generally one of those was an inside-the-park job. Sportsman's Park in St. Louis had a short right-field fence with a tall screen fronting it. One year the Cardinals' general manager Frank Lane had the screen taken down, making right field an even more inviting target for left-handed batters. We came in for the first game of a series and Richie hit two homers into the right-field stands. The next day the screen was back up.

There are a number of stories about Richie, with his great bat control, fouling balls off. One day I was warming up between starts on the sidelines on the mound they used to have in front of the dugout. Whitey came over to stand there like a batter, as players often did to help the pitcher. So I fired one in there and, hard to believe, he took a cut at it. There was one fan sitting behind the dugout, about 15 or 20 rows up. Well, Richie hit a slice up into the stands and, as luck would have it, the ball struck the fan in the face, seriously injuring him.

The Phillies, of course, had to pay the man a substantial settlement. Richie felt very bad about the accident, but after everything settled down I asked him, "What were you doing?" Whitey said, "It looked so good, I had to rip at it." That was Whitey.

He was just as much a competitor off the field as on it. I learned this during our first spring together. One evening we went to a movie in Clearwater. It was a cowboy movie and all of a sudden I heard somebody in the theater say out loud, "Get that dirty rat. Get him. Get him." I thought, "Who could that be?" Then I looked around and it was Richie. I knew right then that he was trying to win everything, even the cowboy movies.

We played hundreds of games of pepper while we were teammates. We played with teammates like Putsy Caballero and Bill Nicholson and would bet a Coke or a dollar. Whitey loved for me to throw to him in those games. It was the only time he swung like Babe Ruth. Boy, were we good at pepper and did we enjoy trying to line a ball off each other's shins.

He was the most obnoxious winner in gin rummy that I ever saw. He also loved to play poker and won most of the time. When the losers complained, Whitey would sing, "Tell Your Troubles to Jesus." In retrospect, I am surprised nobody ever hauled off and slugged him.

Whitey would occasionally call to ask me to invest in some deal with him. One time he called to get me to go in on a store and apartment investment in Nebraska. Then he called back a couple of days later to tell me that it was too good a deal and that he was going to put up all the money himself.

Another time he had a man who wanted us to invest $5,000 in a new insurance company. After we met with the man, my wife said, "I wouldn't give that guy a dime." But Richie and I each gave him $5,000 anyway, and we never heard from him again. Funny, but Whitey never again mentioned that one. To him it was just a bad hand in a poker game.

In December 1962 I received a call from Les Qually, the head of the advertising agency that handled Phillies broadcasting. Les wanted to know if I was interested in retiring from baseball and becoming one of the Phillies' announcers. I wanted to keep pitching, so I thanked Les and suggested that he might contact Richie Ashburn, who I knew was thinking about retiring after playing a season for the original New York Mets.

The next 35 years were, as they say, history. I enjoyed Whitey's broadcasts of the Phillies' games with Harry Kalas tremendously. Whitey never changed from the teammate I had known. The game still was not that complicated. It still was not as easy as it looked from the stands, and the umpires still made bad calls. His dry wit and sense of humor were the same; he was just sharing it with many more people. (Once we played a spring training game against Ted Williams and the Boston Red Sox before a packed stadium in Montgomery, Alabama. Richie hit a homer in the bottom of the ninth to win the game 2 to 1. Afterward in the clubhouse Whitey announced to his teammates, "Ten thousand fans pay to watch Ted Williams, and Richie Ashburn hits a home run to win the game.")

Richie was often quick with a quip. When he played for the Chicago Cubs in 1961 the team was trying a system of rotating their coaches as the manager. As a result every few weeks a different coach would actually be serving as manager. The Cubs even rotated some of their coaching staff with their top farm club in Des Moines. I was still with the Phillies, and when we came into Chicago one time to play the Cubs, I asked Whitey how he was doing. He said, "Not too good. The guy who likes me is in Des Moines."

In the summer of 1997 the Phillies invited me back on the night they paid tribute to Jackie Robinson on the 50th anniversary of his breaking into the big leagues. Whitey and I had probably played against Jackie more than anyone. I remember one night Jackie had driven in all four runs against us and Richie had driven in both our runs. Late in the game a large Dodgers fan jumped on top of our dugout to announce to the entire ballpark that the score was Jackie Robinson 4, Richie Ashburn 2.

On the evening the Phillies were paying tribute to Jackie, I was visiting with Larry Shenk, the Phillies' longtime public relations man, before the ceremony began. From behind me I heard a voice, "Smo, I think you need a new watch." It was Whitey telling me he wanted me to appear with him on his pregame show, where his guests received a watch. We had a great visit talking about some of our memories of Jackie Robinson. The show was far too short; we could have talked all evening.

Two weeks later Richie passed away. Roy Campanella once said that you have to have a lot of little boy in you to play baseball. I certainly believe that was true with Richie and me. Whitey enjoyed life's little ironies, and I suspect that he is looking down with a smile on his face. He knows that I never did get that watch.

* * *

Today when fans talk about a great Phillies southpaw pitcher named Lefty they generally are referring to Steve Carlton. But the first Phillies "Lefty" was my fellow Whiz Kid and longtime teammate Curt Simmons. The Phillies signed Curt out of Whitehall Township High School in Egypt, Pennsylvania, for a record $65,000 bonus in 1947. That was a tremendous amount of money for the time. The minimum major league salary was about $5,000, and veteran players made about $10,000. The average annual income in the United States was less than $3,000, and here this kid had received $65,000 as an 18-year-old.

I mentioned how, because I had signed for $25,000, I couldn't wait to see Curt throw when I reported to spring training in 1948. He certainly did not disappoint, throwing harder and with more movement on the ball than anyone I had ever seen. He also had a peculiar delivery that hid the ball from the batter. It was easy to see why 15 major league teams had tried to sign him.

The Phillies even went so far as to play an exhibition game in Curt's hometown of Egypt, with Curt pitching for the local town team. All Lefty did was strike out Phillies in double digits and lead 4–2 going into the eighth inning when his center fielder and left fielder ran together to permit the Phils to tie the score. It ended that way because of darkness.

Curt and I roomed together for a while early on, and even then after he pitched his biceps would be throbbing and hurting. I was just the opposite. I could pitch a full game and have only a little arm stiffness the next day and have no pain. But Lefty threw across his body and put a lot of strain on his arm. He struggled with arm problems for most of his career, and it is amazing that he was able to pitch for 20 years in the big leagues.

Curt won 193 games during that career. I have often wondered how many games he would have won with four or five days' rest between starts like pitchers today have. In the fifties we pitched every fourth day, and with the strain Curt put on his arm, more rest would have really helped him. If he could have kept the stuff he had in the early fifties there is no telling what he would have accomplished.

But Curt never let anything bother him. He just went about his business and as early as high school began to develop effective off-speed pitches that greatly aided his effectiveness. Curt also has a droll sense of humor. Once in the late fifties he was pitching a great game against the Milwaukee Braves, leading 1–0 in the eighth inning. The Braves had a man on third with one out and Henry Aaron at bat. Lefty threw Henry his big, slow, sloppy curveball, and Aaron swung with all his might and popped it a mile straight up for the second out. Curt then got the third out and won the ballgame.

Nobody threw a hitter like Aaron a slow curve in that situation. At the time, Curt and I still lived next door to each other, and we drove to and from the ballpark together. That evening I was driving us home, and on the way I asked Curt, "How could you get up guts enough to throw that slow curve to Aaron with a man on third?"

His reply was classic Curt. He said, "Have you seen him hit my fastball?"

Curt really did give Aaron fits with his off-speed stuff. Whenever anyone asks Henry who the toughest pitcher he ever faced was, he will always answer, "Curt Simmons." And that was after Curt had his arm trouble and lost his exceptional fastball.

The Phillies released Curt in 1960, but he wasn't out of work long, soon signing with the St. Louis Cardinals. Lefty had what amounted to another full career with the Redbirds. For most of seven years with the Redbirds, he was an effective starting pitcher, mixing speed with excellent control. In 1964, at the age of 35, Curt went 18–9 to help the Cards to the 1964 pennant. He was absolutely murder against his old team, winning 17 of his first 19 decisions from the Phillies. In 1964 the Phillies had a 7½-game lead with 11 games left in the season before losing 10 straight to blow the pennant. Meanwhile the Cardinals were winning eight straight, and on September 30 Lefty defeated the Phillies 8–5 in Sportsman's Park to sweep the Cards into first place. He held his old team hitless for six and two-thirds innings, by which time St. Louis had forged an 8–0 lead.

Lefty finally pitched in the World Series in 1964, 14 years after missing the Whiz Kids' Series in 1950. He started Games 3 and 6 against the New York

Yankees, and, although he did not come out with a win, he gave the Yankees only four runs in 14 innings for a 2.51 earned run average. In Game 3 in Yankee Stadium against Jim Bouton, Lefty pitched a great game, leaving for a pinch-hitter in the top of the ninth with the score 1–1. The Cards lost when Mickey Mantle hit reliever Barney Shultz's first pitch into the stands for a home run in the bottom of the ninth. The Cardinals won the Series in seven games, however, making Curt the last of the five Whiz Kids to play on a World Championship team. (The others were Ken Silvestri for the 1941 Yankees, Blix Donnelly for the 1944 Cardinals, Dick Sisler for the 1946 Cardinals, and Russ Meyer for the 1955 Dodgers.)

Under Eddie Sawyer and Cy Perkins, Curt had been groomed without pregame meetings to go over the hitters. Johnny Keane, his manager with the Cardinals, however, required that the starting pitcher go over the hitters and tell everyone how he was going to pitch to each one. Bob Gibson, who also disliked pregame meetings, told me that Curt just hated having to tell everyone how he was going to pitch each batter. So Curt would go through the lineup saying, "Low and away, high and tight and play them straightaway" for every hitter. Then he would say, "Play the big guys back and the little guys up," or if he got to someone like Hank Aaron, he would say, "Play him a little bit to pull, maybe three steps to pull."

Meanwhile, Gibson would be rolling on the floor, he would be laughing so hard. Lefty would go through the entire meeting and manage to state only the obvious and never say anything about how he really planned to get anyone out. Bob could not wait for Curt to pitch so that he could hear Curt say, "Play the big guys back and the little guys up."

It is hard to imagine that friends as close as Curt and I could have such different personalities. He always calls me "the overboarder." I think he's right. I am always arguing about things and I am stubborn. Curt, on the other hand, never lets much of anything bother him and is flexible enough to change and go with the flow.

I often thought that Curt would have been an excellent pitching coach or even manager. He had a good temperament for it. He was a realist, was always on an even keel, and could make decisions without becoming emotional. I even mentioned my idea to Curt one time when Bob Skinner was managing the Phillies in the late sixties. Bob and Curt were good friends from their days on the Cardinals, and I thought Curt could really help the Phillies by working as Bob's pitching coach. Curt said he wasn't sure that was something he wanted to do. I was still trying to get the Phillies straightened out, even though they really did not want my help, so I mentioned it

to Bob Carpenter. I guess it went the way of most of my suggestions, because nothing ever came of it.

As I mentioned, the Simmons and Roberts families lived next door to each other for many years, from 1952 until 1969. Mary and Curt's wife, Dot, were and are great friends, and our kids grew up together. In the fall Curt and I would be waiting for the school bus to drop the kids off from school so we could play our touch football games. He would quarterback one team and I'd quarterback the other. The joke around the neighborhood was that we were more interested in touch football than the kids were, and that probably wasn't far from the truth.

For many years, Del Ennis, Curt, and I played basketball together in the off-season for the Phillies' basketball team, which Maje McDonnell organized. We played all kinds of opposition—town teams, pro teams, and high school faculties. We won way more than we lost, and in later years retired NBA stars like Paul Arizin, Tom Gola, and Ernie Beck sometimes played with us. Then we were downright invincible.

Curt and I also worked out together in the winter. We would go to a local gym and throw to each other, but we had only a right-handed catcher's mitt. I had a tough time catching Lefty because his ball moved so much even though he wasn't throwing it full speed. I was always amazed that Curt put the catcher's mitt on the wrong hand but still caught me without any trouble. I guess that says something about the kind of stuff he had.

Mary and I finally moved in 1969 because our kids were going to Germantown Academy, which was quite a haul from Meadowbrook. So we moved closer to the school after 17 years next to the Simmons family. Later on I coached the Germantown Academy baseball team for a few years, and Curt's oldest son, Tommy, was my catcher.

Of course, Curt and I ended up together with the Cubs in 1966 during my stint as Leo Durocher's playing pitching coach. Curt came back with the Cubs in 1967 and went over to the California Angels in the middle of the season. We had invested in a golf course together in suburban Philadelphia a few years before. The Angels wanted Curt to come back in 1968, but he was ready to retire and told me, "I think I'll manage that golf course."

So he did, and he has managed the course, called the Limekiln Golf Club, ever since. He is a natural, and the course has turned out very nicely for my family, thanks to Curt's managerial skills. About 10 years ago he hired my oldest son, Robbie, to be the assistant manager at the course, and Robbie has been with him ever since. Curt's youngest son, Tim, has recently joined the

staff as well. It is probably a very good thing for the Roberts family that Curt never pursued my suggestion to him about becoming a pitching coach.

Our families are still very close. We visit the Simmonses once or twice a year in Philadelphia, and every March Curt and Dot come down to Florida to stay with us for a week. I even have a grandson named Curt. My youngest son, Jimmy, named his firstborn, Curtis, after the old southpaw.

It has been a great run for the Roberts and Simmons families. We were both fortunate to be involved in baseball, and our families grew up together. Who would have ever thought that a couple of Phillies bonus babies from the late forties would be longtime teammates and neighbors and still be business partners and friends 55 years later?

Epilogue

Since I was eight years old, when I come home the question to me has always been "who won?" Even today, I'm still playing a lot of golf, so Mary asks, "Who won?" or "How did you do?" when I come in. My life has always revolved around sports in general and baseball in particular. When Honus Wagner was inducted into the Hall of Fame in 1936, his acceptance speech was very short. He said, "Baseball is an easy game if you can play it." Well, I was fortunate enough to be able to play it. As I look back, it was a dream to be able to make a living playing baseball. It wasn't exactly stealing, but it sure beat working for a living, as I later found out.

I have wonderful memories from the game, such as Luis Aparicio throwing from deep shortstop or Brooks Robinson and Willie Jones catching everything at third or Granny Hamner making a relay throw from the outfield. I enjoy remembering Richie Ashburn running the bases, Curt Simmons throwing the ball when he came up, Andy Seminick behind the plate like a block of granite, and Del Ennis showing up every day, never saying much, and playing the game all out.

Because of Cy Perkins, I always appreciated watching talented ballplayers, even those on the other side. The first time I saw Willie Mays, I, like everyone else, knew he was something special. Henry Aaron was so slim when he came up, it was hard to imagine how he could hit like he did. I thought he would hit .400 the way he hit to the opposite field, but he started pulling the ball and did all right hitting home runs. Roy Campanella was a superb catcher; I wish the Phillies would have signed him when they had the chance. Stan Musial swinging the bat and running the bases and Red Schoendienst playing second base are special memories. The classic swing of Ted Williams is hard to forget, even though I only faced him in exhibition and All-Star Games.

Folks often say that Ted Williams is the best hitter ever. That may be correct, but Barry Bonds is walking arm in arm with him these days. In the mid-eighties I traveled down to Miami to do television color commentary for a college baseball tournament. Arizona State was in the tournament and had a skinny 18-year-old center fielder named Bonds. From the outset it was clear he was the best player on the field.

I truly enjoy watching the modern-day players. They are bigger, stronger, and probably faster than we were and take better care of themselves, with better diets and year-round workouts with personal trainers. I enjoyed watching Sandy Koufax and Bob Gibson when I played, but today it is a pleasure to watch Curt Schilling, Tom Glavine, Roger Clemens, or Greg Maddux pitch. For many years after I retired I particularly liked to see Steve Carlton and Tom Seaver throw. I first heard of Seaver by way of Richie Ashburn, who was broadcasting Phillies games. He called one morning in 1967 after the club had been in New York playing the Mets and said, "You won't believe what happened last night. I saw you pitch."

I said, "What do you mean?"

He said, "There's a rookie pitcher with the Mets that throws just like you. His name is Tom Seaver."

Whitey was correct. Seaver had the same drop and drive delivery, and so I followed his career closely. I even sent him a note once later in his career when he was with Cincinnati. He seemed to be dropping down against left-handed batters instead of staying up on top during his delivery. I had done that, too, and remembered getting ripped, so I let him know that probably wasn't a good idea. I'm not sure whether I helped him or not, but I tried.

In spite of my great memories, I do think the game played on the field today is better than ever, even though the games are too long, there are too many conferences on the mound, and the pitchers throw to first base too much. The last two World Series have been simply superb, with the Diamondbacks defeating the Yankees in the bottom of the ninth inning of the seventh game in 2001 and the Anaheim Angels' great comeback over the Giants in 2002 in Game 6 that enabled them to get to a seventh game and win the Series. The Angels epitomized what it means to be a team and had a bunch of fine ballplayers all doing their jobs.

I guess it is obvious that I still enjoy watching baseball. I watch it on television every night. I love the shot from center field behind the pitcher toward the plate; it is almost like I'm pitching again. If there is a game on, I'm probably watching it, and Mary is in the other room because they throw to first too much.

Of course, the game is so different today from the way it was in my time, and not only because the pitchers throw over to first so much. It is not that the game was better then, it was just different. I have mentioned many of the differences, some of which are minor and some more significant. For example, I began pitching in the big leagues when the fielders still left their gloves on the field when they went in to hit. Our uniforms were flannel and baggy, and we had a no-fraternizing rule. An umpire actually sat in the stands watching batting practice, and you could be fined $50 for talking to someone on the opposing team. Some of those old rules were pretty silly.

I recognize that it is easy to second-guess and criticize the current state of the game when you are no longer involved with it and don't understand the reasons the people now involved make the decisions they do. But I do care deeply about the game that afforded me such a wonderful living and believe it can get better. For example, I don't understand why organized baseball does not better support American Legion, high school, and college baseball in this country. The clubs seem to be doing a great job finding and developing talent in Latin America, the Caribbean, and now Asia, but at home many of our best athletes end up playing other sports. Inner-city kids often play little or no baseball, although that situation may be improving. With all the athletic talent in the country, it just seems that the big-league clubs could do a better job helping amateur baseball.

I've already given my perspective on baseball's long history of labor problems. I really do believe that the fans have been left out of that equation. To be honest, the only real regret I have from my playing days involves the fans. Although when I played I spoke at any number of banquets and made many personal appearances, I was so focused on pitching and the competition at the big-league level that I really did not appreciate how important the game was to the fans and how closely my fans followed my career. I guess I didn't fully realize how many people were rooting for me and how my success or failure affected them. I once had a fan named John Druckenmiller send me a beautiful scrapbook with only my wins in it. There was a true fan!

Of course, when people hear the name Robin Roberts today they are likely to think of the attractive female sports anchor by that name. Recently I participated in a celebrity golf scramble, and one of the individuals who had paid to play with me came up and said that he wanted his money back because he thought he was playing with "the real Robin Roberts." He was just kidding. I think.

A number of people actually named their children after me. Over the years, I have met quite a few adult Robins who were born when I was pitching. In fact, I have met a woman named Robin Roberts who is an outstanding artist living in Texas. Her parents planned to name their baby after me if they had a boy, but when they had a little girl they decided to call her Robin anyway. When I would learn that someone had named a baby after me, I would always send a congratulatory card to the parents. A few years ago, I was making an appearance at a memorabilia show in Tulsa, and no fewer than three men in their early forties named Robin came by to show me the card that I had sent their parents shortly after they were born. But as I mentioned, at the time I was playing ball I really did not appreciate how ballplayers and the game of baseball affected people.

Although this is not really a regret, I am not sure my family understood how important they were to me while I was playing baseball. In talking about his success as a manager, Casey Stengel once said that he couldn't have done it without his players. Well, in my case I couldn't have done it without my players at home. Mary and the boys provided the stability that was so important to the success I had. I wanted them with me whenever possible and, for example, never considered going to spring training without them.

The four boys had to put up with an old man who was so competitive he would never let them win. By the time my youngest son, Jimmie, came along and got to be a teenager, he started beating me, and so I stopped playing him. Thanks to them, Mary and I have seven grandchildren to enjoy. As I mentioned, Robbie helps run our golf course outside of Philadelphia. Danny was head baseball coach at the U.S. Military Academy at West Point for 17 years and now coaches in the minor league system for the Phillies. Ricky is doing very well in the restaurant business in Atlanta, and Jimmy is prospering in the banking business in Tampa. Whenever we get together these days, we argue about sports. I know that I must be getting soft. I let them win some of the time.

I know it must have been frustrating for Mary when I was trying to hang on as a pitcher. But she hung in there with me, even though she was ready to settle down in Philadelphia and get on with our lives. So I went to Reading and commuted. Of course, I really thought I could still pitch, although Cy was gone by that time and I may have been the only one who thought so. On second thought, I'll bet Ken Silvestri, my old bullpen catcher with the Whiz Kids, probably thought I could still pitch, too, but Hawk didn't own a team, and you have to have a team to keep on pitching.

I understood from the beginning that I was blessed with a good arm and what they now call a drop and drive delivery. I had good wrist action that made my fastball move, and I had a rare combination of speed and control. Red Schoendienst once said that my fastball acted like it hit a cake of ice when it crossed home plate. Of course, sometimes the ice had melted and the ball went a long way in the other direction.

I did give up a lot of home runs, but they only bothered me if they cost me a ballgame. If I won 6–3 and gave up three solo home runs, I had won the game and didn't give a thought to the home runs. Of course, I didn't know anybody was counting. Maybe if I had known, I would have changed something, but I doubt it.

I was mainly a one-pitch pitcher, although I sometimes mixed in a curveball when I was ahead in the count. I could put my fastball where I wanted it, but I was sometimes criticized for not pitching inside more and not knocking hitters down. Dizzy Dean broadcast the *Game of the Week* on network television during the fifties and every time he saw me he would tell me, "Robin, you've got to knock somebody on their ass." Well, lots of people talked about knocking batters down, but few did it. And it just wasn't me. I just went after people with my best stuff and let the batters hit it if they could. That was my act, and it got me through 18 years in the big leagues.

Stan Hochman was a sportswriter with the *Philadelphia Daily News* while I was pitching. After every game I pitched, whether I won or lost, he would ask, "How are you feeling, Robin? How's your arm?"

No matter what, I would always say, "I feel good. My arm's great." In the years after I retired from baseball, whenever Stan would see me he would ask, "How's your arm, Robin?" and I would respond, "My arm feels great, Stan. I'm well rested."

Well, I am very well rested, but no one has called requesting my pitching services. It looks like no one is going to call. As a result, I want to announce my official retirement from baseball. I will not pitch again. I know I am disappointing my fans, but so be it. I'm moving on.

* * *

One day when I was coaching at South Florida, we won a game with two out in the bottom of the ninth on a bloop hit just beyond the infielder's reach. As Mary and I drove home after the game, she said, "You know, it's all luck." Well, I've thought about that quite a bit, and I think for once I'm going to have to disagree with Mary. I think I agree with Gary Player, the great golfer, who said, "The more I practice the luckier I get." I do know I have been blessed with a lot of good fortune, from the wonderful home my parents provided to Mary and our four boys. Possessing a strong right arm and great delivery didn't hurt any, either. But come on, Mary, surely it wasn't all luck, was it?

Robin Roberts' Career Statistics

Year	Team/League	W	L	PCT	G	SV	IP	H	BB	SO	ERA	BH	AVG
1948	Phillies/N	7	9	.438	20	0	146	148	61	84	3.19	11	.250
1949	Phillies/N	15	15	.500	43	4	226	229	75	95	3.69	5	.075
1950	Phillies/N	20	11	.645	40	1	304	282	77	146	3.02	12	.118
1951	Phillies/N	21	15	.583	44	2	315	284	64	127	3.03	15	.172
1952	Phillies/N	28	7	.800	39	2	330	292	45	148	2.59	14	.125
1953	Phillies/N	23	16	.590	44	2	346	324	61	198	2.75	22	.179
1954	Phillies/N	23	15	.605	45	4	336	289	56	185	2.97	15	.123
1955	Phillies/N	23	14	.622	41	3	305	292	53	160	3.28	27	.252
1956	Phillies/N	19	18	.514	43	3	297	328	40	157	4.45	20	.200
1957	Phillies/N	10	22	.313	39	2	249	246	43	128	4.07	13	.162
1958	Phillies/N	17	14	.548	35	0	269	270	51	130	3.24	20	.202
1959	Phillies/N	15	17	.469	35	0	257	267	35	137	4.27	17	.191
1960	Phillies/N	12	16	.429	35	1	237	256	34	122	4.02	12	.152
1961	Phillies/N	1	10	.091	26	0	117	154	23	54	5.85	3	.091
1962	Orioles/A	10	9	.526	27	0	191	176	41	102	2.78	10	.192
1963	Orioles/A	14	13	.519	35	0	251	230	40	124	3.33	16	.203
1964	Orioles/A	13	7	.650	31	0	204	203	52	109	2.91	9	.132
1965	Orioles/A	5	7	.417	20	0	114	110	20	63	3.38	6	.171
	Astros/N	5	2	.714	10	0	76	61	10	34	1.89	5	.238
1966	Astros/N	3	5	.375	13	1	63	79	10	26	3.82	1	.063
	Cubs/N	2	3	.400	11	0	48	62	11	28	6.14	2	.200
Total		286	245	.539	676	25	4,688	4,582	902	2,357	3.41	255	.167

W = Wins; L = Losses; PCT = Percentage; G = Games; SV = Saves; IP = Innings Pitched; H = Hits; BB = Bases on Balls; SO = Strike Outs; ERA = Earned Run Average; BH = Base Hits; AVG = Average

Index